Improvisation, Inc.

Improvisation, Inc.

Harnessing Spontaneity
to Engage People and Groups

Robert Lowe

JOSSEY-BASS/PFEIFFER
A Wiley Company
San Francisco

 Creative Training Techniques
Press

Copyright © 2000 by Jossey-Bass/Pfeiffer and Creative Training Techniques Press
Jossey-Bass/Pfeiffer is a registered trademark of Jossey-Bass Inc., A Wiley Company.
ISBN: 0-7879-5142-0

Library of Congress Cataloging-in-Publication Data

Lowe, Robert, date.
  Improvisation, Inc. : harnessing spontaneity to engage people and groups / Robert Lowe.
    p. cm.
  Includes Bibliographical references/
  ISBN 0-7879-5142-0
  1. Creative ability in business. 2. Improvisation (Acting) 3. Management games. 4. Employee motivation.
  5. Communication in management. I. Title.
  HD53 .L69 2000
  658.3'14—dc21

Printed in the United States of America

JOSSEY-BASS/PFEIFFER
A Wiley Company
San Francisco

Published by Jossey-Bass/Pfeiffer
350 Sansome Street, 5th Floor
San Francisco, California 94104-1342
(415) 433-1740; Fax (415) 433-0499
(800) 274-4434; Fax (800) 569-0443

Creative Training Techniques
Press

7620 West 78th Street
Minneapolis, MN 55439
(800) 383-9210
(612) 829-1954; Fax (612) 829-0260

www.pfeiffer.com

www.creativetrainingtec.com

Acquiring Editor: Matthew Holt
Director of Development: Kathleen Dolan Davies
Developmental Editor: Leslie Stephen
Editor: Rebecca Taff
Senior Production Editor: Dawn Kilgore
Manufacturing Supervisor: Becky Carreño
Interior Design: Yvo Reizebos
Cover Design: Richard Adelson

Printing 10   9   8   7   6   5   4   3   2   1

This book is printed on acid-free, recycled stock that meets or exceeds the minimum GPO and EPA requirements for recycled paper.

Dedication

Improvisation, Inc. is dedicated to

my son, Jonathan Michael Mawle Lowe;

to improvisers everywhere; to business leaders, trainers,

and people who build and grow things by communication;

to you the reader;

and to God in all His love, wisdom, and mercy.

Contents

PART TWO: IMPROV FUNDAMENTALS

PART THREE: APPLIED IMPROV METHODS

PART FOUR: BASIC GAMES

PART FIVE: ADVANCED IMPROV TECHNIQUES

PART SIX: MAKE IMPROVISATION YOUR OWN

Preface

This book is an introduction to the use of improvisational comedy theater principles and techniques for business and organizational development applications. It covers theory, technique, methodology, and practice, and includes some exercises that can be used in a business setting.

The book is also about tapping sources of creativity, both in your business and in your life. The material is intended to be used by business executives, business owners, corporate career-track leaders, trainers, educators, teachers, presenters of information, and others who understand how important it is to communicate effectively and easily as we face the new century.

It is my prayer that you will think your time well spent reading this book and considering the art of Improvisation. I hope that you will use the theories, exercises, practices, and games to develop your own improvisational management skills and that you will pass them on to the people with whom you work and play. I hope that you will use the information to build creative, laughter-filled environments in all realms of your life. I know that if you do, you will experience an increase in the creativity and spontaneity in both your business and your personal life.

I have worked with a great number of people who have made real and valuable changes in their lives and businesses by exploring Improvisation as a creative tool. Working with this powerful tool will also result in increases in *your* business profitability. It will enhance your organization's development and speed your personal growth.

IMPROVISATION

Most people come to the discipline of Improvisation through an interest in improvisational performance comedy. Today, however, more and more people from business are looking to Improvisation as a source of knowledge and skills. In 1999 it was reported that the revenues of The Second City Comedy Club, an Improv group in Chicago, were expected to be surpassed by the revenues from classes in Improvisation taught to business professionals hoping to loosen up and lighten up to keep ahead of the game.[1]

THE IMPROVISATIONAL EXECUTIVE

Information is provided in this book for any chairman, president, executive, administrator, sole practitioner, professional presenter, consultant, public speaker, supervisor, lead worker, trainer, teacher, sociologist, psychologist, philosopher, artist, poet, or student of human nature.

Your interest may be in the bottom line, the return on investment (ROI), hardware, software, the next generation, the Internet, human relations and management, business communication, industrial development, organizational development, personal development, presentation skills, education, laughter, humor, playfulness, joyous celebration, or delight in living. Whichever it is, you will gain from a knowledge of Improvisation principles and techniques.

All who come to The Improv can find some insight into living, working, producing, and playing more fully, spontaneously, openly, effectively, sweetly and gently, powerfully, and completely. For most, the discovery of The Improv brings a major shift in perspective and insight into understanding themselves and others.

This seems like a lot for a little. Over the years, time and again, people with whom I have worked and played have said the same thing, using almost the same words:
> "I don't want to do this for a living. I mean, I am not a performer, really. But it seems that I am using this stuff all the time in my work, in my daily life, even with my family."

Often the speaker's eyes are lightly glazed over as he or she shares this revelation. This response is what has made me a professional improviser. This is the reason for *Improvisation, Inc.*

1

"CORPORATE DRONES HEAD TO IMPROV CLASS." *THE WALL STREET JOURNAL*, JUNE 15, 1999.

THOSE WITH WHOM I HAVE WORKED

I have been blessed by working with a wonderful range of people and organizations. My work has brought me into contact with business executives, construction workers, computer people, sales folk, moms and dads, clerks, lawyers, teachers, military leaders, nurses, physicians, educators, professors, administrators, social workers, farmers, actors and comedians, radio artists, painters, dancers, potters, and writers. Among them have been some of the most bold and some of the most shy people imaginable.

The information in this book comes from twenty years of real-time experience exploring organizational development and creativity through Improvisation. My work has been developed and presented for sole practitioners and Fortune 100 groups, for service industries—volunteer organizations, medical institutions, prisons, and not-for-profit corporations—in academic circles for teachers, professors, school administrators, school counselors, and social workers, and in public and private schools—kindergarten through university—and in a wide range of open public workshops.

This book is an introduction to the application of The Improv in business and industry. It is, and should always be, a work in progress. You are the primary participant.

Come now and follow me through a set of thoughts and ideas and considerations and stories and delights and experiences. Let me introduce you to experiences, applications, guidelines, parameters, philosophies, and a very few rules that will open new portals to working, learning, and teaching. Follow me into "The Improv," where you may discover unique doorways leading to your own personal best-possible practices.

Robert Lowe

June 2000   Atlanta, Georgia

www.ImprovisationInc.com

Acknowledgments

The contradiction is a funny thing. They say that talk is cheap yet the best advertising is word of mouth. If you ever sit down to write a book you will discover that there you are, all alone, by yourself. There is no one to cheer you on or hold your hand into the long nights and deep parts of your soul. Writing really is a lonely thing.

However, if you ever sit down to thank the people who made it possible for you to write a book, you will find yourself surrounded by people too numerous to name, and by a sea of love and encouragement. Here are most of the names of the people without whom I could not say, "Look at what I did!"

First my family: my wife and friend Dr. Elizabeth Meredith Dowling Lowe; my son, Jonathan Lowe; my step-children, Meredith Dowling and G. Geddes Dowling IV; and my mother-in-law, Ruth Meredith. Next are my mother, Emily Lowe, who taught me love and toughness, and my father, Robert Lowe, who taught me the most about love. He also taught me to write, and more important, to work with an editor. My grandfather, A. C. Warner, carried the genes of delight and passed them on to us all. My grandmother Louvisa Warner gave me keys to the doors of the spirit.

There are the people who gave me guidance when I was young: Vernon S. Cox, who showed me how to live with love and strength on a daily basis in the real world; my aunt Francis Warner, who shared my love of life and laughter; my aunt Edith Bullockus, who had faith in me from the beginning; my cousin Annie Kuoppamaki, who laughed with me through tempest, storm, and gale; and the brothers of Beta Omega Sigma, who continue to give me a continuity. T. J. Mullins and Joe Stanovich gave me direction. A thousand others just gave of themselves.

Where would I be without the work of Viola Spolin, God rest her creative soul, and the wonderful improvisational life and explorations of Keith Johnstone? On the path of The Improv, I owe a great deal to Judith Greer Essex, who taught me Improv dance, and Jon and Jonathan Glasier, who opened the doors to microtonal Improv music. Deep blessings to my first Improv teacher, Don Victor, and to my first creativity teacher, Jacquie Lowell. In my own improvisational explorations, I would never have made it without the love and help of Alan Freedman, Andrew Einspruch and Billie Dean, Chris Kauffman, Alison Mawle, Jerry Farber, Gene Dale, and Jim Sligh. I learned an awful lot about The Improv from all who played with *The Lightside City Players* and especially from Jay Russell, Bruce York, Leslie Truman, Charles Mc-Givern, Chris Passante, Mike Scarbro, Tommy Futch, Emelio Perey, Keith Hooker, Joel Gilmore, Allison Dukes, Marc Farley, O'Clair Alexander, Stephanie Astalos Jones, Deb Calabria, Eileen Kimball, Irv Wardlow, Donna Holland, Phil Tardif, Rich Bailey, Leila L'Abate, Bill Troschek, Judith Young, Pac McKibben, Tommy Chappelle, Carol Haynes, Anna Collins, John O'Hagan Ward, Jeff Lebow, Gil Puffer, Bruce Hansen, Ian Cook, Nick Jameson, Mitch Rouse, Clark Taylor, Georgia Dial Davidson, Janet Wells, and Susan Andrews. Then there are the hundreds of Improv players from *The Next City Comedy Theatre* to *The Let's Try This Players* of Georgia Tech, and the thousands of business and community participants who have played with me over the years.

Special thanks for special reasons are due to Jeff Justice, Frank and Mary Hamilton, John Vitek, John Bolton, Dick Leitgeb, Mark Weiss, Clabe Hangan, Bagavhan Sri Sathya Sai Baba, Baba Gi, Rob Bigalki, Pauline Temple, Mary King, Sondra Ray, Ken and Jane Stanbridge, Janet Grantham, Greg Abbott, Scott Hawkins, Don Mitchell, Diirga Brough, Jean Houston, Edward Haig, Sr. Miriam McGillis, Terry O'Keefe, Dr. Carol Winkler, Emory Mulling, and Dr. Ed Metcalf.

For the Aikido which is so much a part of The Improv I must give personal thanks to my teachers in the order they came to me: Steven Samuels, Fumio Toyoda, Dick Kedlubowski, Kazuo Chiba, Rodney Grantham, Yoshimitsu Yamada, George Kennedy, Daryl Tangman, and Ginny Whitelaw. There are another thirty or more Aikido teachers who have helped me along the way and another thousand or so with whom I have shared time on the mat.

This book would not have been started without conversations between the wonderful teachers and magicians Max Howard and Dave Arch; this followed by action on the part of Bob Pike of Creative Training Technologies, Inc.

I express deep appreciation to all the great people at Jossey-Bass/Pfeiffer, who impressed me as "book people" from the start and gave so much at every step. Special thanks to Matt Holt and Josh Blatter, who believed in me, and to Adrienne Biggs and David Horne who helped so much and with so much heart. A very deep appreciation goes to my developmental editor, Leslie Stephen, who could see the work as it was meant to be. I must express very special appreciation for the help of my copyeditor, Rebecca Taff, who knew just what I was trying to say in spite of my inability to punctuate with "quotations." Thanks to Sandy Dufault at CTTI, and how would you know about this work without my publicist, Celia Rocks?

With apologies to the hundreds of others who have helped and encouraged me in my work and who are too numerous to name I offer special thanks to all who are leading the way toward creativity, spontaneity, laughter, and joyfulness in our world.

Introduction

The purpose of this book is to introduce *Improvisation* as a business tool. Improv techniques may be used in many ways: as an exercise, as a training event, as a vision, as an organizational development mechanism, as a communication environment, or as a presentation form.

THIS BOOK IS ABOUT CREATIVITY

Access to the wealth of your own creativity can give you answers to your most pressing questions and solutions to your most serious problems. You need to generate and release creativity in all aspects of your life and work. Exploration and play with Improv techniques can develop and strengthen your ability to communicate, to think, to act, and to behave creatively. The use of Improvisation has practical and useful applications in many areas of business, such as

- Development and practice in creativity and spontaneity

- Enhancement of communication skills in professional and public communication, interpersonal communication, and quality communication

- Organizational development practice with groups, networks, and individuals

- Community development

- Planning practice

- Training and learning needs

- Measurement procedures

- Analysis of people

- Feedback on effectiveness

- Quality of working

- The need for playfulness

This information is useful for people who have no experience in performance arts. The Improv has many ideas and processes that will be of value to advanced executives and managers interested in organizational and human development. Involvement of key executives, managers, supervisors, and informal leaders can lead to the greatest possible long-term benefits. With Improvisation you may address problems associated with resistance to change, such as adherence to tradition, misconceptions about purpose, "goal denial," unattractiveness of possibilities, and fear of results.

Improv tools can be used to facilitate conflict resolution, problem solving, strategic planning, meeting management, change management, team building, stress management, and program presentation. The introduction of basic games and structures into your practices will result in positive changes in your communication and your organizational development. Most of the tools presented here can be used with little training or practice. The full development of the use of Improvisation in your whole organization can produce long-term benefits.

COMMUNICATION BEGINS WITH PLAYFULNESS

Mammals, especially humans, begin communicating and learning by playful exploration (finding toes, fingers, and belly buttons) and by taking action (wiggling toes and sticking fingers into belly buttons). Among humans the explorations of infants and the playful nature of children are magical events that are the foundation of the basic functions of communication and learning—from walking, to talking, to our most complex patterns of communication and organization.

We know that children learn, grow, develop, and communicate more readily when they are completely engaged by their activities. Training and teaching systems use all sorts of games and diversions, toys, and graphics. Today, in a world in which education competes with all forms of media, educators must also use attractive, pleasant, playful, or at least palatable, ways to make information interesting enough to be noticed and integrated into the learners' memory and behavior.

WE LEARN SERIOUSLY ORGANIZED GAMES

Eventually we give up "hide and go seek" and begin to "play" chess, basketball, tennis, board games, video games, crossword puzzles, social games, interpersonal games, war games, and simulations. Through these we develop the behaviors that help us work well together, follow rules, and solve problems.

Play is also a necessary element in organizational development. If there is no "play" in the organization, it will be too stiff to work well in a changing environment. This is not merely a clever use of words. The relationship is reciprocal. If there is no "play" in an organization, there will be little "playfulness" among the people.

Playfulness itself is often seen as a sign of immaturity and insincerity, and thus is discouraged in many "serious" settings. We are often expected to put away playfulness, along with other childish things.

Yet people need some form of practice in order to work really well together. Playfulness functions as such a practice; it is intrinsic to the concept of Improvisation. Inappropriate playfulness is usually the result of lack of training and practice.

A fundamental theory of Improvisation is that play and playfulness are not "childish things." They must not be put away when we become adults. Rather, playfulness is a powerful element in the communication process. Play and playfulness enhance our organizations and help us to develop people. The Improv is a very useful tool for introducing, enhancing, or reintroducing playfulness we have "outgrown."

LIFE PROVIDES PATTERNS

We live in a self-organizing social structure, working, playing, growing, learning, interacting, organizing, building, creating, and socializing. Our lives are organized in accordance with the conventions of our cultures, communities, families, parents, guardians, friends, and teachers. Our patterns are shaped by the style of our learning minds, personal lives, religious teachings, gender, wishes, thoughts, fantasies, fears, fables, falsehoods, and formulas.

We live in a self-organizing human body—emerging according to a DNA encoded pattern. Cells form, divide, and differentiate, creating structures, systems, *soma,* relationships, needs, and responsibilities. These eventually result in a unique human. Each human can be, in most ways, functional, in many ways beautiful, in some ways powerful, and in a few ways incredible beyond belief.

> *Soma:* "The body of an organism (the heart, the lungs, the brain, the lymph system) or an intoxicating plant juice of the milkweed family used in ancient India as an offering to the gods as a drink of immortality by worshipers in Vedic ritual and worship as an Vedic god."

Without our knowledge, we follow the patterns laid down before us as we develop our crawl, walk, stumble, or run. We establish and follow patterns as we learn sounds, signals, signs, symbols, syntax, and language.

Before we know it, we are molded by the patterns, codes, and conventions we have learned and inherited into a personality—a person with a name, identity, and *persona*. In short, before we gain any real power or control over ourselves or the world in which we live, we are patterned by our tribes, our experiences, and our genes.

Persona: "The role in life that the individual is playing."

—CARL JUNG

We demand our individuality in our adolescence and, if we are loved and lucky, we are educated, we are trained by a reasonable code of values, ethics, and morality, and we receive a functional and human set of basic patterns of behavior. During our young adulthood, we (one hopes) strengthen our individuality as well as our commonality, and we come to some sense of an integrated personal identity. It is this identity that we take to our professions and to our work.

We are creatures of patterned behavior. It is common in business at every level to hear that things do not change, that they change too slowly, or that they change in the wrong direction. Tradition can keep change from happening. Disbelief can make things change very slowly. Bureaucracy and error can make us change in wrong directions.

Improvisation can help us to keep and institute strong, viable tradition while allowing for change. It can help us address and dispel disbelief. It can shine light on inefficient bureaucracy. It can not forestall error, yet it can encourage feedback and honesty of analysis to help discover and correct error sooner. Improvisation will also help us laugh and be real and to get on with what must be done once errors have been discovered and addressed.

In all of our activities, we have little formal, structured practice in the arts of communication and organizational development. In human development as in business development, the pace of growth and change is fast. *Improvisation, Inc.,* explores the use of practical Improv techniques that will help us deal with this pace.

RESISTANCE TO CHANGE IS NATURAL

Planning, creativity, training, development, organization, growth, invention, and dealing with the future all require making changes. Resistance to change is a continual challenge in most business settings, yet *Improvisation, Inc.,* can give you some tools and can lead you to an organization more willing to accept change and more willing to confront resistance to change. The following are just some of the reasons you will want to use Improv techniques:

- Resistance to change stems from *unfamiliarity,* and hence it appears unattractive. Improvisation helps us become familiar with new concepts and thus helps to overcome resistance.

- *Misconceptions* build walls of resistance. Improvisation helps us communicate at higher levels so that misconceptions can be exposed and addressed.

- *Disbelief* stops people from moving forward. Disbelief is almost always based in mistrust, which is based in lack of knowledge and communication. Improvisation creates channels of communication that lead to new levels of trust.

- *Fear* is also a major stumbling block. We will talk extensively about fear in Chapter Seven.

Resistance Is Not All Bad

Resistance can be a reasonable response when we face youthful or inexperienced thinking. Off-handed change can be an unsafe thing. Thoughtless destruction pf patterns can unweave useful and complex tapestries.

Our ways of adhering to patterns, scientific constraint, developmental planning, and deference for precedent are not all bad. In fact most of these processes have had fabulous results. They have allowed us to meander rather freely between order and chaos. We have created a world filled with health, promise, possibility, and magnificent products of the imagination. All have been set into motion by our patterns and designs.

For the past two hundred years or so, our sciences have been based on principles of experimentation known as "the scientific method." This method restricts us to knowledge that can be weighed and measured. We must produce and publish protocols (how we did it); we must be able to duplicate our results; and others must also be able to duplicate our results. Then we can call our findings "true."

With the scientific method we have created systems, structures, business and economic practices, machines, buildings, tools, medicines and treatments, plans, and blueprints, all based on past proofs that work safely and well, time and time again. A great many of our patterns are useful and powerful forces.

I do not wish to fly in airplanes built by improvisational methods. I do not wish to undergo surgery with "playful, experimental physicians." I do not wish to have my financial analyst ignorant of trends and patterns in the marketplace.

Improvisation Can Be Learned

Improvisation asks that we look for the patterns that can and must be challenged. Improvisation can be used to help challenge patterns in need of change with enthusiasm and openness.

Even when we are working with plans and designs, we tend to improvise regularly and often. When our plans do not go according to predictions; when our tools or resources become depleted; when the knowledge is not available or has failed; when long-held ideas become challenged by new data and circumstances; when competition, downsizing, reorganization, re-engineering, disaster, and other external pressures are applied, we either must exhibit the essential ability to improvise or our plans will miss their mark.

The heart of the problem is that we have not actually studied and learned the art and science called Improvisation. We have merely experienced it in the midst of disaster, on the factory floor, in the classroom, when our children become teenagers, and by the seat of our pants. We have had to adjust to The Improv in the atmosphere of chaos. This is not necessary. Improv techniques can be learned.

Improvisation provides a mechanism by which we can practice challenging our patterns without breaking the machinery. It provides a system with which we can practice handling change in positive and effective ways. Improvisation can be understood, it can be learned, it can be taught, and it can be applied to a wide variety of situations. Improvisation is an invaluable tool for all who must manage, grow, solve problems, build teams, resolve conflict, organize, lead, teach, or learn. The wonderful side effect is that Improv skills are developed along with solutions to the problems at hand. With this in mind, it is time to start learning about Improvisation as the art of communication.

PART ONE

Introduction to The Improv

CHAPTER ONE

What Is Improvisation?

As you explore the idea of using Improvisation as a serious business and developmental tool, read this book with delight in the human spirit and in the search for your own creativity. Also consider the following good advice:

"Let me absorb this thing. Let me try to understand it without private barriers. When I have understood what you are saying, only then will I subject it to my own scrutiny and my own criticism. This is the finest of all critical approaches and the rarest."

JOHN STEINBECK[2]

2

JOHN STEINBECK AND EDWARD F. RICKETTS, *THE SEA OF CORTEZ: A LEISURELY JOURNAL OF TRAVEL AND RESEARCH.* MOUNT VERNON, NY: APPEL, 1941.

IMPROVISATION IS THE ART OF COMMUNICATION

During the past twenty years, I have been using Improvisation as a business and communication tool and as an organizational development technique. The formal use of Improvisation is a new development in the management of business interests. It is a complex concept. It can be seen as a technique, a tool, a state of mind ("The Improv"), a frame of reference, a method of being and thinking, or a technology.

Improvisation is also a process. It is a form and format for transformational experiences in business, learning, relationships, and life. Improvisation is both a technology and a discipline. It is a professional level mechanism for the development and enhancement of effective communication among people.

> *Improvise:* "From French, *Improviser;* Italian, *Improvvisare;* French, *Improvviso:* sudden; Latin, *Improvisus:* unforeseen.]" *To Improvise:* "To make use of the tools and resources at hand without reference to expected results; to improvise, *to deal in the unforeseen, to take part in the act of creation.*"

This marvelous human skill is learned by some at an early age by disposition or by training. Most of us learn about the skills through experience, living life, and responding to a changing world. We learn to improvise when our plans or tools or resources fail. This means we usually are introduced to our Improv skills during crisis. Because humans are very good at being human, this on-the-job training often works fairly well and teaches us something about Improvisation in general.

The interesting thing about Improvisation is that it is a real tool, the use of which can be learned rather easily. It can be taught. It includes skills that can be studied, practiced, developed, and polished by anyone with a good book or a good teacher and the desire to learn.

You Can Use Improv

• As a communication model • As a method for creating models • As a teaching technology • As a transformational learning tool • As a spontaneity generator • As a participation generator • As a feedback development mechanism

Improvisation Can Be Experienced

• As a creativity paradigm • As a method for creating perspective shifts • As a group analysis device that surpasses some of the most sophisticated organizational and personality testing systems • As an interactive benchmarking mechanism

Improv Can Be Used

• As a source of inspiration and laughter • As a source of energy • To brainstorm a solution to a problem • To define a problem • To isolate a problem • To analyze a problem • To model a problem • To test a problem • To play with a problem • To monitor group dynamics • As a barometer of group purpose • As a tool to determine risk-taking ability, and manageability of a group • As a tool for breaking deadlocks, resolving conflict, moving past stalemates, easing tensions, opening new directions, and bringing people together

Improvisation is a self-teaching, self-organizing, virtual-reality, participant-centered force for learning and remembering. Improvisation is a tool-making tool.

You can go anywhere you would like by using Improvisation. You can make it yours as an organizational development tool, an executive development program, a training philosophy, a presentation enhancement device, a toy, a plaything, or a lifetime of work and play.

N O T E

Throughout this book, you will find three words that can be used interchangeably at some level. In general, the following distinctions may be helpful.

Improvisation: The concept of using Improvisation as a tool for generating creativity, communicating, learning, growing, exploring, and teaching people to think quickly and with delight.

Improv: The technique used in an Improvisation process or exercise or idea.

The Improv: The special state of consciousness that spontaneously occurs when Improv technique generates the best and most honest Improvisation.

WORD FOR WORD EXERCISE

Improvisation begins as an exploration. To begin our understanding of this exploration we will look at a simple structure called *Word for Word*. The game is studied in detail in Chapter Thirteen.

This exercise requires about half an hour and works best with some serious concentration. If you do not have the time right now, read quickly through the description below and then set the time aside later to concentrate on it. The exercise can be done any number of times with new and interesting results each time. It works best if you are in a comfortable, private setting with few distractions.

PREPARING FOR THE EXERCISE

Move away from your desk, keyboard, workspace, or television so that there is nothing directly in front of you. Set everything aside physically and mentally and sit up straight in your chair with nothing on your lap and nothing in front of you.

- *Be prepared to have a little fun.*

- *Your feet and legs should be relaxed and not crossed.*

- *Relax your whole body.*

- *Try to find your body's natural center of gravity, below your navel and midway inside your body.*

- *Take a deep breath and exhale slowly. Take a deep breath and exhale slowly.*

- *Take a deep breath and exhale slowly.*

If you can snap your fingers with either hand, practice snapping a few times, switching back and forth from right to left. If you are not very good at snapping your fingers, you can pat your knees, left then right, one at a time back and forth. Practice snapping or patting for a moment. Try to do this without thinking about anything.

Rest your hands on your lap for a moment as you consider a question. A simple open-ended question will give you the best results. Start with something simple, such as, "What is the weather like today?" "What does it look like outside right now?" "What is my favorite vacation activity?" or "What do I like best about fine art?"

Now, think of your own question and let the snapping of your fingers or patting of your knees work as a signal to speak each word out loud. Use a single word for each snap or pat. The goal is to let a sentence form.

Example: If the question is "What is the weather like?," snap right "the"; snap left "weather"; snap right "is"; snap left "just"; snap right "fine."

After you have made a sentence or two, try the same question again to see whether you can get different answers. Now try for a third, then a fourth answer. Seek more serious and practical answers. Practice as necessary. The goals of the exercise are to learn two skills:

- *The ability to ask yourself a simple question without answering it automatically*

- *The ability to allow the words to form a sentence prompted by the snap of your fingers*

| **Practice** Ask and answer at least three questions besides the ones suggested. | **Practice** Try the exercise again with a different, a more serious, or a more complex question. | **Practice** Ask more serious and personal questions. Try to come up with several answers. |

EVALUATING AND ANALYZING

Take a deep breath and exhale slowly. Take a deep breath and exhale slowly. Take a deep breath and exhale slowly.

If you did this exercise easily and without confusion or distraction and you would like to do it again, you have done well. If you did it with some laughter and joyousness, you have approached the state of "The Improv." You can gain more insight into this process by doing the exercise again and again over a period of time. If the exercise was not easy and fun, keep reading and come back to this later.

PRACTICAL APPLICATION EXERCISE

This exercise may take from thirty to forty minutes. If you do not have time right now, mark this place in the book for later exploration.

You will need blank paper and a pen with black ink. Do not use a word processor or a typewriter. You may wish to use a tape recorder later in the exercise. Find a place you can sit quietly and write in response to the instructions you are about to read.

N O T E

Your particular business focus will be unique. You may choose to focus on the development of creativity, as used here, or you may choose to focus on other points, such as executive development, management development, human resource management, strategic planning, personal development, organizational development, or teaching and training skills. You may do this exercise for each of the above and you may add to the list.

Keep the following questions in the back of your mind as you proceed: "What do you want in return for your time spent reading this book and learning new skills?" "What can you accomplish by learning about Improvisation?"

STARTING THE EXERCISE

- *Take a deep breath and exhale slowly. Take a deep breath and exhale slowly. Take a deep breath and exhale slowly.*

- *Make a list of seven ways you would like to develop your creativity. Do this quickly. Do not stop to think about it; just make the list.*

- *Add three more items to the list.*

Improvisation, Inc.

- *If you did not come up with ten items for this list very quickly, try using the game Word for Word that you learned earlier. For example, try saying, "A way I would like to grow in developing my creativity skills is to [snap-word, snap-word, snap]."*

- *Add five more items to your list.*

- *Look over the completed list of fifteen or more ways in which you would like to develop your creativity. Quickly circle seven that seem the most important to you. Be sure to do this quickly.*

- *Of the seven items you have circled, pick four and write them on a different sheet of paper. If you are not good at writing things down, you may wish to use a tape recorder for the next instructions.*

- *Consider each circled item and ask the question, "What must I do to grow in this area?" Use the technique Word for Word, as described above, to answer this question at least three times about each item.*

- *When you have written or recorded three answers in response to each item, answer the question in regard to each item one more time, honestly seeking a new, simple, creative, and thoughtful answer.*

- *Write your new answer; now write it again with your left hand instead of your right—or with your right hand if you are left-handed.*

SOME OTHER THINGS TO DO

Try the *Word for Word* exercise while speaking into a tape recorder. Do the exercise while standing up and walking around and stamping your feet. Do it again with your eyes closed. Do it while walking backward. Do it while turning in a circle. Try it some new way you invent. A breakthrough is available if you work for it. If you have been working for half an hour or more, it will help to take a break.

The exercise has nearly infinite possibilities and applications. As you work in The Improv it is a good idea for you to keep a list of key issues for later exploration. Your list should include personal development issues and issues involved in the development of your business. Review your list regularly.

Improvisation is the art of communication—first, last and forever. It is a state of mind and a state of consciousness different from the normal. It takes time, work, playfulness, and discipline to begin using Improv techniques effectively and efficiently. The exercises and games are progressive and build on one another. Your willingness to play develops a further willingness to play. Playing develops skills. The development of the skills makes you want to play more. The more you want to play, the more you will want to play with other people. You can begin using Improv principles and practices now, slowly and step by step, for your immediate benefit. The following chapters will help you make this tool your own. Proceed and you can open the doors to your deepest creativity.

CHAPTER TWO

Open the Doors to Your Creativity

The first requirement in the use of Improvisation is *being completely in the present moment*—to learn and change by opening your own mind and spirit. This is also probably the only requirement in its use. Everything else is merely a guideline, a suggestion, an idea, or a technique. It is not a matter of being an open-minded person. Ask yourself whether you are currently attending to the doors and windows to your mind and soul. Are you actively engaged in a discipline that will open you and keep you open to the current moment? It is said that, to walk in another's shoes, one must first remove his or her own shoes. I suggest that you start out barefooted and see where it leads.

Organizational development for groups, for networks, and for individuals begins with opening doors—to the personal creative initiative that can enhance all efforts in human organization, to new ideas and methods that create group participation and encourage crews, teams, and project groups. Opening doors between people is a key to communication. Before we can learn or teach anything new, we must have openings.

Consider the simple act of putting something new into a container. The container must be open. If you are careless, you may have to deal with spills or a broken container.

Broken containers may no longer be able to hold the "something new." Try to open a soap bubble to put in air. Try to put a thought into a soap bubble without confining the thought.

The mind is like a partially closed container when enmeshed in patterned responses. It is often lithe and loose when open. It also can be as fragile as a soap bubble or brittle as glass. For a bubble to bounce, it must be filled with something hard, as is a golf ball. When the mind or the heart is closed, there is confusion and stress, especially about "new" stuff we don't know about.

"If I don't know I don't know

I think I know.

If I don't know I know

I think I don't know." [3]

R. D. LAING

NEW STUFF IS A CAUSE OF CONFUSION AND A SOURCE OF CREATIVITY

A sign on a door says, "I don't think I am here. If not, I have gone to look for myself. If I get back before I return, please let me know where I am so that I may assist you as soon as I am there."

A note is left for a friend saying, "I was here but you were gone. Now you are here and I am gone."

These thoughts are like Zen teaching stories or "koans." They are designed to create a confusion of possibilities to help you reach for another level of listening, experiencing, observing, and understanding. The confusion of possibilities is a foundation upon which The Improv operates. If I lead you or your organization to the confusion of possibilities, the doors to creativity will open.

R. D. LAING, *KNOTS*. NEW YORK: PENGUIN BOOKS, 1970.

Because creativity happens in the state of confusion, you must learn to take small, successful, incremental steps in the direction you want. Because people are so wonderfully complex and rich in possibility, the size of the steps they take is relative to what is happening in the present moment.

After creating an open mind and spirit, you must strive to become completely aware of the present moment. You must try to work and act in the present moment only.

Stay in the Present Moment

Being completely in the present moment is a key feature of the use of Improvisation as a business tool. Study and practice are required to learn how to stay in the present moment. This is the same kind of "being in the present moment" that the pilot of a military jet must achieve. It's not just a "be here, now" abstract, philosophical construct. It suggests a focus on the realities of functioning in the current moment—at high speed, high altitude, high tech, high concentration, striving for Olympic quality.

This kind of attention must be given to an infant in your care, to a child who is talking to you—the kind of attention you like best when it is being given to you.

Get into the Present Moment

In order to use Improvisation most effectively, it is best not to assume that you are operating completely in the present moment. It is good to seek a physical discipline to help you avoid pursuing a purely mental perspective. Dr. Ginny Whitelaw tells us that the mind learns from the body.[4] If you already engage in a discipline that gets you into and keeps you in the present moment, revisit your art and consider your practice in the light of Improvisation.

Your ability to communicate well is part of your ability to learn and grow. Some disciplines that can be used to keep you in the present moment include: active meditation, craft building, physical arts, many sports, a number of forms of physical training, many martial arts forms, making music, singing, dancing, and all kinds of fixing, building, making, and growing things. Other recommendations include physical prayer—prayer

FOR A FULL EXPLORATION OF THIS IDEA AND A VARIETY OF EXERCISES THAT WILL AID IN ACHIEVING THE COMPLETE STATE OF BEING IN THE PRESENT MOMENT, SEE THE MARVELOUS WORK OF DR. GINNY WHITELAW IN HER BOOK *BODYLEARNING*. NEW YORK: PENGUIN PUTNAM, 1998.

while walking, biking, canoeing, and so forth—focused community service, active participation in a hobby with children around, and practice, practice, practice.

Most really deep training requires that you periodically use and learn new methods and techniques and that you add them to your practices. Your disciplines must be effective, easy to get to, clear, simple, and something you do really often—perhaps every day. It is nice if your disciplines are personally rewarding; better health, self-defense awareness, increased balance skills, improved interpersonal communication skills, strength, confidence, better self-awareness are all available from such practices. However, personal gain is not a requirement.

> ### KARMA YOGA
> Karma Yoga is a meditation form in which you may achieve a high state of consciousness by performing menial labor in aid of the general good, while focusing only on both the fullness of the moment and the emptiness of the moment. If this can be done anonymously, it is even more valuable than simple personal gain.

EXERCISE IN THE PRESENT MOMENT

This is an exercise for developing the skill of clearing your thoughts and bringing yourself completely into the present moment. The first time you do this exercise it may take as long as an hour. It has three phases. Variations on this exercise may be used to review and analyze various aspects of your life and work, your future, your goals, and your objectives.

If you do not have the time to do this now, bookmark it and make a commitment to try it soon. If you decide not to do the exercise right now, try the following instead: Put the book down and give someone a gift of a laugh. Another alternative is to call someone close to you and say just how much you appreciate him or her. Better yet, tell someone how much you love him or her.

USING THE EXERCISE

Sit in a quiet place and read the instructions below. It can be even more effective if you have someone else read the instructions to you. I encourage you to

Improvisation, Inc.

record the instructions on tape and then go through the exercise, rather than having to read the instructions aloud. Keep the tape for future use.

Some Working Rules

- *Do not interrupt the exercise once you have begun.*

- *Do not stop to take notes nor to focus on any particular thought that comes to mind.*

- *Always start the exercise from the beginning and complete it in a single, uninterrupted session.*

- *If you find you must stop, take care of the matter that came to mind and then ask yourself how you came to be interrupted, even though you were going to set aside enough time before starting.*

N O T E

This exercise is a great first step in bringing yourself completely into the current moment so that you may do a review of your life or any aspect of your life or business. However, it is very important to note that this is not a "life review" process.

Get set to record the session from "Beginning the Exercise; Releasing the Past." Watch out for notes that tell you what to do. At first the instructions will be very detailed. As you proceed, how often you repeat the process will be left up to you. You may use more or fewer repetitions depending on your purposes and progress.

BEGINNING THE EXERCISE; RELEASING THE PAST

* * Begin recording. * *

Sit with your eyes closed, your legs uncrossed, and your hands neither clasped nor touching. There should be nothing in your lap or in your hands.

Relax for a moment while you breathe in deeply, then breathe out slowly. . . . Breathe in deeply, breathe out slowly. . . . Breathe in deeply, breathe out slowly.

If anything comes to mind and does not immediately go away, acknowledge the thought and release it. Take a deep breath and, in your mind, say, "Thank you," then move on to another thought—breathe, release, and move on.

Now let's explore.

- *Think for a moment about what has been happening around you during the last few moments. Whatever comes to mind, let the thought go.*

- *For a moment consider anything that has happened during the past fifteen to thirty minutes. If nothing comes to mind, that's all right. As thoughts come forth, release them quickly with a "Thank you."*

- *Think about something that has occurred during the past hour or two. Release these thoughts. Move on.*

- *Consider any thoughts about things you have done or thought during this whole day—from the time you woke, through the day up to this moment. Breathe, release, and move on.*

- *Now allow the events of last evening to come into your mind. Any thoughts? Any memories? Now just let these thoughts and responses go.*

- *Think back to yesterday. What happened yesterday? Now think of anything that happened during the past few days. Remember last weekend. Breathe, release, and move on.*

- *Consider last week. What comes to your mind when you think about last week? Anything at all from the beginning of last week until now. Breathe, release, and move on (BRM).*

* * It is up to you whether you record the Coaching Notes or not. * *

COACHING NOTES
Breathe, Release and Move On. Make the sounds of saying BRM, BBRRM, BBRRRMM, BBBBRRRRRRMMMM aloud. It is fun to add a guttural "g" sound between the R and M (BBBRRRgggMMMMMM). (Remember that this book is also about having fun.)

* * Start recording. * *

- *What has occurred during the past two weeks? What has happened during the past month that still comes to mind?*

- *Has there been any event in the last few months that has a place in your mind just now?*

- *Quickly review the past year, season by season. Is there any other thought that comes to mind to be honored for a moment and then released? Note that any thought is worthy of thanks and blessing for its presence and its reminder.*

- *As you consider the past year, think about special events or special moments. Bring to mind Christmas, Hanukkah, Kwanzaa, Ramadan, New Year's Day, Easter, Valentine's Day, Memorial Day, summer vacation, Labor Day, Thanksgiving, Halloween, Michaelmas, birthdays, and anniversaries. Consider them, breathe in and out, let them go.*

- *Breathe in deeply. Breathe out slowly. Breathe in deeply. Breathe out slowly. Breathe in deeply. Breathe out slowly.*

- *It is time to take a look at the previous year. Is there anything that comes to mind?*

- *Let the time frames become a little fuzzy. Let the thoughts go without worrying whether they were last year or the year before or in the summer or the winter. Keep breathing slowly.*

- *From the past couple of years what comes to mind? Let the thoughts come quickly and release them quickly. Fill in the blanks in the next sentences:*

  "Over the past five years I can think of. . . ."

  "If I think back over the past ten years, I remember. . . ."

- *Let the thoughts arise on their own. Let them go. Think back to graduate school . . . back to college . . . back to your first job . . . back to high school . . . when you were a small child.*

- *Relax. Breathe in. Release it. Relax. Breathe in. Release. Relax, relax, relax, relax completely. Keep breathing. Move more quickly now. Stay only a moment in each place. You are not exploring. You are mind surfing, head gliding, flying though time.*

- *Do you have any remaining thoughts from your past, your family's past history, or human memory that can be brought to the surface for a brief look and a quick farewell? Think about them now and let them go.*

- *Relax and breathe for a moment. Let the past go completely and fully. When your mind is clear of the past, it will be time to come back to the present for a moment.*

* * Stop recording for a moment. * *

COACHING NOTES

Please do not stop the process now. If you feel you must stop now, when you return please go to the beginning of the exercise and do the whole thing over again from the start.

I will never know whether you have followed these instructions, but you will know. If you do not follow these instructions, you may wake up one morning at 3:00 a.m. saying, "Oh, no! I cheated and lied to myself."

You have been through the process of breathing, relaxing, and letting go, so you know how to BRM (breathe, relax, and move on). I will not repeat the BRM instructions during this next exercise phase. It is up to you to take the reins and do it for yourself. The instructions are presented in terms of time frames. Move quickly and smoothly, with a sense of playfulness and exploration.

RELEASING THE FUTURE

* * Begin recording. * *

- *Do not open your eyes. Do not look around. Get ready for another journey.*

- *What are you thinking about doing after you finish this exercise? During the next couple of hours? How about later tonight?*

- *What have you planned for tomorrow? Who do you have to see? What do you have to do? Consider the coming weekend. What will be going on then?*

- *What about next week? How about the next couple of weeks. What about next month? Think: "During the next two months I must. . . ."*

- *What season, holiday, devotion, or celebration comes next? When is your birthday? What does it bring to mind? What is an anniversary of any kind coming up?*

Improvisation, Inc.

- *What are you going to do next year? How about the year after that?*

- *Fill in the blanks.*

  "During the next five years I hope to. . . ."

  "In ten years I would like to. . . ."

"Twenty years from now I would like to be. . . ."

"Before my life is over it would be nice to. . . ."

"For my children there should be. . . ."

"My grandchildren will need. . . ."

"The next generation really needs to. . . ."

"Far into the future I know that there will be. . . ."

- *Let all these thoughts go. If they are really important, they will come back. For now, just let them go.*

- *Take a deep breath. Relax. . . . Relax. . . . Relax. . . . Relax. Prepare for the next journey in which we will explore the present.*

EXPLORING THE PRESENT

- *Keep your eyes closed for a few moments and slowly begin to increase your awareness of your immediate surroundings.*

- *Feel the temperature. Is there a breeze? Can you feel the air on your arms or face or hands?*

- *Without using your hands, feel the clothing on your body. Can you feel your glasses or your hair on your face or neck? Feel the weight of your body. Feel your shoes on your feet.*

- *Listen to the sounds around you. Try to hear the obvious sounds first: air conditioning, voices, traffic, the sound of your own breathing, the little noises around you.*

- *Can you feel the air moving in and out of your mouth or nose? Are your teeth together or apart? Can you feel your tongue in your mouth?*

- *Now notice any tension you may have in your neck, your hands, your jaws, your back, the rest of your body.*

- *Can you smell anything pleasant or unusual? Can you smell anything at all? Can you feel anything else?*

- *Now, very slowly, open your eyes and look around. Look around the room. Look up and down. Look from side to side. See the ceiling . . . the floor. Look at your hands and arms.*

- *Look around again and find something you have not noticed before.*

- *Breathe. Relax. Let go of any thoughts you have right now.*

- *At this moment you may wish to rub your hands together or slide your feet back and forth on the floor in order to bring yourself back into normal consciousness and into this room at this time on this date. Breathe in your surroundings and let yourself be in this present moment completely.*

- *Keep breathing.*

- *You can set your present level of awareness into your physical being. Rub the back of one hand with the fingers of the other. Repeat this same small action at a future time to help you return to this level of feeling completely in the present moment. If you have fully engaged in this exercise, you may be more fully aware of the present moment than normal. Notice the feeling. Relax into it. Choose to be here. Revel in being completely here.*

* *Stop recording. * *

LET'S DEBRIEF

If this exercise was hard to do, confusing, jumbled, or just did not make much sense right now, please do not give up. If you have never done this sort of work, there may be a lot of housecleaning that needs to be done. After you have had an opportunity to consider the thoughts and emotions that did come up, try doing the whole exercise again. Your next effort will be easier and will take less time. It will continue to become faster and easier each time you try it. You will become more proficient, and the process will give you new insights at new levels each time you practice.

As you work with this idea and this exercise, you will be able to get yourself into the here and now more quickly using less of the exercise. Eventually you will be able to simply say something like, "Clear the past. Clear the future. Notice your surroundings," touch the back of your own hand, and you will become truly "present."

There are few rules to opening the doors to your creative self. If you are earnestly on the path to these doors, you will go through some levels of confusion. You will need to work hard to get yourself completely into the present moment. Working with all the doors and windows open is the essential element of creativity and of The Improv. If you do not have the discipline to help you do this, use the above exercises as often as necessary. Committing to such a discipline will help you to learn and to practice the basic Improv principles.

CHAPTER THREE

Basic Improv Principles

Community and *communication* can be seen as interchangeable. In both our individual differences can be set aside in favor of a higher order. Without community or communication, our focus tends to be centered too much within our "selves." With strong community, we can garble our speech, misspeak our words, and stumble across our ideas, and allowances will be made in deference to the sense of community. Without community, elements of disbelief and misconception interfere with our ability to communicate. The Improv itself is composed of values that create strengths of community among the people participating. The practices and principles of Improvisation create strengths of communication among the people playing. As we play together, we grow together.

Many people have explored the use of Improv tools and methods in a wide variety of non-theatrical applications. Some who have adapted Improv methodology to non-performance venues have expressed thoughts about how and why it works. A few have used it in business settings. A few books and articles have documented uses of Improvisation outside the theater. The principles I present here have proven valuable to me, over time, in developing creativity and using Improv methods in business and professional settings.

FOUR IMPROV PRINCIPLES

I find these ideas so compelling that I call them *principles*. With Improvisation, all "rules" are subject to challenge, scrutiny, and laughter. The principles I propose here are grounded in teaching Improv skills to business and professional people with no theater or performance background. These principles are as valuable for professional presenters and trainers as for experienced Improv players. They also apply to real situations.

The best Improvisation happens when there are four basic Improv principles at work. This is so whether you are working with executive skills, general management problems, organizational development, personal development, or training and education.

First principle:	Second principle:	Third principle:	Fourth principle:
You must strive to come completely into the present moment.	You must strive to become completely honest with yourself.	You must learn to become honest with at least one other person.	You must put your work out for public view.

First Improv Principle

You must strive to come completely into the present moment. My first Improv principle is a key to what makes Improvisation work in complex and real settings. We are in the *here and now* when we are most effective, most clear, most alive, most joyful, and most fun. It is also the state in which we can make the greatest change, fight the best fight, do the best work, take in the most information, and enjoy the greatest retention of new information.

The very fact of being completely in the present moment is a creative act in itself. New thoughts, new ideas, new solutions, new creations, new pathways, new images, new visions, new directions, new programs, new devices, new relationships, new applications, and more can come from the process of simply being completely in the present moment.

A STORY

A friend of mine once had the great pleasure of meeting Margaret Mead, one of the most extraordinary anthropologists of our century. The setting was the non-public area of a large meeting hall where Ms. Mead had spoken to several thousand people. My friend spoke with her for about five minutes and never forgot the experience. He said, "She was completely with me. It seemed that there was no one else in the world, she had nowhere else to go, no one to see, nothing else to do, and there was nothing else going on. I was the center of the universe." His eyes were a little shiny as he remembered the experience of being with someone who was completely present in the moment.

Others are very good at being aware when we are *not* present with them. Few, however, will mention the problem. One can verify this with children. Little ones will whine and howl to get our focused attention. Nine-year-olds will tell us truths about ourselves if we are somewhere else when dealing with them. Adolescents will write us off or even become dangerous to themselves and others in an atmosphere in which adults are "absent" in their presence. They do this even while doing all they can to drive adults away.

In business, it has been noted that one of the first and most important reasons for job dissatisfaction is the feeling that "no one is listening," that "people are not really there for me."

In handling customers, if you are completely present with the client it is possible to say, "no" and yet to retain both the customer and the customer's goodwill. In the same setting a "yes," given in an absent or vacant spirit, can lose both.

To say you want to live or work in the present moment and actually living in the moment can be two different things. Getting there (here) may require discipline and hard work. It need not be so hard; yet if it is hard, that is certainly normal. It is also worth the work.

Second Improv Principle

You must strive to become completely honest with yourself. This is a tricky principle. Personal honesty is a private matter. This discussion may be merely a doorway into a lifetime of exploration. Only *we* know our own motives and motivations. Only *you* know whether you are being honest with yourself.

Many life struggles come from not being honest, first with ourselves—and then with others—about our own errors and weaknesses. Real honesty requires that we look at the world with true eyes. When we do this we often see things that we do not wish to see. Our world also sometimes seems filled with inequity and corruption, stupidity and error, meanness and obstinacy, ignorance and violence. Often we close ourselves to these truths in order to protect ourselves from such harsh realities.

But there are other truths as well. The world is also filled with wonder and delight. There is kindness and compassion, there are miracles and saints, there is laughter and joyfulness. In order to maintain our sense of truth, we must look at both sides of everything and seek to understand the balance between chaos and order. We must do this when considering our own balance as well.

To use Improvisation to its best advantage we need to try to overcome all these influences and pressures and work on being as honest with ourselves as possible. Being honest with yourself begins with operating in the current moment.

NOTE

- *We hold to the basic rule that anything being done is being done for the first time.*

- *We cannot use an idea nor a "line" that is not being generated by the current event.*

- *As leaders we must demonstrate this value and we must lead our participants in this direction.*

Improvisation is a uniquely human event, as is any complex communication. It helps us to look at and understand ourselves as human beings. We need to allow that during any event we may be afraid or elated, we may be confused or inspired, we may be right or wrong. We must strive to be available to these truths, and we must seek them and act on the knowledge that we are human as well. One of the most powerful comments from people who have done Improv work is the statement, "I have learned that it is OK to make mistakes! It is *not* OK to ignore them."

Improvisation does not require that you become a completely honest person immediately and suddenly. Nor does it assume that you are a dishonest person now. But it does require that you explore and develop your ability to stay totally honest with the moment at hand. This is true whether you are a facilitator, a director, a student, or a player.

The deep concepts of being true to yourself and of being consistent within yourself are the subject of almost all the religions and philosophies of the world. For The Improv, all you must do is strive to be honest about what you are doing in the present moment and not bring in words from the past.

Third Improv Principle

You must learn to become completely honest with at least one other person. We live in societies that tacitly condone "little white lies." Sometimes we are allowed a little lie, to be kind or to protect one another. Sometimes we tell little lies to ease our own paths or to get our own way. We expect our government leaders to withhold certain kinds of information and often to compromise their own personal values in favor of the general good. Sometimes this is for the sake of "national security," sometimes it is for public safety management, and sometimes it is simply outright dishonesty. In business we are under many constraints in openness and "hard line honesty" due to the existence of business operating secrecy. Certain meetings must be held in secrecy, and certain information cannot be shared with a work force, the general public, or competing organizations. A lot of information must be released in portions over time in order not to place either the organization or its people at a disadvantage. Laws of disclosure do not allow us to share our joy at good fortune if doing so constitutes insider trading.

Being honest with one another is also a general life principle. It would be lovely if we could be completely honest with all people at all times. It seems, however, that this is simply not practical nor possible in all situations. When there is a real emergency, especially if there are young children present, we must often hide the truth, monitor our words, and inhibit our emotions in order to protect the people in our care. Sometimes great honesty could hurt us personally. Telling an armed robber that we think he or she is a jerk or where the jewels are kept might not be in our best interest. It is probably not best to share too many personal truths with our own supervisors and managers. When others irritate us due merely to differences in style, it is not always necessary to tell them so—and to do so may actually be harmful to those concerned.

However, many systems suggest that complete honesty with at least one other person is a path to personal development and correction of error. The Catholic church has advanced the value of confession for a very long time. Twelve-step programs all advocate honesty with at least one individual. Having a friend to tell about the trials and tribulations of our truths is a wondrous thing. At the least a person can become completely honest with God or Spirit in the form of prayer. Possible confidants are a spouse or a best friend or any person who will support your efforts to achieve the goal of achieving honesty with at least one other person.

Find some confidants, people with whom you can be completely honest. The greater the number of people you have in this category, the better will be your Improvisation. I also think honesty is related to happiness. Whoever has the least to hide has the most to share.

There is a difference between permanent confidants and temporary confidants in Improvisation. The Improv principle is that you must learn to be honest with *one other person*. The first candidate for this position is a person with whom you are working at this time, the most closely, the most personally. If you are lecturing, choose at least one member of the audience, if only in your mind. The next-best candidate is anyone among the people with whom you are currently working. In the Improv theater, this is the person who is on the stage with you right now.

When managing or teaching with Improvisation, it is sometimes possible to recruit a specific member of your audience to serve this function temporarily. It may be that you will need to recruit someone in private or bring an ally with you for this purpose in special cases. In any case there must be at least one other with whom you are learning to be honest during the Improv experience.

Fourth Improv Principle

You must put your work out for public view. Improvisation is based in activity. It has intellectual components, yet it cannot be done entirely in the mind. At the same time, Improvisation is a thoughtful process that requires great personal exploration that cannot be accomplished in private.

The Improv manager and the Improv facilitator must stand up in front of others and engage them in the exercises. This is the core of "participant-centered training" and of participant-centered change and development as promoted by training pioneer Bob Pike.[5] Without interaction with the outside world, all experience can be self-managed, and therefore ignored, stifled, or redirected from within. Thus the possible changes in behavior can be lost or veiled in apparent change.

When you plan a process, you bring order to its development and can accomplish much more than you could with chaos. However, a plan, by definition, automatically limits the product. The perfect plan perfectly executed will give you what you expected or hoped. A plan will give you more only if there is a component allowing for the unknown within. This tactic is similar to Improvisation, yet it will not usually invoke the same level of extraordinary possibilities.

This does not mean that you can avoid work and preparation. It just means that you have to use the Improv process to do the Improv process, so you have to put your work out into public view.

BOB PIKE, *CREATIVE TRAINING TECHNIQUES*. MINNEAPOLIS, MN: LAKEWOOD PUBLICATIONS, 1994.

Improvisation, Inc.

A STORY

One of my early Improv training contracts was for a regional meeting of professional executives of the Girl Scouts of America. They were gathered from nine Southern states at a prestigious and elegant meeting facility. I found myself at the crossroads of my Improv principles. I was being offered a large amount of money for a small amount of time with a very important client. The schedule gave me three months to "think" about it.

My first response was to begin planning. I started making outlines and listing the games I would use. I thought of clever lines and interesting progressions that would bring the crowd to me and to my work. After about three days I realized what I was doing and stopped. I was doing all this in private. I was doing everything Improvisation advises against.

Improvisation was my craft and I knew it inside and out. It did *not* include planning the steps I would take three months hence. From that moment forward when a thought came to me I gave it full consideration and then let it go. Each day I reminded myself that I was an Improv artist and pioneer with full knowledge of his craft. I could not decide what techniques would be most appropriate until the moment of the gathering. The people with whom I would be working would lead the way and it was my job to follow them. It became the core of my discipline.

In the meantime I also read every training manual the Girl Scout organization had available. I studied not only the professional adult training materials but the manuals and materials for the volunteers and the children. This was in addition to a review of my lifetime as a volunteer and my credentials as a professional volunteer organizer. By the time of the event my knowledge of the organization was as great as it could be for me as an outsider.

Upon meeting the participants on the morning of the presentation, my mind was a blank sheet. I did not know what would be the first words out of my mouth. I did not know where we could go. This resulted in participants operating at the highest levels of creative interpersonal cooperation. By the end of the day someone said, "We are working at a level that we usually do not get to until the end of the entire conference."

This was the result of staying in the current moment throughout the developmental and actual phases of the program. This was the result of building it while putting it out there. This was the result of following "Improv principles."

A PHILOSOPHY OF IMPROVISATION

My research sample is small in terms of the human population. My protocols are not written. My research is not finished. However, my experience with improvisational management and business Improv principles has included work with around five thousand individuals. Counting larger gatherings, the number I have observed has come to perhaps 30,000. Time and again I have come to this working philosophy: "With some assistance, everyone can be spontaneous and creative, and everyone can love it when it happens."

The following is offered as a way to think that will help you learn and develop the skills of improvisational management.

THOUGHTS

Improvisation is a discipline. It can be taught.
Improvisation is a state of mind. It can be learned.
Improvisation is a tool. If used correctly it always works.
Improvisation is an ancient art form.
The Etruscans did it first.
Improvisation is a process.
It works in steps, one at a time, over time.
Improvisation is an art.
It takes desire, practice, and experimentation.
Improvisation is a technique, not a thing of itself.
It is a way of doing things.
Improvisation is a craft.
It has rules that will produce desired results
if they are accepted.
Improvisation is a frame of reference.
One can learn by watching,
by thinking, and by doing.
Improvisation is a science.
It has predictable elements and
verifiable and reproducible results.
Improvisation is a way of being.
It is a way of being present in the moment
while being externally focused.
Improvisation is a gift.
Improvisation is a relationship.
It is a relationship with oneself and with others.
It is a gift given and received and given again.
Improvisation is a natural event
for all conscious beings.
Improvisation just is.

As a general rule, it is not true that the ends justify the means. Nor is it always true that the means will achieve the ends desired. The true balance of life comes from understanding the fact that the means and the ends are all of one fabric. Improv form and spirit are as important as the goals or objectives of the practitioner. This truth is at the heart of Improvisation.

As you explore and practice the work of improvisational management, you will discover your own principles and thoughts. As you earnestly implement Improv practices in your business and in your daily life, you will see and hear the changes in yourself and in the people with whom you work. As you discover more and more practical applications of Improv methods, you will find community and communication growing before your eyes. It will take work and play to achieve these results. It will take earnest, honest, self-evaluation and organizational evaluation to walk this path. If you apply the principles and think the thoughts, Improvisation will work for you. You must also seek more deeply into the look and the feel of The Improv at work.

CHAPTER FOUR

The Improv at Work

Improvisation is more than a free-form, free-for-all. It is more than "flying by the seat of your pants," more than making things up as you go along. There are guidelines to follow, axioms to learn, suggestions to be considered, work and preparation to be accomplished if it is to work. Mental preparation is required. You need to know your audience. You must know what you want to accomplish. There is even planning to do.

You must do much of your planning and training before you begin the Improv activity in order to be prepared to make full use of the communication and community being developed.

A very important element of planning and training is involved in exploring and developing human feelings. If you do not feel like learning, you probably will not learn all that much. If you do not feel like changing your behavior, you probably will not change your behavior. If there is not passion in your goals and visions, there may be a lackluster performance. If there is little feeling, there tends to be little creativity in the person or the organization.

Keith Johnstone considers the frame of mind required for good Improvisation to be a special, separate, and distinct state of consciousness. He calls this state of consciousness "Impro."[6] This state is filled with feelings and emotions. "Impro" is achieved by entering into Improv discipline with a full commitment and effort. To get yourself ready for excellent Improv management, it is a good idea to review your feeling—both your emotions and your sensory perceptions.

6

KEITH JOHNSTONE, *IMPRO, IMPROVISATION AND THE THEATRE*. ROUTLEDGE, NY: THEATRE ARTS BOOKS, 1979.

Understanding the role that the senses play in Improvisation may help you to understand their role in communication and organizational development in general.

THE PHYSICAL SENSES

Improvisation requires the use and activation of combinations of the senses. This is true of all exceptional work. When the Improv state is achieved, it tends to generate various and deep reflections in the participants. For this reason it becomes necessary to examine the feelings and to begin to engage the senses more fully and easily. It is good to engage in this process enthusiastically, for your own sake as well as for the development of the people with whom you are working.

Engaging more full and complete feelings is partly a matter of using a number of senses at a time. The more senses involved in an event, the more completely and deeply it may be experienced. The five or six or seven senses that humans use are basic, and expansions of synergy must be considered as well.

To See

"To see" is a complex and miraculous event.

See: "[ME: seen; French, AU, *seon*; akin to OHG *sehan* to see and perhaps to Latin, *sequi*, to follow. To perceive by the eye, to perceive or detect as by sight, to have experience of, to come to know, to be the setting or time of, to form a mental picture of, to perceive the meaning or importance of, to be aware of or imagine as a possibility, examine or watch, read, to read of, to attend as a spectator, to take care of or provide for. . . ."[7]

- *To see* includes internal vision, with mental pictures and movies, symbols, and recognition.

- *To see* deals partially with memory: what we saw and what we thought we saw, what we think we thought we saw, what we would like to think we thought we saw, what we would like to think we thought we may have seen.

7

MERRIAM WEBSTER'S COLLEGIATE DICTIONARY, 10TH EDITION. SPRINGFIELD, MA: MERRIAM WEBSTER, INC., 1993.

- *To see* has a future tense that is linked to memory. What my experience tells me that I think I might see is what I believe comes next.

- In the past tense, "been there, seen that." *To see* has a wondrous and blank past tense: "Never saw it. I have no memory of that person, place, thing, number, movie, date, formula, question, book." *To see* may be influenced by others: "Did you see what I saw?"

To have seen, in a past tense in the French, is expressed in the term *vu*. *Deja vu* means "seen before"—the sense that one has seen a thing before. *Praesta vu* means "never seen," suddenly noticing something that has been there all along, yet was never seen by you.

JUST FOR FUN

Deja you: "Haven't we met before?"

Deja who: "I'm sorry, you are. . . ?"

Deja do: You know this one. You get out the front door or into your car and remember that you have forgotten something. You go back and get it, and as you go out the door again you say, "Didn't I just do this?"

Deja clu: "I haven't a single idea regarding your comments."

Deja boo: "That's really scary again."

From flashes of light to flashes of word fancy, the idea of "to see" brings up a rather large number of factors and elements of its own. The more of these we engage and consider, the more fully we "see" and the more fully we feel. The Improv process works with and engages sight.

To Hear

"To hear" is a lot like "to see," with different mechanisms. To hear can be thought of as a branch of touch, as hearing is done with the feeling and decoding of vibrations.

The sound transmission medium itself is one of the miracles of the world. The ability of biological creatures to use sound and its dynamics as a feedback device is astounding.

The diversity and range of hearing is an epic adventure of its own. From bats using ultrasonics, to dogs hearing above the range of human hearing, to the songs of whales audible over hundreds of miles, to the fabulous extensions of hearing in recording and electronic transmission, sound surrounds all we do.

Although it is not yet possible to create a picture in perfect holographic detail, a perfect recording and reproduction of a symphony is very near. It is the nature of sound to be reproduced and mimicked. We can make many sounds that are close enough to fool humans and other animals. We have not yet made pictures that can actually fool an animal.

We talk to ourselves. We hope this is internal sound. My friend, Jeff Justice, a professional speaker and consultant, is known to ask a crowd, "Who here speaks to him- or herself?" When some do not respond, he says, "Those of you who failed to raise your hands, didn't you hear a little voice saying, 'Not me. I don't talk to myself.'" Our internal voices can allow for and encourage laughter. They can also encourage depression and separation and other foolishness and fantasy.

Sometimes we talk with many voices. Sometimes we talk back to ourselves. Sometimes we talk back in what we think is silence, yet it is audible to all around. The power of what we say and hear is tied to the foundation of civilization. The difference between, "What did you say?" and "What did you mean by that?" can be the difference between negotiation and war.

"To hear" is at least as complex as "to see." The Improv manager must strive to engage the sense of sound.

To Listen

Listening is very, very important. If people are not effectively listening to one another, things do not work very well. You must confirm, think about, and remember what is being said in order to listen well.

In the Improv structures, players may experience the effects of not listening and can realize, in public, the results of their own failure to listen. Some players may actually observe themselves in the act of not listening and may come to know the silence that results. Some of the people begin to feel the "not listening" going on in themselves and in others.

In the Improv form, the underlying nature of the game comes back to the participant and generates a true interest in listening more carefully—with all the senses. It is good to hear our internal voices tout the values of listening for all aspects of management and learning.

To Touch

The sense of touch is a key to the reason that Improvisation works. When we are affected by our surroundings, we often say we were "deeply touched"; people who walk to the beat of odd drummers are sometimes thought of as "touched"; being lightly brushed by providence or good luck is to be "touched" by an angel.

Touch is personal. No other person can actually feel what we do. Empathy is as close as we can come. Touch is both direct and indirect—both giving and taking. It operates at both a gut level and a mind level—somatic and intuitive. It is emotional and rational ("I feel a tack in my foot" versus "I feel sad"), proactive ("I take your hand in mine"), reactive ("I feel your hand on my arm"), specific and general, internal and empathetic. Touch can encompass dozens of responses. When the maximum number of these aspects of our sense of touch are engaged, our feelings are more powerful and more clear.

Improvisation helps to activate the sense of touch. Improv systems work at a speed that requires more than mere thinking about solutions. It is necessary to activate other channels and systems. Activating feelings helps us work at speeds equal to or faster than thought.

To Smell, to Taste

The senses of smell and of taste are related to those of sight, hearing, and touch. The vast arena of recollections dominated by smell and taste can fling us around in time and space. We all are aware of smells that may take us far away in an instant. Try smelling crayons without recalling your childhood. The mention of certain foods can cause involuntary salivation and journeys of the mind to past places. As The Improv engages us fully, it heightens our senses. The forms help us activate our senses. Full use of the senses brings us into current time.

To Sense Surrounding Space

Another human sensory field is known as *proxemics* or *kinesthetics*. This sense tells us when someone is looking over our shoulder. It is also experienced as stage sense or sports sense, whereby players automatically stand in balance with one another and the area of the stage or move automatically in concert on the playing field.

In Aikido this aspect of human awareness is called *maai,* the art of being at the perfect distance from another for the purpose at hand. It has aspects of sight, sound, touch, and smell. This sense is at work in elevators, where people automatically face forward and divide up the exact amount of available space more or less equally. We do this also when waiting in lines.

As we enter The Improv state with all of our senses working together, literally dozens of sources of information and action become available to us. The more senses we activate, the more alive and in the moment we become and the more our learning and development stay with us. The more alive and in the moment we become, the more we can be with others, the more we can engage one another on the same quests. Our plans and organizations work better and more efficiently when the emotions are fully engaged.

THE SPIRITUAL SENSE

Beyond the physical senses is a realm of exploration that adds a new dimension to all aspects of The Improv. The sense of spirit is vital to complete understanding of the look and the feel of Improvisation.

The nature of Improvisation suggests that you work in the spirit of play and fun and safety for all. To understand the meaning of this, we must look into the nature of the spirit and the spiritual aspect of human interactions. When we bring people together, more happens than meets the eye.

Very little in our world is truly known to us. Visible light is only a fraction of the electromagnetic spectrum. Sound that is audible to humans involves a small percentage of the available vibrations. Our internal structures are out of sight. Our cells are to be seen only with extraordinary optics. Atomic elements can only be seen with even more extraordinary optics, and subatomic particles are not within the arena of sight except by the paths they trace in cloud chambers and the minds of mathematicians.

We certainly cannot look into tomorrow nor into the heart nor mind of a friend. We cannot see behind ourselves, except in a reflection. The thoughts of others are not ours to know. Our thoughts and fears and hopes and dreams are all beyond vision.

This leads us to the realization that a large part of what we deal with is out of our sight, but in the level of available energy, of invention and creativity. It is also at the invisible spiritual level that the greatest resources exist. Spirit is the source of everything. It may be the only place in which anything really exists.

In view of the resources in the realm of the spirit, we should practice our arts with some reverence. We need to be gentle and thankful for all our blessings. We should be forgiving of one another and of ourselves. Whether The Improv is a matter of the spirit or whether it is only a form in which spirit is revered means the same thing. With an understanding of the spiritual nature of all things, this art may help you to reach deeply into your sense of communication and organizational development and generate a truly creative approach to your work.

YES, AND . . .

"Yes, and . . ." refers to both verbal and mental responses to the suggestions, ideas, presence, opinions, and viewpoints of others. This subject is discussed here rather than in Chapter Nine about language because it touches a very subtle aspect of how we feel in a communication situation and how we encourage others to feel about our interactions. Always remember that the use of this phrase can enhance every aspect of your communication.

We will look at its opposite, "Yes, but . . .," first. When did you last hear someone use the expression, "Yes, but. . ."? These words are a common part of our speaking and communicating patterns. When did you last hear someone say, "Yes, and. . ."? Unless you are in a community skilled in Improv techniques, you probably will not hear these words at all.

Consider the message behind "Yes, but. . . ." As you may know, if you tell a computer "yes" and "no" at the same time you will hear an annoying little beep that means, "You have broken a rule of logic." I have my computer programmed so that my errors activate my son's voice saying, "Silly Daddy." That way I do not feel quite so cyberdumb when I make mistakes. In some circumstances you will experience a crash of a whole computer program, or your computer may lock down as it runs back and forth between the conflicting messages.

You may know that if you tell a child to stop and to go at the same time you will soon be dealing with confusion, frustration, and tears. The phrase, "Yes, but . . ." says yes and no at the same time. It is a *mixed message,* a positive and negative at the same moment. Mixed messages do not serve us well.

In the world of Improvisation, many advocate the use of "Yes, and . . ." as a standard response to all incoming messages. It is important for the phrase to become an automatic element of the verbal, mental, and emotional environment in which Improvisation is being used.

In some gatherings, this conversation can bring up a great deal of resistance. Telling people that a favorite phrase, unconscious as it may be, is a mixed message can be a serious challenge to their language skills. It can feel a lot like criticizing a person's accent or the way he or she is raising children. I have had participants defend the use of "yes, but . . ." as the only way to say something. It is one of the miracles of language that there is always more than one way to say anything.

USES OF "YES, AND . . ."

A conversation about this phrase can provide an opportunity to evaluate the effectiveness of a communication environment. If someone has an extraordinary amount of resistance to the idea, there are probably deeper problems in the group with which you are working.

The following exercise can help people to replace the words "Yes, but . . ." with the words "Yes, and. . . ." It can be simple and difficult at the same time.

EXERCISE IN USING "YES, AND . . ."

Have the participants mill about making simple statements to one another, with the requirement that all of their responses begin with "Yes, but. . . ." Then have the participants do the same thing, but respond with "Yes, and. . . ." Encourage people to go through the cycle at least four or five times. You may need to repeat and reinforce the instructions as you hear people saying things such as, "Yes, and, but . . ." or "Yes, uh, but, and. . . ." Listen carefully for people who may be avoiding following the instructions. This is different from *misunderstanding* the instructions.

Often the gathering will get the point almost immediately. In this case, briefly encourage the elimination of "Yes, but . . ." in favor of "Yes, and . . ." as a general practice. If there is resistance or difficulty during the exercise, spend some time in open discussion of the process and the feelings engendered by the words and the exercise.

You may try instituting "Yes, and . . ." hours in a given day or perhaps a whole

"Yes, and . . ." day in your organization. During these times the words "Yes, and . . ." must be the first words out of anyone's mouth in response to any idea, comment, or suggestion. If this is done playfully and in the spirit of Improvisation, it can make some real and positive differences in the ways in which people communicate.

A STORY

Once I worked with a conference center. The senior salesperson came to an Improv workshop. When asked if she thought the "Yes, and . . ." theory was clear, she said, "Yes, but it is not practical."

In her business, potential clients often complained about price. She felt that hearing a customer say, "Your prices are just too high" and responding with the words, "Yes, and . . ." was not acceptable.

Not long after the workshop, she had a very important prospective client call and say, "I am sorry your prices are just too high." There was a great deal on the line. She could not say what she wanted to, which was something like, "WHAT!!! Are you out of your mind? Do you have any idea what you are saying?"

She took a deep breath and stepped into The Improv. Her mind went blank as the words came forth: "Yes, and well, uh, if you consider the, uh, the value of our personal services, food, coffee, water, fruit, and ambiance and, uh, if you factor them into the price you will find, um, that our real cost per square foot is more than competitive."

The potential customer said, "I will look into it in those terms. Let me get back to you." He did the numbers, came back, and signed the contract. This woman now says, "Yes, and . .," if only in her own mind, to almost anything anyone says to her.

"You are an incredible fool!"

"Yes, and . . . let's talk about the word 'incredible.'"

LET'S DEBRIEF

The idea is that by first saying "Yes!" you acknowledge what has been said. You actually begin to create a positive atmosphere regarding the position of the other person.

You do not have to *agree* with the other person. You simply use the affirmative "Yes!"—indicating that the other person has made a statement and has a right to do so. Your next word is a commitment to add something. The word "and" commits you to something more that is an *addition* rather than a *substitution*.

I sincerely ask you to change your use of the language. When someone speaks to you about something with which you may disagree, take a breath and say, "Yes, and . . ." with the commitment to fill in the blank with something. I really just mean "something." Not something excellent, nor something noble, nor even something good and wise—just something. The wisdom and goodness and truth can come from the feeling that you are actively involved in creating a positive feeling in and around your organization. It is especially important to do this when you may disagree with the speaker or the circumstances or if the ideas being presented are new or different.

Imagine what life would be like if every time you spoke you were assured that there would be, first, an affirmation and, then, a commitment to add something to what you had to say. An environment dedicated to listening would be established—a feeling of positive cooperation.

The look and feel of Improvisation at work will lead you to your own philosophies of The Improv. It is an entire philosophy and way of life. The improvisational way of life is filled with emotion and passion. It is filled with perceptions of the senses. The ways of creativity are also filled with sensory perceptions. It is incumbent on you to explore and develop the emotions and senses as much as you can. You can use an Improv path to do this.

As an improvisational executive and manager, you will be served by promoting the values of being in the present moment and engaging the senses completely. You will explore and discover processes and work with gentleness. You will seek balance and develop listening skills; you will encourage speaking up, laughing, and delighting in differences; and you can gain a deep understanding of living in the spirit of the moment.

As you gain a full appreciation of this great art, you can begin to use Improv fundamentals for making greater connections with the people in your life and in your organization.

PART TWO

Improv Fundamentals

CHAPTER FIVE

Greater Connections with Others

Making greater connections with people is a primary product of the Improv path—actively exploring the uses of Improv techniques, theories, principles, ideas, suggestions, exercises, games, and tools. When working in business development situations, Improv methodology is effective in making subtle and fundamental connections. Over the years I have created a poem I call "My Improv Axioms." These axioms will be useful to you as an executive or a trainer, as a presenter or a manager. These thoughts can become vital to your organization, to you, and to the people around you.

As you read my Improv axioms, allow the words to bring your own images to mind. These ideas are presented in poem form because it is so easy to rush over ideas in a list. It is my hope that you will return again and again to read these axioms, both for the sound of the words and for the feeling of the ideas.

MY IMPROV AXIOMS

STRIVE TO BECOME

Strive to come completely into the
present in this precious moment.
Striving to stay here and now.

Attempt to be honest
completely with yourself,
honest, completely
with another.

Have you heard before,
or said or read,
considered, thought,
or noticed, an idea?
Then do not use it now.

Keep them clean and fresh,
your words and thoughts,
staying upon the high road,
the tougher road,
the road more fun.

Use the magic words
whenever you can,
"Yes, and" "Yes,
and," "Yes, and . . ."

Deny not. Say not no,
a thing called blocking.
Commit and give something
new to each new moment.

Think not, first. Act first.
Respond before reacting!
Act not as though
you did not hear, not see,
though maybe you did not.
Act not as though
you are confused,
even if you are.

Improvisation, Inc.

This works best
in games and play,
yet you must consider
how it applies to
real life as well.
Listen. **Listen**. *Listen.*
Listen. Listen. Listen.
Listen. Listen.

If you become too reckless,
your effort may die.
If you become too safe,
your effort may fall.
Give more
than you take
as you seek
balance.

Breathe.
Stretch your body,
mind, voice, and spirit.
Stop writing in your head.

Create relationships.
Seek not a laugh.
Seek laughter,
joy, fun, and light.
Avoid the pun.

Establish first,
who you are,
where you are, and
what you are doing.
The language of your body
composes most of what
you communicate.
Use it carefully.
Your presence
is a great deal of
what you say.
Express it freely.

Reach for the stars.
Should you fall short
you may merely
catch the moon.

A
risk
A path
A game
A technique
A path to trust
A methodology
A positive approach

An ancient theater art
A state of mind
A way of thinking
A frame of reference
A way of not thinking
A process
A pleasure
A discipline
A team effort
A living thing
A way of being
A current event

A matter of timing
Unplanned
Scene work
Spontaneous
Out of control
A lot of laughs

A
Gag
Jokes
Mean
Negative
Scatological
Role playing
Potty humor
Script writing
The easiest path
Stand-up comedy
A one-person show
That which was said before
That which was done before
That which was heard before
That which was thought before

Play.

Give.

Listen.

Receive.

Support others.

Engage in feelings.

Relax, enjoy yourself.

Accept what is going on.

Even now keep yourself saying

"yes," and "Yes," and "Yes and. . . ."

Add something each time you act or speak.

Say yesss. Keep saying yes. Inside and out.

The Improv

works best

when everyone

is trying to make

everyone else look good.

"Resistance is useless."

Respect and acknowledge all words and ideas.

Bring your yourself into the present moment.

Be honest about what is going on now,

with yourself and with others.

Laugh again and again.

Laugh some more.

Be respectful.

Be care-ful.

Be playful.

Play.

CONNECTIONS WITH PEOPLE

Making greater connections with people and maintaining those connections is a most important factor in excellent leadership. Excellent leadership is a key element in organizational development and training. It is also a key element in successful Improv management. Each time an organization experiences a change in programs, directions, materials, structures, personnel, or procedures, the job of maintaining or remaking connections becomes the next priority. Each time subject matter is added or changed in your presentation or work, the job of re-establishing or reinforcing connections comes next.

If there are great connections between you and those in the organization, whatever you introduce has a better chance of working. Learning is enhanced. When there are great connections, feedback becomes overt and readily shared and the involvement of people working well together increases. When there are great people connections, problems that are encountered surface sooner and solution thinking is usually activated at the same time. When people connections are greatest, resistance is reduced, communication is clear and open, and all efforts are more productive.

If the connections are weak or incomplete, new things can be very hard to introduce. If the participants have no sense of connection among themselves or between themselves and the leadership, whatever work or learning you have to do will be more difficult. Students in groups who get to know one another earn better grades than do students in groups in which there are no connections made between the individuals.

People do not make great connections at the level of the mind alone. Ideas may gather us together in a forum, yet the ideas alone have no power. They must be learned and turned into behavior or there has been no training. It takes action and interaction to bring people together and to integrate information. It is our feelings about our ideas that open the doors that bring us together.

The Improv process works on a level of activity and interactivity that automatically brings people and their minds together before the arena of ideas is engaged.

DATA VERSUS PROCESS

One of the reasons that people have trouble making connections is that the data is given too soon in the communication. We tend to present our ideas planned out or mentally written out.

It is easy to get ahead of ourselves. It is easy to become so focused on our goal, or on the vision, that the participant loses value. It is easy to become caught up in the idea that the business, or the program with which we are involved, is more important than the people who make it work.

When working in business or with real materials, a vision *and* a process are necessary, and the process must still be considered first. When working with buildings, plans are quite important; but unless the process is clear and easy, the building itself can be cumbersome and stiff.

A STORY

For many years I worked in the Marin County, California, Civic Center, the last public building designed by Frank Lloyd Wright. It was beautiful and a marvel of architecture. The building was built after his death and was originally designed to be constructed in the desert of the Southwest. It was placed in coastal Northern California and its functional internal layout was designed by people who did not fully consider process. The place was cumbersome and made many services virtually inaccessible to those who needed them. The people working there often found it just as difficult and confusing.

LAST, MOST IMPORTANT

The following is an Improv concept as well as a basic tenant of public speaking and of general communication:

"Information is the last, most important element in a communication."

This statement makes some people shudder, while others seem to go quite mad: "How can you say such a thing about my precious information." or "I have spent years learning this information; how dare you challenge it?"

This statement is not a challenge. It is a functional frame of reference. Let us assume that your information is right, good, true, and *very* important. You must put the information from your brain into the minds and lives of others or it has little value.

AN ANALOGY

Consider the computer as a means of communication. No matter how good your information, if the computer is not plugged in, you cannot access this wonderful tool. If the computer is plugged in and there is no power to the outlet, bad luck. If you have power but your keyboard is not plugged in, it does you no good. Have you ever had your fingers positioned one set of keys to the right or left on the keyboard? It gives you an opportunity to work with "babble." If your fingers are shifted to the right, your next words will look something like this: "eo;; ;ppl dp,ryjomh ;olr yjod." If you have no monitor with which to see your information, it is very difficult to proceed. If you have neither printer nor modem, you may as well have your information locked up in your head.

If there are problems with syntax or definitions, how quixotic will your ex-substantial delictions be incredulated? If your punctuation! clearly, cannot allow: the true" meaning of } your words? to appear—what will(; others make of.' your meaning!?!?!?

A STORY

A good friend was with his five-year-old daughter. They had to wait for the mom to finish an errand before they could do other things. Andy said, "We will go to the store as soon as Mommy is finished. In the meantime let's play with your toys." She looked at him through the corner of her child's eye and said, "Daddy, why do we always do things in the mean time? Why don't we ever do anything in the nice time?"

The more important your message, the more important for you to understand that:

"Information, or data, is the last, most important element in a communication."

BONDS MUST BE CREATED

A connection is a form of bonding that has a kind of magic to it. We talk of something that "resonates" with us. It vibrates at some compatible frequency. In music this is called harmony. In Spanish the word *simpatico* touches on the idea. It translates roughly as "agreeable" or "pleasant," yet it connotes more than that. In French the term *je ne sais quoi* means literally, "I know not what." The sound, the facial expression, and the gesture that accompany these words say as much as the words themselves.

There is a laboratory experiment that illustrates a point about bonding. Two pieces of living heart tissue are placed near each other in a petri dish. They are not touching nor connected by any material that conducts electricity. When one piece of the heart tissue is given an electric stimulus that makes it pulse, the other, if it is close, will pulse as well. The same experiment done with brain tissue or bone tissue produces no such response.

There are studies that indicate that bonding between mother and child may have a great deal to do with the proximity of the hearts in utero and during breast feeding. A good, full-bodied, hug can produce mutual palpitation without regard to the relationship between the partners in the hug.

When there is a bond, it is not necessary for two parties to be in the same room, nor even the same town, to feel connected. As a matter of fact, it has been suggested that when the involved parties must be present to one another it is an "attachment," rather than a connection or a bonding. Attachment behavior can be the basis of dysfunctional relationships.[8]

Understanding connections at the level of the heart makes the introductions of new leadership, new material and new programs, and new systems easier. Creating a connection at the heart level makes motivation easy. Heart-level connections make everything easier.

The four Improv principles are essential to making connections with the heart. Remember that these principles suggest striving toward being present in the moment, being honest with oneself, being honest with another, and putting yourself out there for public view.

Among the best ways to make connections is the sharing of stories from your own life and experience. To find the best stories, you must search honestly through your own life and reflect on and record what you have learned. Look especially for odd, strange, and silly and maybe some young or dumb things. Stories that are the most important are not merely ones that illustrate your point. More important are the stories that tell who you are.

JOSEPH CHILTON PIERCE, *THE MAGICAL CHILD MATURES*. NEW YORK: BANTAM BOOKS, 1985.

Improvisation, Inc.

Besides leading us into wonder and delight, Improvisation exposes us to fear, failure, silliness, embarrassment, illogic, and confusion. Stories that demonstrate that you are human and that you too have been embarrassed, lost, confused, and sometimes just plain wrong are particularly powerful. Chapter Sixteen explores Improv storytelling more fully.

CONNECTIONS REQUIRE US TO SHIFT GEARS

In my younger years I was hitchhiking in California. I caught a lift with a truck driver who had dropped off the trailer, the back portion, of his eighteen-wheeler and was taking the cab back to his original destination.

I got into the cab and he said, "Hang on, young fellow, this here rig ain't got no brakes." He proceeded to take me forty miles, through six or seven small towns, including a good number of stop signs and stop lights, using only gear shifting up and down. He never even touched the brakes.

Making connections with people in organizations is helped by appropriate and successful speeding up and slowing down. Successful acceleration and deceleration in The Improv requires moving smoothly between the changes. To be off the ideal speed is to be out of current time. You must move quickly, yet not too quickly. Go slowly, yet not too slowly. This idea holds true in working with people in any capacity. It is true whether you are working with one or with many.

The skills that make and keep strong connections with your participants include easy acceleration, thoughtful action, clear consciousness, good listening, sensitive feeling, quick learning, fast decision making, reasonable planning, easy slowing, smooth acceleration, quick gear changes, and trained reflexes. These skills are used to manage speed changes and are imbedded in Improvisation.

Speed

Speed is a straightforward thing in nature. Light has a constant speed (mostly). Sound has a predictable speed, depending on the medium in which it occurs. A falling body has a constant acceleration in reference to the larger body toward which it is being attracted. A projected object has a predictable rate at which is slows based on gravity and the laws of aerodynamics. (Keep in mind, however, that according to some laws of aerodynamics, the bumblebee cannot fly.)

Acceleration by biological entities is a fairly clear matter. The top speeds of most living things have been measured or calculated. The top speed for an unaided human being is currently 27.89 miles per hour (mph). The cheetah moves at 70 mph, the lion at 50 mph, the hyena at 40 mph, the domestic cat at 30 mph, the black mamba snake at 20 mph, the chicken at 9 mph, and the garden snail at 0.03 mph.[9] Slowing down usually has to do with either getting tired or running out of fuel—or with no longer needing to run for your food or your life.

In living things, speeding up and slowing down is a straightforward matter. Adding or subtracting energy speeds us or slows us the same way a dimmer switch turns a light up or down. In mechanical things, we must learn to deal with the shifting of gears. Human interaction and communication move at the speed of thought, at the speed of group dynamics. Some theorize that these velocities may exceed the speed of light. We must attend to our accelerations.

Acceleration

Improvisational work can accelerate in a variety of ways. During a specific game, the gathering can "get it" and spontaneously begin to change levels of exploration, understanding, application, and interaction. Issues that have previously inhibited the organization can suddenly disappear. People can begin to desire work in larger settings in which there is more public exposure. Another response is that participants can become more comfortable with smaller sets, in which issues of intimacy are more critical. Risk may become suddenly easier. Ideas may begin racing through participants' heads. Conversation, problem solving, and brainstorming can erupt among the participants. Sudden and unexpected feelings of well-being may appear. There can be a sudden rise in the general energy level of the organization. New channels of communication and new levels of interpersonal comfort can suddenly appear. These are all signs of acceleration.

Gear Shifting

A realistic question is, "Do you really want to accelerate?" If you are going downhill on a slippery road with a heavy load of precious cargo, you may not want to go any faster. It may be necessary to slow down.

Whether accelerating or slowing down, it usually becomes necessary to shift gears along the way. When changing gears we may go into a stall. We may break the trans-

THE WORLD ALMANAC AND BOOK OF FACTS, 1998 EDITION. NEW YORK: WORLD ALMANAC BOOKS, K-III REFERENCE CORPORATION.

Improvisation, Inc.

mission or engine by operating at a speed that is too fast for the vehicle. We may lose people or tax ourselves and our participants to exhaustion and burnout, or we can merely become less and less efficient and, as in an automobile, fail to get the mileage that is possible from efficient running.

When we change gears, we must first decide whether our purpose is to slow down or to speed up. Sometimes in order to speed up we must first slow down, shift into a lower gear, speed up in that gear, and then shift again into the next higher gear.

Shift Gears with People Too

When shifting gears with a group of people, the initial introduction of an idea or a start-up game is first gear. Adding details to the idea or asking for basic feedback will function as second gear. Having the participants become physically active or interactive touches on third gear. Having them play a game at higher levels or with more relevant or risky topics is fourth gear. Giving the process to the people to let them run with it is fifth gear.

Neutral

When working with groups of people, it is a good idea to go through neutral to get from one gear to another. Without going into neutral it is difficult to get out of the gear we are in. Moving into neutral is not necessarily an easy thing. For humans, getting into neutral can be a physical, mental, emotional, social, and a spiritual event. Each step requires complex levels of thought, action, compassion, and communication. To begin we must listen, consider the past, consider the goal, participate, work as an individual, and work as part of the group.

When working with people, it is good to lead by doing. When you come to the conclusion that you wish to shift gears, you must make the decision as to whether your goal is to speed up or slow down, to gear up or to gear down. You need then to take an action that moves you through your own personal state of neutral.

You need to be compassionate with yourself and with your audience. Some leaders and trainers become upset with themselves when they have to change gears suddenly. Some executives become upset with their workforce simply because gear changes become suddenly necessary. Being upset is not a neutral position. You must focus entirely on becoming disengaged.

You may warn the participants that you are about to change what is going on. You may ask them to shift into neutral with you. You may allow them time to get into neutral and help facilitate this by the way you move and act. Your posture, your gestures, the position of your head, the set of your mouth and jaw, your expressions, and the gestalt of your physical being must all express and signify neutral.

Neutral really means you are neither adding energy to the system nor taking it away. On a flat or uphill road, a car in neutral will slow down by itself. On a downhill road, a car in neutral will tend to pick up speed. An audience in neutral will do the same. You, as an individual, may do the same.

Managers sometimes try to get into neutral by explaining things, by analyzing the situation, or by changing the set structure. These are all additions of energy. These all change the level of the road or the amount of gas. They do not bring us to neutral.

Some try to get into neutral by calming the audience down. This can be an addition of energy. Trainers sometimes try to get into neutral by asking questions or setting up new problems. These are all *additions* of energy. To achieve neutral it is necessary to reach deeply within one's self and come to the point of neither adding nor taking away energy.

People often slam on the brakes when they wish to change gears. This is not neutral. It is the *removal* of energy from the system. Tapping the brakes, giving the vehicle a little gas, and engaging the clutch may be interim steps in achieving neutral. Slamming on the brakes is not.

If you do not feel calm, peaceful, content, at ease, and happy, you are probably not in neutral. If you do not feel as though you are in neutral, you are probably not in neutral. If you feel that you are accelerating on an uphill road or slowing on a downhill road, or vice versa, you are probably not in neutral.

If you have a sinking feeling that you are not in control, you may not be. If this happens when you are trying to change gears, you are probably not in neutral. If you cannot say, "I think that I am just going to let providence, or the universe, or chance, or God, take over for a moment," *you are probably not in neutral.*

If you are not in neutral, your gathering is not in neutral, so changing gears is going to be a problem. If changing gears is a problem, there will almost certainly be problems in efficiency and difficulty in keeping the connection with your group.

The Fast Lane

In the movie *Star Wars* the Millennium Falcon space ship jumps into "hyper-space" on a screen filled with extending lines indicating that the ship has gone into some new dimension and crossed vast distances of space in a moment.

A similar event in the human being is a cognitive leap. Religionists tell us of a transition that is called an *epiphany,* a sudden manifestation or perception of reality. Events very like this can happen in The Improv with a sudden breakthrough experience into new levels of understanding.

Beyond mere acceleration, an organization, or a training session, the same sort of event can happen. I call it "moving into the fast lane." The gathering has been learning well or the organization has been working smoothly, there is healthy laughter, the participants are following directions with little effort, moments of brilliance have become common, shy participants seem to be coming out of their shells, difficult or strong participants seem to relax into easy cooperation, and suddenly there seems to be an internal flash of bright light—"kazaam," warp speed.

The participants become calm and relaxed at the same time as they are being energized by new feelings and understanding. Suggestions are readily accepted by all, the members of the gathering take control, and the activity moves to levels that could not have been planned. The happening is generally unpredictable.

These events usually have elements in common. The executive leadership is relaxed and confident and operating in the *perfect present moment.* The facilitators are focused on relationship and take delight in the people with whom they are working. There are feelings of safety and security. There is a sense of seriousness of purpose accompanied by a feeling of playfulness and fun. Participation is near 100 percent. People are either active or very attentive. Energy has been growing on its own. The state of "Impro" has descended on the organization of the meeting.

Achieving the Improv fast lane is an objective, yet it cannot be the goal. It seems to be a product of generating a critical mass of Improv elements engaged in by a critical mass of the participants, functioning with a critical mass of feeling, led by an Improv executive encouraging excellence.

It has been said there are a number of things that are difficult to achieve or hard to sustain if directly sought for their own sake. Among these are fame and fortune. The

Improv "fast lane" can be added to this list. We can hope that it will come, yet a direct grab often seems to keep it just out of reach.

CONNECTIONS AMONG PEOPLE

The pace at which your organization moves involves a variety of measures. Smooth and quick movement indicates that the connections are strong and building. Jerky or slow response tells us that a connection is breaking down. Carefully observe the people with whom you are working. How quickly are they warming up to you? How fast are they accepting information? How quick are they to complain? How quickly and smoothly are they taking part in activities? How fast are they moving physically when they are shifting to new positions or locations? How quick are they at understanding instructions? These are some things you must know to track the connections among people. Add to the list as you continue looking for other indicators.

Making greater connections with people is not only a physical matter. Joseph Chilton Pierce makes the case that if physical presence is not necessary to maintain a connection, the relationship is "bonded," that is, strong, and supple, healthy, and healing. In a *bonded* state, difficulties can be worked out or can even correct themselves. When people must be in the presence of one another in order to be connected, there is an attachment relationship that can be difficult and unhealthy. Being in the presence of another can be either physical or emotional.

My Improv axioms support bonding between people. Bonded relationships have the strongest connections. Understanding the relative position of the information or data involved in our communication helps us to maintain our connections to people rather than merely to ideas.

If we remain conscious of the speed and tempo of shifts in events and organizations, this will help us to maintain, develop, and enhance bonding among people. To build and keep bonds, and therefore to make greater connections, we must do *real* things at the physical, social, spiritual, and emotional levels.

When you are dealing with physical, social, spiritual, and emotional elements among people, you will run directly into patterns in behavior. Some patterns are good, but many are not. We must learn to attack patterns actively in order to make change.

CHAPTER SIX

Patterns and Changes

Patterns can be useful and are necessary to accomplish some things. Patterns work best when the environment in which the patterns were created can be duplicated or has not changed too much. Patterns can help you make good use of your past experience. Patterns are also capable of strangling creativity. Patterns may also inhibit bonding and reinforce attachment behavior.

When working with people and their patterns, you will need benchmarks and other measures. When working with people, measurements are more difficult than they are when working in more concrete areas. In businesses, measuring performance and identifying and measuring the best available business practices is very important. Observing people in the act of Improvisation will give you valuable insight to the patterns of communication and interaction that are active. Improvisation can be used to measure human performance, and thus to develop all-important best practices.

Qualitative research is recognized and viable for discovering truths and verifying reality. Improvisation is such a qualitative measurement system. It can be effectively used to keep track of the way people respond to slowly increasing levels of instruction, responsibility, freedom, creativity, pressure, and confusion. Improvisation provides an excellent device for measuring the capacity of people to change, to challenge patterns, to grow, or to work together in new situations and environments. It is a good device for measuring communication and listening skills. When this information has been gathered, we can begin to attack our negative patterns and to make positive changes.

Almost any pattern can become a problem if we hold onto it or find that we cannot let go. If we, as leaders, hold onto our old patterns, our participants will follow.

We know that it is impossible to add to a full cup. In the same way, it is very difficult to introduce change or to give people new information when either giver or receiver is holding onto an old pattern. Letting go, however, is sometimes difficult. Changing patterns and accepting change are not necessarily natural things.

The human body and mind are built to hold onto things and to grasp tightly. The body's physical structure curls into itself. Our fingers can grasp and cling until they are frozen in position, incapable of opening without pain. Our bodies and minds can settle into cramped positions, making it difficult for us to move or stand. Our muscle tissue and our connective tissue are designed to clamp down and hold tight. Attacking patterns and making changes are learned skills. Use of Improvisation will help develop these skills.

WE CHALLENGE SOME PATTERNS

In some of the fine arts we begin to approach the idea of challenging patterns. We "let it all hang out." We search for "it." We reject analysis and allow for exploration of feeling. Even in the arts, however, there is an amazing adherence to form, pattern, convention, and function.

In writing we explore poetry, fiction, science fiction, fantasy, and invention. Still the words must be spelled "correctly," except by the occasional Mark Twain who "never could trust a man who wil spel a wrd the same wae twize."

Our grammar and punctuation are required to be carefully organized and developed following acceptable forms. The exception is the occasional e e cummings.

Stories about artists are filled with tales of those who challenged the patterns of convention—and starved or lived outcast lives, in body (Gauguin), in mind (Van Gogh), or in soul (Bosch). Our musical greats have led us through fascinating paths, ranging from great pattern consistencies—Beethoven, Mozart, and Liszt—to extraordinary pattern innovation—Charlie Parker, Duke Ellington, and Django Reinhardt. Western music, which includes a lovely amount of improvisation, is imprisoned in the model of a twelve-tone scale. Deep work in Improvisation has challenged the field of music with the microtonal work of Harry Partch and Jon and Jonathan Glasier.[10]

Dance has generally been dominated by adherence to the patterns of ballet, ballroom, folk and international folk, cultural dance, swing, or country line dancing. Even with personal variations and innovations, these all have set patterns on which they are based. In the field of dance there have been pattern challenges in the forms of jazz and modern dance inspired by such wonderful people as Isadora Duncan, Merce Cunningham, Twyla Tharp, and Mikhail Baryshnikov.[11] Pure improvisational dance has also appeared with the work of Susan Greer Essex with her "Movement Choir," with improvisational dance theater, and Contact Improv Dance, which has become a worldwide event.

The 20th Century experienced a steady attack on conventional patterns in representational art. There were been "happenings," performance art, ice sculpture, and junk sculpture. Salvador Dali madness and M.C. Escher perspectives delighted and confused us in the directions of pattern manipulations and destruction.

In daily life, abandonment of patterns by breaking rules and standards runs rampant in our schools, on our streets, and in many of our institutions. With Basquiet, heroin-inspired graffiti was lifted to the level of museum art. Yet there is little that is truly *new* in these things except perhaps in the negation of convention, which is actually a pattern of its own.

10

THE HUMAN EAR IS ACTUALLY CAPABLE OF DISTINGUISHING UP TO FIFTEEN HUNDRED TONES WITHIN A SINGLE OCTAVE. THE ORGANIZATION WITH WHICH WE ARE FAMILIAR AS THE TWELVE-TONE SCALE (A, B FLAT, B, C FLAT, C, D FLAT, D, E, E FLAT, F, G, A FLAT) IS A LIMITED AND ARBITRARY MECHANISM. FOR AN EXPLORATION OF THE EXTRAORDINARY RANGE OF INTERVALS AVAILABLE WITHIN A SINGLE OCTAVE AND THE VAST FIELD OF MUSIC BEYOND THE TWELVE-TONE SCALE, SEE *GENESIS OF A MUSIC* BY HARRY PARTCH (NEW YORK: DACAPO PRESS, 1974). ALSO SEE THE WORK OF JONATHAN GLASIER OF SONIC ARTS GALLERY, INCLUDING THE INTERACTIVE PROGRAM CALLED "THE IMPROVATORY: THE OPPOSITE OF CONSERVATORY," AND *THE INTERVAL: JOURNAL OF MUSIC RESEARCH AND DEVELOPMENT*, PUBLISHED QUARTERLY BY THE INTERVAL FOUNDATION, SAN DIEGO, CALIFORNIA.

11

THERE IS AN EXCELLENT PBS VIDEOTAPE OF THE BARYSHNIKOV DANCE "PUSH COMES TO SHOVE," CHOREOGRAPHED BY TWYLA THARP.

In order to attack our patterns and make real changes, we must first *learn to let go*. Then we must train in and practice the art of letting go.

A LESSON IN LETTING GO

I grew up where there was no snow and it rarely rained. When the rain did come the roads became slick with a layer of mud that was like driving on ice. Drivers went a little bit mad. The skids would be accompanied by panic, hands gripping, feet stomping, overcorrecting, frantic attempts to regain control, more panic, and the crashing and littering of cars, monuments to those who did not know how to handle skids.

My father took me out into the rain to teach me how to handle a serious skid before I got my license. He taught me that the trick to controlling a skid was in learning when and how to let go. Let go? Yes, let go! Let go of the steering wheel and take your feet off the pedals. To demonstrate his point he stomped on the brakes and put us into a major spin. As a passenger I nearly panicked. His hands never completely left the wheel, they simply let go; and though his feet left the pedals for a moment, they were back almost immediately. He was tapping the brakes ever so gently, adding gasoline carefully as he brought the skid completely and effortlessly under control.

The first time I put myself into a practice skid I started to experience the pattern I call LMOLPC (loss of control, manic attempt to control, overcorrection, loss of control, panic, crash). Thanks to the early lesson from my father, I intervened just before "overcorrection." I let go, and there was no crash.

Over time my body began to respond to the simple command, "LET GO." The first time I faced a truly unexpected skid I really let go. There came a wonderful sense of relaxation, calm, and freedom. I learned to let go with my real body in a real situation and it worked. Since then I have experienced this feeling of freedom most often working with people in The Improv.

The feeling is that of "popping into current time." I have become aware of and comfortable with the fact that I am not really "in control" of anything. Letting go requires that I enter into a real-time relationship with my surroundings. The result is most startling.

Over time I have learned to give the people I work with as much freedom, respect, responsiveness, and consideration as I give an automobile and the road. I have learned to guide and direct, as well as to let the people do their own work with their own relationships to time and space. I have learned to let go of my immediate control and goals in order to reach a true and natural destination with everyone aboard.

If you have been moving too quickly with your associates or you have changed lanes too quickly; if you have become distracted for a moment and have lost control; if you have overestimated or underestimated the capacity of your participants or the gathering, you may experience dangerous skids. The only answer is to become extremely honest with the situation and with yourself and to let go in order to regain control.

"There's a signpost up ahead."

ROD SERLING

Rod Serling made this phrase famous in the TV program "The Twilight Zone." It is a warning that we are entering new and interesting and perhaps difficult and confusing territory. As one works with Improvisation it is a good idea to keep this in mind.

Of course, the best way to keep out of trouble is to see the trouble coming. There are signposts that an Improv process provides by its own form. The first of these signposts is silence. The next is lack of healthy spontaneous laughter. Another is odd laughter. See Chapter Ten, *Wholesome Laughter Leads the Way.* Next comes resistance by individuals or sets of individuals. Then look for failure of physical participation. Listen for chatter or noise or unrelated conversation on the part of the participants. Notice confusion on the part of any of the participants. Obviously, hostility or direct challenge to the manager or trainer, the information, or the process give you clues that there may be trouble ahead. Use your own experience to add to the list of signposts.

When you see a signpost be prepared to let go. Let go. Take a step back. Slow down. Change form. Let go of the goal and focus on the process. Just let go.

WE BLAME PARTICIPANTS

The pattern of blaming the people with whom we work can occur in all leadership, teaching, and training situations. The pattern may come from the executive, the manager, the leader, the supervisor, the trainer, the participants, or even from the corporate or organizational culture.

The moment you think of placing blame on the people with whom you are working, stop, look, listen, and reconsider your position. Assigning blame to others is a very important signpost. When you observe yourself engaged in this behavior, you should immediately do something to let go of the ideas behind it.

The moment you begin to blame the gathering or the participants you are more than likely involved in some pattern of your own. Perhaps it is a pattern of your own creation; perhaps the pattern was created by others. It does not matter. You are now in it and it is your pattern. You need to release it. Also release the thought that something outside yourself is to blame.

> **N O T E**
> If there are real problems with individuals or with an organization that is operating in a self-destructive manner, you may not be able to engage effectively in deep Improv games with the gathering. In this case you must learn to apply these Improv lessons to your own personal life and interactions.

> **A N O T H E R N O T E**
> Even if others are the problem, you are the only one you can work on, so start with yourself anyway.

Ups and Downs

Improvisation is not only about laughter and success. As with any serious work, there are ebbs and flows. In Improvisation it often happens that several really good units of activity will be followed by a slow or difficult set. The participants do not laugh as much. There may be a sense of struggle or resistance. In these situations it becomes very easy to blame the participants.

It may be that a deep level of reality has been reached and that internal work is being done by a significant number of the people with whom you are working. Because of the nature of Improv work, it may be that the group has pushed past a barrier, has reached a plateau, has touched a hidden nerve, or has activated some dormant resistance. It may be that people are becoming tired or are merely distracted by having been so completely in the moment. These are all among the important elements of Improv process.

The difficulties may be individual and personal, or there may be resistance to the material, the organization, the trainer, the gathering, or life in general. Whatever the source or the nature of the apparent problem, it must be handled first by letting go of the impulse to blame the gathering.

THE TRULY NEW

People have an automatic sense of confidence in an experienced guide. Your stories and memories can make you an authority even before the journey begins. You can draw maps and paint pictures. Paths and mountains may be named after you. If you have actually been somewhere before then, people can hear you say such things as, "Come, this is the way, I remember it well," or "Ah, it is as lovely as I remember. Come with me and I will show you." It can be easy to lead others to places you have been before. Leading into the truly new has none of these perks. New is . . ., well, new. This is simply the truth. If no one has been there before, then how do you *lead* others there?

In the martial art of Aikido, there are unlimited numbers of response options to an un-limited number of attack situations. This is also the reality of life. With Aikido we deal with the infinite possibilities with focus on a defense technique called *ikkyo,* meaning "first teaching" and a mode called *irimi,* meaning "to enter." We go back to *ikkyo* and *irimi* again and again over many years. It can take a lifetime to master either. As practitioners of Aikido return to basic technique, as musicians return to basic scales, Improv executives need to go back to simple games, to first principles, and to basic techniques in order to reinforce the foundations.

We can begin by understanding that Improvisation is an ancient art used to generate creativity. It creates true, real, deep, personal, wholesome, healthy, vital, delightful, fascinating, powerful, long-lasting, and sometimes frightening creativity. The territory being explored is new to everyone, including the leadership.

As we deal with ups an downs, it is the job of the Improv executive to lead the par-ticipants to the next level. The next level is, by definition, truly new.

Leading into the truly new is the great work of Improvisation. One leads into the truly new by taking *small, successful, incremental steps toward a vision.* This requires starting with the creative challenge and use of patterns that ultimately must be abandoned. Leading Improv gatherings requires us to make great connections with people, building on disciplined patterns, letting go of the patterns, and then walking fearlessly into the truly new together with our co-workers.

Being Together,

Moving Together

Into the Truly New

Being

Being? Being what? What being?
Together? Too gather? Two gather? Together.
Moving! Moving into! Moving in two!
The truly new? The newly true?
What is true and what is new?

Make the change—let go. Make the commitments—let go. Make the connections, engage in mutual goals, allow for spirit, open doors, invite creativity—let go. There is that higher state of consciousness that we describe as "The Improv" or "Impro" or Alpha state—or just being hot! The use of Improv principles can help us get hot more often.

Having made the commitments, you can also help your organization achieve the condition we call "together." As an organization or gathering separates into factions, it becomes increasingly difficult to operate in this state. If we separate into groups, we must implement management activity to overcome the natural separations. In Improvisation these management activities are called games, techniques, exercises, playthings, axioms, rules, suggestions, directions, and instructions.

You are the first participant in The Improv. You, the executive, manager, leader, mentor, presenter, teacher, or trainer—you are the primary leader in the reality that *we are all in this together*. Being in this together is about more than attending a meeting or a conference. It is about more than being part of the same company, the same business, the same industry, or the same educational organization. It is about being humans and working and living at the highest possible levels.

We all live on a tiny planet inside a delicate, small, and profoundly interconnected biosphere. We are all connected by the magnificent mystery of life. We are all defined by mysteries of DNA coding and learning styles. We are all associated by our similarities. We all have bodies that must breathe, drink, and eat. We are subject to health and to illness. We are families, communities, and peoples. We share the abilities of our emotions, our joyousness, and our fears. We live in alternating light and dark. Brilliance is followed by confusion, by moments of clarity, by strengths, weaknesses, hopes, and dreams. These are also the things that bring us together.

Sometimes during our busy and complex days, we forget that it is the similarities that make it possible for us to allow connections and thus to share information and experience. It is in our connections that we can do business. Walking our lives and talking our lives—with the deep self-assurance that we are truly in this together—can provide enough of an example for the entire gathering to begin operating as a unit. This is how we lead into the truly new.

HUMAN TOOLS

Complex modern communication tools include availability of paper, pens, pencils, drafting and graphic tools, electricity, projectors, screens, phone lines and phones, cables, keyboards, printers, copiers, computers, radio and television transmission stations, microwave stations, cells, and satellites. These items do not have free will. We do not have to ask them to participate. We do not need to explain that they are parts of a network. We do not need their cooperation to function. They must simply be technically introduced with correct interconnections, then we turn them on and off.

Communication between people works in a system that includes mind and brain, memory and language, numbers and symbols, emotions, meanings, voices, ears, and fingers. People have personalities and free will. We must be asked to participate. We are unlike machinery in that we must be reminded that we are part of a network or we can tend to drift away.

Start the Moving

Once Improv basics and communication elements are in place and working, we can best begin moving together into the truly new by asking for permission. Simple words should be used, such as:

"Shall we go to the next level?"
"Are we ready to try something new?"
"Shall we see where this leads?"
"Let's see what there is to see."
"Let's try this."[12]

THINGS CAN GO WRONG

If we miss or ignore signs and signals and try to push our original goals, sometimes it works. Often it does not. Leaving gaps in Improv methodology will usually make things go wrong. Sometimes we try to skip to another process, leaving a miss or a mess behind. We may try to leap across gaps, catch up later, let time heal small wounds, or simply let holes in the process stand. In organizational development these events can cause structural damage to the fabric of the connections. This can be dangerous to the development of basic understanding and behavioral change. A great teacher taught me that if I read something that does not make sense I should go back over it to look for any word I do not fully understand. She said I must then learn the meaning of the word and read the passage again. She said that with difficult materials it may be necessary to do this with each word we do not understand completely, even when we know the basic definitions. Sometimes we must go over words we really think we know. It is a great exercise for an individual or a group to look up such simple words as "the," "at," "in," or "play." There is much to learn. We cannot afford to leave gaps of reality in our work.

Responding to the Response

Remember that listening is extraordinarily important. Responding to the responses of your participants is a form of listening. Sometimes an executive or presenter will ask questions and neither respond nor react to the responses. It is best not to ask questions merely for the sake of form.

When we move into the truly new, a form of consensus is required. There must be 100 percent willingness to go along.

12

THE IMPROV ORGANIZATION AT THE GEORGIA INSTITUTE OF TECHNOLOGY, FOUNDED BY THE AUTHOR, IS OVER TEN YEARS OLD. IT IS CALLED "THE LET'S TRY THIS PLAYERS."

"100 percent willingness?"

"Yes, 100 percent willingness."

"Are you crazy?"

"Maybe."

Willingness to go along merely means that there is enough understanding, agreement, co-operation, and willingness that the organization can move forward with everyone aboard. If you cannot generate this level of consensus, you may be taking too large a step. Consensus does not mean that everyone *agrees* on every point. There may be—in fact, probably will be—resistance, fear, timidity, ambivalence, doubt, and even grumbling.

- You may need to scale back and ask for a smaller step.

- You may be accelerating too quickly.

- Your set design may need to be altered to create more safety, comfort, and network alliances. (See Chapter Eleven, *The Size and Design of Creativity.*)

- You may be working too far ahead in your language. Imagine describing a kiwi fruit in order to convince a person to set muscle and tools to work in order to cultivate land and to plant seeds. It is a little like trying to convince an executive that a single ropes course will help the bottom line.

- You may not have made the personal commitment to take the step yourself.

- You may not have demonstrated the need to take the step.

Improvisation works best with small, incremental, successful steps toward your goal. It is not necessary to obtain acceptance for your whole program. All you need is 100 percent willingness on the part of the participants to enter into the next arena. With careful work you can establish an attitude of willingness to participate within the gathering.

A DESIRE TO PARTICIPATE

Extraordinary clarity, confidence, charisma, and charm can be enough to compel a crowd to go along with you for a little way. Generating wholesome laughter as you proceed will accomplish miracles in helping people follow.

The simple technique of asking the audience to stand up and then sit down again can begin full participation. You may say, "Stand up, turn around to the left, then turn around to the right, and then sit down." Having the participants stand and introduce themselves to someone next to them serves purposes both of icebreaking and of generating activity on the part of all the participants. As you do these things, you must be careful to note whether there are any members of the group who do not take part in such a simple exercise. With resistance you must work the smartest.

Asking questions and requesting that hands be raised in response is an easy method of generating physical participation. Ask a simple question such as, "How many people here have been through a corporate reorganization? Let me see a show of hands." Notice how many hands are raised. Then ask the opposite to the question, "How many people here have *not* been through a corporate reorganization?" Notice the hands again.

Even if you are absolutely certain that 100 percent of the participants raised their hands for one of these questions, say something like, "OK, how many have been through too many corporate reorganizations and are just too tired to raise your hands?" Then say, "Anybody who has not raised your hand yet, do so now."

It is often good to discuss this question process with the participants in order to make the point that you want full participation and that it is important to you, to them, and to the process.

At later points in your work you can start the question process as a gentle reminder. You will usually get some laughter when the gathering recognizes the pattern. If you do not, it may be time for a break.

Another set of techniques for obtaining full participation uses pen and paper. Ask the participants to take out pen and paper. This is a 100 percent activity all on its own. Ask them to *print* one goal, vision, or dream on a single sheet of paper. If they go along with this, ask them to print *two* goals, visions, or dreams on another piece of paper. If this works, ask them to print *three* of each on still another piece of paper. There should be no names on the papers. It is important that you ask them to *print*. There are a number of things you can do with these papers.

- Gather them up and redistribute them randomly.

- Gather them into stacks for random review through the day or week or month.

- Tear them into little pieces.

- Ball them up and have a paper snowball fight with them.

Each of these activities will generate energy and will create small participation steps. These simple steps can be used and reused with many variations. If you need more ideas about generating participation, refer to the work of Bob Pike, of Creative Training Technologies International in Minneapolis, and the work of Dave Arch, of The I Can Factory in Omaha.

DO AS I DO

Simple demonstrations of Improv techniques will accomplish a great deal in helping people move along with you. It is usually best to use simple steps. Present a demonstration yourself, then let the group play a little; demonstrate with an assistant, then let the group play again. Then have two participants from the audience do another demonstration. These demonstration processes will help to create unity between you as the leader and the group. Once this process has been done, it becomes easier to move forward together.

Attacking patterns and making change require careful selection. Patterns are often necessary for building and growing things. However, when your patterns are negative or produce unwanted results, you may need to identify and attack your own personal patterns in order to lead the way for others. As you develop the use of Improv methodology, you will need to let go of many of your own ways. As you lead people through these explorations, you must not place blame on others who may be holding onto patterns of their own. When you are moving into that which is truly new in your organization, you need to bring people together and help them to move together. When things go wrong, you can fall back on the great connections you have made and work to make greater connections. Generate cooperation and participation by the way you act and by your own example.

Once we are moving together, breaking non-working patterns left and right, we can move unhindered into the truly new. The only thing that must be dealt with then is *fear*—of change, of the new, and of fear itself. Improvisation can help you learn how to better manage these fears.

CHAPTER SEVEN

An Exploration of Fear

The use of Improv methodology creates change. Change can generate fear. Fear can interfere with or even destroy our connections with other people. If we are afraid we tend to fall into patterned responses. Because fear is unavoidable, we need to learn to manage our fears.

Management of fear has three major elements. The first is *admitting the fear, bringing it to the light, and exploring the fear.* The second element requires *working through your fear in the present moment.* The third element calls for *using a discipline as a structure on which to hang your fears as you work through them.*

BRING FEAR TO THE LIGHT

To manage fear you need to bring it into the light. You can use Improv techniques to learn to take small, successful, incremental steps that allow you to bring up fear in portions that can be handled. The principle of putting Improvisation out for public view is part of bringing fear into the open where it can be managed.

- The more serious the subject matter, the more there will be fear.

- The more difficult the subject matter, the more fear it will bring.

- The newer the subject matter, the more fear.

- The more complex the subject matter, the more fear.

- The more personal the subject matter, the more fear will be imbedded.

- The more abstract the subject matter, the more fear.

- The more taboo, the more fear.

- The more real, the more fear.

- Fear factors can be increased or decreased according to the size of the gathering.

- The more public, the more fear.

- Some fears are phobic and without rational sources.

- Some fear is internal and without discoverable sources.

- All fear is in the mind and body of emotions.

- We measure things in order to know them and thus be less afraid.

Measurements

Time and motion studies early in the 20th Century helped factory managers promote more efficient work processes. Even some of the physiological responses to fear can be measured, but the communication and interactions of people are simply too personal and too complex to study with simple time and motion measurements. People and organizations are living, changing, holographic, analog organisms. They can be observed and annotated, recorded and viewed; yet chart and graph measurements do not give us complete enough pictures to quantify organizations and people in motion in a realistic way. Improvisation can function as a methodology for conducting qualitative analysis.

Improvisation provides living, changing, holographic, analog processes that you can observe, record, and compare. You can change various elements at will and record the responses. From the very first exercise, you can observe, and reliably measure, the abilities of the group and of individuals to move together, to change, to communicate, to laugh, to cooperate, to learn, and to alter behavior. You may even be able to observe aspects of direction and speed.

If you wish to learn about the effect and effectiveness of any Improv activity, you can move to the next level of complexity or the next level of seriousness or reality, and there will be observable response. You can see what real changes have occurred in the group's ability to work together. You may then move back to a previous level of complexity and seriousness to compare and verify your results. Simple changes in your presentation will give you the ability to move back and forth while observing the response of the group. If you can demonstrate faith in the group as a learning and changing entity, the levels of fear that are present will be diminished.

As you learn about your fear, you bring it into the light. In the light you can manage the fear; you can call on allies to help you; you can begin to work through the fear; and you can lead your organization through the fear.

WORK THROUGH FEAR IN THE PRESENT MOMENT

Clear analysis and understanding of reality are difficult in the face of unmanaged fear. Understanding information gathered from study and research can also be difficult when one is afraid. Management of fear is rarely taught and seldom practiced. Fear is usually handled personally and covertly in the real world, which can be a difficult and expensive training ground. Some games are serious enough to simulate fear so that its management can be practiced in an artificial setting. As a naval officer, I was placed in frightening and dangerous simulations during fire-fighting training in order to practice prior to a real crisis. That sort of system is usually a little drastic for those working in offices and boardrooms. Outdoor challenge programs and "ropes" programs have been used to "build teams" and to give organizations practice dealing with the unknown and with fear, but these require extraordinary surroundings. Improvisation has been called an "indoor ropes course" by some of my participants.

- Improvisation provides a practice tool for real-time training in fear management.

- Improvisation requires working in the present moment.

- The management of fear requires discipline. Improvisation is a good discipline. It operates at a different level than does an exercise or a philosophy.

- The rules and attitudes that need to be followed and practiced while playing with Improvisation can be used as a daily discipline in fear management.

- The practice of observing the people in your organization can help you improve your skills in observing and measuring fear-management realities.

- The games can be used to address the specific topic of fear management, as well as other general concerns based on the business matters at hand.

HANG THE FEAR ON A STRUCTURE

The third element in managing fear is using a structure on which to hang fears as people work through them. It is simple truth that fear is a difficult aspect of life. Improvisation is a microcosm of life and has within it both fear and its cure.

As an Improv executive you are going to say such things as:

> "Please, stand up with a group
> of the people around you.
> I have no plan nor idea of what
> you will be asked to do or say next.
> We are going to work on real issues
> and real problems together.
> We are all going to watch together
> as we work our way through the problems.
> We will talk about what we have done and learned.
> We will create plans to implement some of the new skills
> or good 'bits of information' that we have observed.
> We will measure and benchmark ourselves
> to see how we have improved.
> We are going to bring fear into the present moment.
> We are going to bring fear into the light.
> Together we are going to learn to manage our fear."

- Playing the games and working with the exercises, in scheduled and monitored real time, with real people and real feedback, is an activity of Improv discipline.

- Integrating Improvisation into your daily personal life is another form of the discipline.

- Integrating the attitudes and ways of Improvisation into your family and community life is the work of the discipline.

- Bringing the activities and techniques, the philosophies and agreements of Improvisation into the daily life of your business practices is the value of the discipline.

- Improvisation engages creativity.

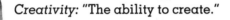

Creativity: "The ability to create."

By engaging in this discipline you will create a structure on which fear may be placed on display and managed by the whole gathering. Improvisation goes beyond the things humans generally fear—public speaking, falling, death, the dark, spiders, and snakes.

The fourth Improv principle suggests that you put yourself out for public view, although *fear of speaking in public* is very strong. If you try something new and it does not work, we say that you "fell on your face." This is the *fear of falling*. The processes and games create results we cannot see, even though they are right in front of us. This is certainly like *fear of the dark*. Comedians talk of trying to be funny in front of people and having the attempt fail. They call this "dying on stage," which equates with *fear of death*. I guess that just leaves fear of spiders and snakes.

Improvisation is, by definition, the act of entering the truly unknown. *We fear the unknown.*

> *"The only thing that makes life possible is permanent intolerable uncertainty—not knowing what comes next."* [13]
>
> **URSULA LE GUIN**

13

I HAVE HAD THIS QUOTE ON A NOTECARD ABOVE MY DESK FOR MANY YEARS. WITH APOLOGIES TO MS. LE GUIN, I DO NOT KNOW ITS SOURCE.

OVERCOME FEAR WITHIN THE IMPROV

The ability to be afraid is a strange and wondrous thing. Fear is a primary emotion, along with hope and determination, that has helped humans to thrive in a hostile world and against all odds. At the same time, fear can stop us in our tracks and cause us to freeze in the face of real danger. All kinds of fears show up in life and during an Improv process.

AFRAID? OF WHAT?

Fear of being looked at, fear of being seen,
fear of being noticed, fear of not being noticed,
fear of being embarrassed, fear of being bold,
fear of being extraordinary, fear of being common,
fear of judgment, fear of self-judgment,
fear of feeling alive, fear of feeling not alive,
fear of letting go, fear of holding on,
fear of knowing, fear of not knowing,
fear of being wrong, fear of being right,
fear of having a good time, fear of having no time,
fear of freedom, fear of change, fear of failure, fear of success,
and fear of fear, or of no fear of fear.

DISTINGUISH GOOD FEAR FROM BAD FEAR

Extraordinary things have been accomplished because an individual has been fearful of loss or failure, while equally great plans have never gotten off the ground for fear of loss or failure. We are often as fearful of success as of failure. Success means that people will really notice us. Success usually requires that we repeat ourselves, and then success is expected even before we begin. A single success may have been luck. What if we are found to be lucky instead of good? Success can also generate jealousy and competition.

The worst aspect of fear is that it begins deeply, in the quiet darkness of our insides, with a tightening of the blood vessels, and changes in the heartbeat. It comes with constricted breathing. It begins to change its nature as it travels along the nerves and makes the skin tingle, the palms sweat, and the mouth dry. At this point we can know it for what it is—just plain fear. It creeps into the mind and we then have two choices. The first is to send the fear back into the dark internal world where it can hide and grow evil, like Shelob in her lair (from Tolkien's *The Lord of the Rings*), or we may bring it out into the light.

Improvisation, Inc.

Good Fear

Fear is a powerful force in real life. It gives us warning of real danger and eminent consequences. It comes with, or is caused by, a flow of adrenaline, giving us extraordinary strength or speed. Adrenaline can help us to deal with real or imagined emergencies. My very tiny grandmother once rescued a fifty-pound barrel of nails from her burning house. After the fire she could not even move the barrel. (She was never able to explain why she chose to save nails. Perhaps it was an affinity of toughness.)

Good fear can also be a valuable motivator that forces us to reflect carefully on choices and on consequences of wrong or slow decisions. Here the adrenaline may help us to think more clearly and more quickly. Fear may startle us out of inaction or lethargy when consequences may not be extremely serious yet lack of action would create uncomfortable results. Improvisation helps us practice working with fear at these levels as well.

Good fear may be valuable as a motivator that can push us slowly out of patterns, beliefs, and behaviors that may have taken a long time to develop or cause problems in our lives.

A PERSONAL STORY

For years I had insisted to myself that I was terrible at math. I had allowed this belief to keep me from several goals. When I was young and working for a manufacturing corporation, in spite of my "math disability" I did complicated financial analyses of prospective customers. My work was good, my results excellent, and as my responsibilities increased, the complexity of the work increased, so the company purchased an expensive correspondence course in "Financial Analysis and Risk Projection." I received the first lesson, saw that the math was difficult, and set the lesson aside to try later. Lessons piled up on the "to do" shelf.

The final unit arrived and I had one weekend left in which to have all the lessons done and into the mail. If they were not done, all I had to do was explain to my next prospective employer what had caused the termination from my last job.

"Good fear" set in, and when I sat down to work the math suddenly seemed simple. A greater fear had driven a lesser limitation from my mind. I put the whole series of lessons into the mail on Monday morning and graduated with honors. My math skills have been just fine since that day.

Fear and Learning

On the other hand, a great deal of learning difficulty is based in fear. There is the fear that you cannot learn, fear that you are not good enough, fear that you will forget, fear that you will fail when tested, fear that you will remember the wrong things, fear that you should have known it already, fear that someone will discover that you do not know what you should know, fear that it doesn't really matter anyway, and many other forms of just plain fear.

All these aspects of fear take us out of the present moment. They all create distractions and inhibit focus. The stronger the fear, the more likely it is that surges from the endocrine system will stress the body and mind into the posture of "fight or flight" and we will run rather than learn or change.

"Not Good" Fear from the Past

"Not good" fear is sometimes in league with good fear. It comes from another dimension. "It is a dimension neither of sight nor sound, but of mind."[14] It is also a dimension of time. "Not good" fear comes also from both the past and from the future. It clouds the thinking and slows the reactions. It is a little like neurosis. It speaks to us in voices from our heads, and those voices often have little or no association with reality. An understanding of Improv process will be served by a further look into these fears.

Fear of Public Speaking

Fear of public speaking makes me tilt my head in wonder. All speaking is public speaking unless we are talking to ourselves. Yet we have learned that fear of public speaking is near the top of the list of fears, just after death. Some of my students claim they have placed fear of public speaking in front of fear of death.

Some people must certainly have been humiliated at early and impressionable ages in public speaking situations. I suppose that many more have watched such an event and have learned fear from that. Some of it seems to come from the "ether." I have been speaking in public for forty years and for more than twelve years have taught public speaking classes at Georgia State University. I have never seen an audience

$\underline{14}$

FROM THE TELEVISION SHOW, *THE TWILIGHT ZONE*, WITH ROD SERLING.

attack a speaker. I have watched people sit down, after excellent presentations, with their breathing heavy, hearts racing, and lips swearing that they will never do that again. It is interesting to note that most often in these situations the audiences demonstrated high levels of support and appreciation, in direct contrast to the feelings of the speaker.

A reality of the fear of public speaking is that it requires one to be removed from present time in order to do its job. When people are in the present moment, they forget this fear. *There actually is no fear in the present moment. We fear what may be and what has been.*

Fear of the Unknown

Fear of the unknown also confuses me. It is a simple matter that we cannot really predict the future. Horse races and dice games have been proving the unpredictability of the future since humans had a minute to spare on frivolity. The weather service comes to mind. It has been suggested in chaos theory discussion that even if we had a grid of weather data receivers stationed one foot apart, completely covering the globe, we still could not reliably predict whether there would be rain in a certain place four days from now.

The closest we can come to predicting the future is to analyze as much data as we can gather (in supercomputers and on the Internet we are creating and linking extraordinary amounts of information) and to put our trust into the possibility of pattern repetition. Then we can hope that statistical odds help us out. If the odds are in our favor and the predicted event happens, we can take credit for our knowledge.

Always, and all the time, the next moment is unknowable. Life is the next moment revealing itself again and again. Fear of the unknown is fear of life. This is a "not good" fear. As with all such fear, it is a waste of time at best and can be destructive if allowed to grow. It takes us further and further out of the current moment and robs us of our strength; it robs us of The Improv. I call fear of the unknown "tomorrowphobia."

Learning, Memory, and Not Good Fear

When the people with whom you are working are essentially attentive and the communication methods are realistic and reasonable, poor retention of information is the result of at least two things: lack of relevance and fear. Fear is the more destructive. As easily as fear can implant a memory as a phobia, it can also wipe out recall of information and experience.

"Not good" fear starts in the guts and expands to fill the available space. Some of the first space filled is that reserved for memory. The next space to be filled is inside the person's body, and then it expands to that which can be touched. Fear can fill the area surrounding the body with fear. It then spills over to another body and from there to fill a room, a business, a town, or a nation. It can become infectious to the point of uncontrolled mob violence. "Not good" fear is the product of imagination and memory. Not good fear comes from a time other than now, a place other than here. It is the antithesis of The Improv.

Fear in Reality

My fears, whether they are real or not, good or not good, use all the same channels to get to me. Unless fear comes from a real source of danger, we are jumping at shadows and leaping into old patterns of fight, flight, grapple, diminish, resist, and struggle.

In my Aikido practice, I teach classes, present public demonstrations, and show my ability in periodic public tests. At the higher levels, these tests include attacks from four or five trained people at one time. This process is called "randori" which translates as "seizing chaos." These tests are performed in an arena of peers and before a panel of senior teachers. The single most important and most difficult skills are the abilities to relax and to become fearless in the face of real danger. This fearlessness must be developed by real-time training and practice of the principles and techniques of Aikido. Improv work will give you real-time training and practice in learning to relax and to become fearless in the face of business realities.

ACCEPT YOUR FEAR

As executives, managers, trainers, presenters, teachers, and leaders, we have faced all our fears and have put them aside. We have managed our fears of success and of failure and are focused completely on the needs of our participants. As my eleven-year-old son says, "Yeah, right!"

Each time you enter the arena of your work, you face higher levels of expectation. You often impose these expectations on yourself more than others impose them on you. You can become expert in hiding your fear. You can begin to believe that if people feel your fear they will think of you as incapable or incompetent—if they know you have fear, they will become fearful. This is far from the truth. The denial and ignorance of fear infect others' surroundings.

If you do not acknowledge your fear, at least to yourself, you also teach those you influence to hide their fears. If you are not fearful in new and challenging situations, you may teach your participants to think of themselves as beyond such human frailty as fear. This either alienates or intimidates others and teaches them to value things that are not true.

Acknowledging your fear does not require that you fall apart and collapse, nor suddenly become a fearless superhero. However, those who say fear is absent in their lives generally are admitting the absence of feeling or the absence of awareness and common sense. This is especially true with Improvisation.

If I am never afraid, then there is an assumption that I am not being challenged beyond my sense of comfort. If you do not challenge yourself enough, you must ask, "What is really being learned? Am I leading participants into a failure to challenge themselves?"

As an executive leader using Improvisation, you must allow yourself to know and to experience your fear. You must admit that the fear can be real and that it is normal—and that by acknowledging it there is a possibility of working through it. You must also admit that the fear can be unreal and that it may not be normal—yet it can still be acknowledged and worked through.

The second Improv principle is to strive to become honest with yourself. If you are trying something new in public and there are consequences for failure, it is probably irrational *not* to feel some sort of fear. You must be honest with yourself about this reality.

The third Improv principle suggests that you learn to be completely honest with another person. You may accomplish this if you will tell someone when you are afraid. Better still, tell the whole audience and move ahead anyway. You may as well "shout it from the highest hill." It is your job to create an environment in which fear may be released into the light and laughter of the moment.

Whatever You Call It

Fear or trepidation or hesitancy or resistance or unnamed discomfort or timidity—or any other name for fear—has to be acknowledged by both the executive and the participants. It must be brought into the light to be worked through by all who would learn a new thing. If this is not done, it is very difficult to accomplish learning or behavioral change.

Sometimes, as leaders, we find ourselves in the interesting position of being afraid to generate fear in our gathering. Sometimes when fear does surface in our participants, we become co-dependent and attempt to "fix" it, to make it better for them. Both these responses result from an attempt to become comfortable. Pretending to be comfortable, we teach comfort; everyone remains comfortable; comfort begets comfort; and nothing changes at all.

EXPLORE THE FIELD OF FEAR

As executives and leaders, it is good to realize that people can be filled with fear, surrounded by fear, motivated by fear, stopped by fear, and lost in a universe of fear. Our minds, the media, our friends and family, our co-workers, and our culture sometimes seem to conspire to focus on that which is fearful.

We live on a planet on which an undefined thing called gravity holds us upside down and sideways, on a thin layer of loose dirt and rock that is spinning rapidly through space, propelled by some unknown force. We live in a body that is but a single heartbeat away from stopping. Our bodies are made of more than five billion cells, and only a single cell gone wrong can create a life-threatening cancer. As you can see, some fear is rational under the circumstances.

Our entire culture is built on the idea that a percentage of error is acceptable. In any given year there should be 35,000 automobile deaths, so many airplanes are expected to crash, and lightning may strike at any place or time. Terrorism stalks us, financial disaster lurks, technology looms, and fate laughs. "Yet, for today, for this day's task, let's put that all aside and pretend that we are not afraid." I don't think so.

Improv techniques and process can activate our sense of fear. If the various levels of Improv fear are not acknowledged and brought into the light, the people with whom we are working will do the same thing with Improv fear that they do with life fear. They will either submerge themselves in it or ignore and suppress it. They may steel themselves in the face of fear, freeze before it, forget everything that happened while it was present, or let it control their next steps. It is a job of Improv executives to be alert and aware of this phenomenon.

Fear is cumulative and contagious. Sometimes, the larger the gathering the more potential there is for fear. It is also very interesting to note that the larger the crowd, the greater the tendency for people to either suppress or expand their fear. Sometimes, the smaller the gathering the more the potential for fear to be recognized and dealt with.

In "civilized" meetings, where our purpose is general, the odds of the fear growing wildly or getting out of control are pretty slim. It is possible to generate an atmosphere in which resistant participants seem to gain control of the gathering, yet that is about the worst we will experience.

I do not know of a business meeting that has turned into a mob or a riot or a panic, even when I have witnessed people paying lots of dollars for small return. Of course, if you work or teach in the public schools—secondary, elementary, university, or trade—there is a growing chance that an act of violence will occur in response to fear. I guarantee that violence is the result of fear at some usually complex and cumulative level.

Outside the possibility of violence, the normal experience in reaction to fear in a large crowd will be suppression, which will cause a great numbness and peer pressure toward covert isolation. This will eventually allow the entire group to deny that anything is going on.

It has been said that there are really only two emotions: love and fear. If we are not actively working in the direction of love, we will drift in the direction of fear. If we hide and suppress fear with effort and care, the people will smile and express gratitude for a good time had and done by all, and everyone will go home much the same way they arrived, untouched by the experience or the information. Sometimes they will be so pleased with their comfort and lack of change that they will plan an even larger program, just like it, for next year.

USE LAUGHTER AGAINST FEAR

The best Improv fear management tool is the use of laughter. More common methods of managing fear include avoidance, resistance, and suppression. Running away is sometimes mistaken for fear management. Improvisation offers laughter as an alternative approach that allows for rational fear to be present and managed at the same time.

Laughter is a natural product of Improvisation. By encouraging wholesome laughter, we have a natural balm for the fear that occurs when we deal with learning and growing in public. See Chapter Ten, *Wholesome Laughter Leads the Way,* for a discussion of this wonderful healing aspect of Improvisation.

Most kinds of laughter help to dissipate or reduce fear. Hearty laughter may actually release internal chemistry that counteracts fear. Original and spontaneous humor carries a power beyond that of a joke or a story. Its suddenness and the fact that it must be based in current relationships gives it even more power to act positively on fear.

Even when fear is based on reality, laughter can relieve some of the stress and can help restore perception and perspective. When fear is in the mind (the imagination or memory), laughter can actually relieve the fear completely and permanently. When I teach self-defense classes to teachers, I suggest that running from the building to the car in the dark can be made more safe by laughing loudly and joyously along the way. Whistling is also nice if done with assurance and power.

While Improvisation may bring some fear, it is also a generator of spontaneous, relationship-based, hearty, wholesome laughter. Managing fear can be a simple matter of walking through it. One of my many teachers once described fear as "a film like the surface of a soap bubble." She said that all one must do to get past it is to walk through the film. The hard part is taking the step. Getting through is easy. How does one take this step? It is a little like letting go. You lift up one foot and put it down in front of another. Repeat the process until the fear is gone.

Fear has the capacity to paralyze you and me. Walking through the bubble of fear requires movement. Improvisation generates movement. I have seen boardroom executives and middle-school children walk through their fears using an Improv format. They usually step through without noticing the fear, which is wrapped in wholesome laughter.

If you stick with principles and make emotional commitments, The Improv will provide the environment needed to bring you together with your co-workers, your visions, and your goals. Being together helps us to create a safe environment in which we laugh together without regard to our differences. Laughter and laughing together are forms of internal movement that help us to move forward as individuals and as a group. Given an Improv process, the paralyzing effects of fear can be overcome and the power of fear can lead us to fearless action. When the walking begins, the bubble of fear can be very easily pierced.

With the light, with the power of the present moment, with discipline and practice, almost all fear can be turned into good, clear, real, motivating fear. By accepting the facts and realities of fear, we can approach the entire field of fear rather than single, isolated moments that can lock us in place. With playfulness and laughter, we can learn to walk through the bubble of fear and on to the business of life. When we have cleared away the fear, it becomes possible to find the feelings and feel the way into creative Improv management.

CHAPTER EIGHT

Feelings and Emotions

Managing with the creativity of Improvisation involves exploring your feelings and emotions. A lot of our time is spent in our minds. We consider our problems and difficulties, dream about and plan the future, think over the past, and consider problems. We spend time learning, remembering, analyzing, collecting, and organizing data. The unfettered, free expression of emotions is generally not acceptable in a business setting. Feelings and emotions are often difficult to deal with in *any* setting. Our feelings can be confusing and complicated. Emotions are usually activated before logic. Because of this, our feelings are suspect in most formal settings. It can also be difficult to distinguish thought from feeling. All of these realities help to repress the presence and use of feelings in our most serious situations.

At the same time, it is clear that "gut level" feelings are a major tool of creativity and effective management. Invention, implementation, adjustment, problem solving, and crisis intervention are often the result of activating feelings after the statistical and logical factors are interpreted. It also happens that the logical solution, the one that ought to have worked, that was planned and made ready, simply did not work.

In order to develop the best Improv management skills, it is a good idea to feel your way through the realm of feelings and emotion, beginning with thoughts and a survey.

THOUGHTS ABOUT THE WORD "FEELING"

Consider again the sense of touch: pleasure, pain, pressure, temperature, vibration, tickling, soothing, stickiness, and oiliness. The memory of any of these feelings may be activated by any of the other senses. Such memories are thoughts. The memory can actually cause a physical response such as a tingling or even a rash. It is still a matter of thought.

Another level of feeling is known as *somatic*. This has to do with the way whole body systems respond. Examples of somatic units and their responses are: the whole body (it can shudder as a unit or may experience a hot flash or a chill), the skin (it may tingle or "crawl" as a unit), the stomach (it can tighten or churn with tension), the heart (it can beat quickly or palpate), or the jaws (they can tighten). Also, the head aches, the hands shake, the blood boils, the ears ring, a muscle cramps, or the lungs fill. Each of these events may also be triggered by thought.

Another kind of feeling is made of the emotions themselves. When asked how you feel, you may respond with such abstract and subjective words as "I feel sad." Some other abstract, feeling words are tired, bored, happy, sad, frightened, crisp, and clear. As the words become even more abstract and personal and thus less generally descriptive, the line between feeling and thought becomes more unclear.

Another level of what we think of as "feeling" is purely in the mind. It is indirect and abstract. When asked how we feel we may respond with words that have no meaning beyond some personal thought process. We use such words as, OK, fine, good, so-so, bad, upset, silly, or lost.

A SURVEY OF FEELINGS

The following may be done as a personal exercise or used as a group development tool. The purpose is to allow your thinking to open to a *range of feelings and emotions.* The exercise is best done with paper and pen. It can take as little as fifteen minutes. I suggest that you do not spend more than thirty minutes at a time working in this area.

Improvisation, Inc.

Go through and fill in each blank once. Then fill in each blank four more times.

I feel_____

I am_____

Fill in each of the following blanks as you come to them.

My feet feel like_____

My hands feel like_____

My stomach feels like_____

My mouth feels like_____

My_____feels like_____

My_____feels like_____

Fill in each blank below once. Then return and fill in each blank four more times.

I am_____

My feet are_____

My ears are_____

My nose is_____

My toes are_____

My eyelashes are_____

The most pleasant feeling I can remember is when

_____

The worst pain I can remember occurred when

_____

After you have completed this chapter, I encourage you to come back to this survey. I also suggest that you do it again after finishing the book and after your experiences using Improvisation. Fill in the blanks in different orders and a numbers of times. You may also use this exercise before you begin working with people in an organization.

Analyze Your Answers

Take some time to reflect on your answers to the questions in the exercise above. Especially observe differences in the kinds of words you used in the various question formats. Notice what categories of words you have used in describing your sense of touch. Consider your thoughts and reactions to these responses. Are there differences between your thoughts and your physical reactions? Are you willing to share any of your responses with others?

This exercise is intended as a mental focus process that will help you and your cohort group to begin learning with more of the physical body involved and with more honesty. This exercise can also be developed into an entire business session with discussion and feedback groups, which requires a high level of facilitation skill.

If you choose to have participants share their responses and reactions, the gathering may take on a life of its own. You may need to be prepared to abandon some of your earlier goals for the session if this happens.

PARTICIPANT CENTEREDNESS

Complete understanding of feelings also requires Improv executives to be, or to become, fully participant centered. Many people become self-centered when faced with an audience or an organization. Self-centeredness is a primary source of the fear of public speaking. It is also the source of the droning informational meeting or discourse and of strict adherence to an agenda, script, or plan.

If you do not use your material as a buffer between you and the people with whom you work, then you are liable to feel quite vulnerable. You are vulnerable to error, to challenge, and to being or seeming foolish, overcommitted, or out of control. All of these feelings require that we open ourselves to change, to being affected by our relationships and our surroundings. Becoming focused on and centered in the participants in our lives is the resolution to this vulnerability.

NOTE ABOUT FEELING FOOLISH OR OUT OF CONTROL: The states called "foolish" or "out of control" are more normal than not. Our history, our science, our institutions, our forms, our failures, and often even our successes all tell us that "foolish" and "out of control" are not only normal, but they are the majority experience of most people much of the time. It is interesting to note, however, that this reality is rarely admitted by the people who are actually involved in the experience at the time it is happening. This is the stuff of which human folly is made.

"You do not need to worry about making people think you are foolish. They will do that without any help from you."

JEFF JUSTICE

When doing work with Improvisation and feelings, you need to be able to laugh at, and with, yourself. This is part of the reason The Improv works. Improv events help us become comfortable with a reality—that life and culture are not ours to command completely. Life and culture are ours to experience, to become part of, perhaps to influence, and from which we may learn and, maybe, teach.

THE WONDERFUL FEELING OF CONFUSION

We are often distressed by confusion. Our highly structured lives and systems are a tribute to our dislike of disorder and confusion. In contrast, it is true that embracing some level of confusion is among the requirements of deep learning, of clear reflection, of personal change, and of creativity. Disorder requires reorganization. Reorganization leads to new perspective, invention, innovation, insight, re-evaluation, introspection and, ultimately, to learning and change in behavior.

Confusion is a relative of fear and it too can lead to immobilization. It can also lead to hostility or aggressiveness, to calcification of our ideas, to holding onto old forms, to repetition of erroneous patterns, to disorientation, and even to a general reinforcement of the negative. Confusion can be pretty nasty stuff.

In order to avoid confusion, many people do a number of interesting things: refuse to participate in the moment, fail to listen, listen selectively, interpret selectively (understanding only that which agrees with their current ways of thinking), devalue selectively (the presenter, the information, the experience), forget, forget selectively, and avoid being present in the moment in a variety of creative ways. A thing I do in the face of confusion is to argue, either overtly or covertly. We may also discount ourselves, or the other participants, or life in general.

The Art of Being Confused

The Improv way to deal with confusion is to accept it, then to relax into it and allow it to be part of the natural process of organization and reorganization. We must learn to distinguish confusion that comes from reaching into the real change and learning centers of the participants from confusion caused by errors in timing and focus.

As Improv executives and leaders, it is good to learn and understand how you feel and respond when you are personally confused. A good way to do this is to do things that will give you practice in the art of being confused. A primary reason that travel broadens us is that it provides practice in confusion and its resolution. Attending places of worship that are not our own or public gatherings that are outside our norms can also provide such broadening practice. Improvisation is also a good source of practice in being confused.

AN EXERCISE IN TIMING

Make a list of things you could do to place yourself into confusion without placing yourself in physical danger, for example, walking around with your eyes closed in a safe place, perhaps with a guide. Attend a meeting of an opposing political party. Attend a function with an age group that is twenty-five years older or younger than you are. Attend a children's movie on Saturday morning by yourself or with a new friend. Find a big field and spin around and around in circles until you are dizzy and can hardly stand up. Call a stranger on the phone and generate a conversation about life. Make up a "confusion challenge" of your own.

Practice and training are done to improve timing, as well as strength and a number of other attributes of excellence. Usually our experiences with confusion come in the middle of the crisis, just when we feel that we need our wits about us. Usually we face the issue of confusion at critical moments when family, friends, business, time, and money are at stake. It is better to become good at handling confusion in practice settings. This is an almost hidden attribute of working with Improvisation.

Emergency Training in Managing Confusion

My background includes mountain search and rescue and rock climbing training, suicide intervention and crisis counseling, welfare crisis intervention, martial arts training, first aid, water safety, CPR training, and U.S. Naval Line Officer training.

Each of these experiences included dealing with serious consequences and serious states of confusion—my own and that of others. In order to deal effectively with the various aspects of emergency work, it is necessary to experience higher and higher levels of stress and confusion, along with increasing numbers of choices. The success comes not from surviving the confusion but in thriving on it and making it a source of reorganized information.

Confusion, by its nature, comes from there being too many choices or no choices at moments of crisis. For moments of too many choices, time spent "practicing" confusion teaches surveying, analysis, prioritizing, selection, and commitment to a course of action. If there are no choices, practice teaches patience, personal control, inventiveness, and creativity.

When groups practice the human phenomenon of confusion, the lessons take the form of cooperation, teamwork, interdependence, problem solving, "crew response," resource management, open communication, sharing, and basic connectedness.

Improv form includes and requires practice in being confused. Confusion is a good thing unless you are operating at high speeds or far above the ground. Fear of confusion can inhibit learning and teaching. Failure to approach and embrace confusion can render learning and change ineffective.

A FEELING CALLED BLENDING

Blending is more than just becoming "one" with something outside yourself. Blending results in synergy, that state in which the whole is greater than the sum of its parts. Blending requires that the teacher or trainer do more than merely accept his or her own confusion. You must actively present your open confusion as the realm in which the greatest possibility of blending lies. It also requires that the trainer request, accept, feel, and thus blend with the participants' confusion.

As with all Improv principles, blending is so simple as to be complex. Blending is more complicated than merely mixing. Objects mixed together usually can be easily sifted or separated. Blending is less strong than bonding.

The Improv Chef

In cooking we use the term blending to describe components being brought together under the influence of an outside agency. Under the influence of milk and heat, we find that flour and sugar blend nicely to make pastas and pastries. This is a lot like the process of working with people!

Improvisation, Inc.

Sometimes people want someone to come in and change their culture or solve long-festering problems by devoting only a few hours to the process. This is a bit like wanting bread to appear by mere mixing and stirring, without allowing for blending, kneading, rising, and cooking. Kneading is a blending activity. The whole process takes time.

Rising and cooking are biochemical. Blending does not usually have the harshness of chemical reactions nor the permanence of biochemical changes. Blending is softer and more gentle. It is more interactive and less sudden. Rather than creating a release of energy, there is a gathering of energy—a creation of potential energy. If you have never kneaded bread with your own hands, I recommend that you do so at the next opportunity.

Sand Castles

Something creates the magic that appears when everyone is suddenly on the same wave length, we are walking together, as individuals and as a gathering, and miracles seem to happen. What makes this happen?

Considering the sand castle may help us understand. There is an interesting thing about sand. Clean, pure silicon crystals (sand bits) are completely free and loose particles. Dry sand slips through the fingers and flies easily through the air. Each particle is disconnected from all others, beholden to none. But these sand particles can be heated to high temperature and melted into uniform crystalline structures of glass, where the unique character of each particle is lost to the whole form.

Wild sand, however, the kind found in nature, has fine dust mixed with it. The dust is a key component in a powerful process. When blended by the agency of water, the sand crystals and the dust complement and enhance one another. As in Improvisation, they create a relationship. The wet dust becomes mortar, a temporary binding for the sand particle structure. With this fine and simple blending, we can create sand castles. We must also continue to add water or the sand castle will turn again to dust.

People can be like crystals of sand. We can be hard, and jagged, and separate, and isolated, and irritating. We also may be melted into unrecognizable forms with our individuality as invisible as glass. We can be brought together for higher purposes that do not destroy our individuality, yet create more than the individual can create alone. We too can be blended into sand castles. We too must be replenished with a magic binding.

When working with people and Improvisation, the binding materials—the liquid that brings and holds people together, the magic that blends—is consciousness, attention to detail, care-fullness, laughter, kindness, self-awareness, and ultimately nothing less than love in its most wondrous forms.

LOVE, LUV, LOVE

"Perhaps love is like a resting place, a shelter from a storm. It exists to give you comfort. It is there to keep you warm."

JOHN DENVER

Ai is a Japanese word that expresses the feeling that there is a real bonding between people. The word is pronounced "eye." It forms the first part of the word "Aikido." "Ai" means harmony, balance, compatibility and reflection, relationship, or (dare I say it?) love. The words (ai and love) invoke the powers of mutual respect and awareness. Ai suggests honoring, encouraging, allowing, and encompassing difference. There is a gentleness as well as a firmness in ai. Ai speaks of overview at the same time as detail.

Ai describes the harmony inherent in the relationship of the fingers to the thumb while making a fist or the cooperation of clasping two hands with intertwined fingers. It includes grasping, clinging, and letting go. It may note the holding of hands by couples or the holding of hands by people in a circle. Ai expresses itself in such forms as the clapping of hands, the snapping of fingers, the beating of drums, or bodies with hands and arms weaving and intertwining in the complexities of dance.

This ai (harmony, balance, or love) acts like water with wild sand. It is a unifying influence that allows for blending between humans and encourages our very distinct individuality and uniqueness.

BLENDING AS AN EXECUTIVE TEACHER

Practice in the blending of Improv activities establishes connections between people. These connections stay in place for a long time in an Improv environment, an organization that promotes the philosophies and practices of Improvisation.

In training and classroom settings, I tell participants that the most common teaching format describes one teacher with some number of students. A better way is to see the gathering as having all the people in the room be teachers, all students. If I am truly to be a student, I must allow myself to be altered and affected by all my teachers. The more students, the more teachers, the greater the probability of real change, of real learning. This requires teaching by example. As a teacher I teach participants to teach. As a "student" I teach my students to learn. As an educator I must do both.

IMPORTANT NOTE
One thing required of teaching by example is actual participation in the games being used. Improv games are so powerful as agents of change that the leader or facilitator may be seen as a manipulator unless there is personal participation.

LEADING AND LEADERSHIP

There is a difference between *leading* and *leadership.* The idea of leadership tends to identify someone who is in charge, one who holds responsibility, one who makes decisions, one who tells us where to go and what to do next. Overly strong leadership can actually inhibit learning and change. A teacher who seems to know too much can actually destroy a participant's motivation to learn. This does not mean that we should abdicate leadership, only that we must put it in a proper perspective.

Lead: "From the Old English, *lithan,* meaning to go."

Leading is a complex thing and is, of course, the base of all leadership. All the skills of the effective executive are grounded in leading. All the skills of management, supervision, development, production, organization, reorganization, communication, learning, and commerce are grounded in leading.

To lead is to go. This means that we must go where we ask our participants to go. Having been there before is not enough; even when we have been there time after time, we must go there again with new sets of people with whom we are learning or developing an organization.

Go where? Too often we think that this means only that we must go to the end of the trail, at which point the job will be done. Yes, and goals are great for tracking and seeking benchmarks, for correcting and motivating, and for getting the job done. However, with Improvisation there is no end point. There is no final goal. There is only a *process* that grows as the participants grow. It is truly limitless in the extent to which it can be explored. It is more than a skill. It is more than a craft. It is an art. Perfection or an end point are not within its aims. Leading, like Improvisation, is an exploration and an experience that can be enhanced by a personal training system such as Aikido, meditation, tennis, or volunteer work.

The Improv moves us into a state of mind in which we learn by doing. We must be active in the use of Improv principles and processes time and time again, and we must lead our participants by our personal example. As with other aspects of Improvisation, leading has a mental component, an emotional component, a physical component, and a spiritual component.

Mental Leading

Mental leading requires composing one's mind. This usually takes some disciplined practice, such as breathing, focused reading, prayer, exercise, stretching, mental gymnastics, listening to music, or meditation.

Mental leading is a matter of creating an attitude of possibility. It requires knowing that the work can be done and that the goals can be reached. This position must be based in reality and honesty and must be continually re-evaluated.

Mental leading has a lot to do with language-based communication skills. I recommend that you read *Language in Thought and Action* by S.I. Hayakawa and Keith Johnstone's *Impro, Improvisation and the Theatre* for developing these skills. Both are listed in the Bibliography at the end of this book.

Mental leading also has to do with time and place and preparation. Chapter Nine, *Language Is a Funny Thing,* explores being on time and in time.

Emotional Leading

Emotional leading also requires preparation and disciplined practice. The preparation discipline may be the same in both cases.[15] An early problem in emotional leading is

15

AS A MATTER OF FACT, ANY PHYSICAL OR TRAINING PRACTICE MAY BE ENHANCED BY GIVING IT A FOCUS. FIVE MINUTES OF MAKING MUSIC, MEDITATING, OR RUNNING, OR DEVOTED TO EACH ASPECT OF BLENDING AND LEADING WILL RESULT IN THIRTY MINUTES OR MORE OF PRODUCTIVE WORK.

Improvisation, Inc.

in identifying our own emotions. We must have a command of the field in order to lead. Just naming the emotions gives us some power over them. As you may have noted in the earlier exercise, naming your own emotions may be more difficult than one might expect. In an Improv game called *Emotional Symphony,* players call out the names of emotions and make sounds that might accompany them. When I first began working with this game, I would line up six or eight people and ask them to name some emotions. I was fascinated to discover that people began to run out of names for emotions when the group reached seven or eight of the most basic emotions, such as fear, hate, love, anger, lust, and joy.

My father was convinced that there were only thirty-two human emotions. He never gave me a list, yet it is probable that I had accepted the limit of his thinking. I could not imagine the limitation of people who could think of only eight or twelve ways to describe feelings. Once a participant arrived with a list of one hundred names of human emotions. Later I discovered a chart in the office of a psychologist that presented an array of nearly two hundred names for the ways we feel. I have since found a computer brainstorming program that very kindly, capriciously, whimsically, idiosyncratically, eccentrically, and humorously presented just over 2,700 descriptions of emotional states.

Whatever we are feeling as we face participants in an Improv session, it is good to be aware of as many names and descriptions, variations, and subtleties as possible. The next exercise will help you find your own list of possibilities.

YOUR OWN LIST OF EMOTIONS

Make a list of all the emotions you can name. Do this in a single sitting and note the number you can generate from your own, unaided vocabulary. Keep the list and add to it over time. It is very good to work with the list before and after sessions in which you use Improv skills and techniques. Check how many emotions were evoked or used. Also take note of the levels of emotional intensity experienced. If there are few emotions or few highs or lows, the depth of your work may need more attention. Do the same after work that achieves breakthroughs, insight, or enlightenment, or in sessions in which you have experienced stress, difficulty, or failure.

Try to come up with thirty-two names of emotions to start (in honor of my father). Note that "OK" or "fine" are not names of emotions. If you have such words on your list, replace them with words that describe a real "feeling" that happens when the words "fine" and "OK" come to your mind. Hunger may be an emotion, hungry is not. Begin to observe yourself and your activities in relation to your list of emotions. Use a highlighter to note the emotions you most often experience or express most easily.

Make a note of the emotions with which you are least familiar for later personal work. Over time, explore internally for feelings described by the emotions with which you are not familiar. If you cannot get to the feeling of unfamiliar emotions, try imagining what kind of situation might generate such a feeling in yourself or in others.

When you use feedback forms or evaluations in your group work, place your list of names of "emotions" on the evaluation form. Ask for distinctive names of emotions. Ask the participants for the number of these emotions that they have experienced. Ask about the intensity of various emotions. The exercise will help you and your organization to become increasingly aware of emotions and where the effect of emotions—or lack of them—is impacting your work.

Emotional content enhances learning and retention and encourages change in behavior. Random, unnoticed, ignored, suppressed, co-dependent emotional content can also stop development or twist it beyond recognition. Improvisation will touch on the emotions of the participants. Effective teaching with emotional content requires that you continuously lead the way in this exploration, before, during, and after your organizational and presentational work.

Physical Leading

Leading physically is another complex concept. At its most basic level, it simply requires that you put your own body on the line and that you physically do the same things that you expect other participants to do.

Sometimes this can be done by merely standing up and sitting down. When working with people, it often means giving up such crutches as podiums and notes. Sometimes it means taking a physical hand in moving the furniture around in the room to make it work better. It certainly has to do with being present on time and in time and in your own physical body. When working with children, I find that I must often ask them to "stay inside your own bodies." With adults I must do the same thing, but more subtly and more gently.

Physical leading requires the use of your own laughter. Sometimes physical leading requires feeling and sharing more of your own true emotions. Emotional control may indicate strength in some circles, yet it does not necessarily create a leader. As a matter of fact, it may teach the participants to withhold the emotional component of their own work.

Very often leading in the physical arena requires open sharing of your own weaknesses, errors, limits, mistakes, and personal evolution. Children learn a great deal from the sharing of the foibles and mistakes of their elders. Adults do the same, yet tend not to admit it. Adults usually have trouble sharing their weaknesses with others. This results in lost resources for everyone.

We really do respect people who have learned from their own mistakes, so it becomes necessary to present yourself as being experienced, having accomplished enough to have made mistakes, and being smart enough to have learned something from them.

People tend to want to know about people who have had real experiences and who have overcome struggles. In leading with Improvisation, we must learn to share our struggles so that others may make use of them.

Aikido

I have mentioned the wonderful martial art known as Aikido several times. Aikido is a Japanese martial art developed entirely on the premise of defense. There is no hitting nor kicking, hurting nor harming in Aikido. The art of Aikido is founded on the principle that violence begets violence, and therefore violence cannot be effectively managed by the use of violence. I have studied and taught this art for twenty years and I am still learning to comprehend basics.

Aikido is the practice and study of a wide range of physical movements. The mind is trained to be focused on, and to function from, the center of balance of the body, especially in motion. You may locate your center of mobile balance most easily when you are standing, relaxed and balanced on both feet, with hands resting at your side. The center, or "hara," is then located about two inches below the navel and midway between your front and back.

The "hara" or center of mobile balance is also considered to be the center of the will—the will to be, the will to do, the will to influence, and the will to create. Understanding our "center" is part of the heart of leading and leadership.

It takes consciousness, practice, and discipline to locate the center and then to learn to move with and from there. In an Improv gathering there is a center of balance of the group as a whole that is interdependent with the centeredness of the organizational leadership and the individuals. Centered leading and leading from the center by the facilitator are important ingredients in using Improvisation as a business tool.

RELAXATION AS A TECHNIQUE

Anything that must be done for a long time or must be done repeatedly has be accomplished in a state of relaxation. Activity actually requires a state of relaxed tension. Relaxation in the body of an active leader inspires confidence. Tension in the same body inspires tension, fear, or even anger among the participants.

Complete relaxation requires consciousness, practice, and discipline. In any exercise it is good to relax as completely as you can in between moments of muscle and body tension. While you are learning new movements, you may be fairly tense or awkward. This is partially because you are using your mind to do the learning. As you begin to let your body take over the learning and the practicing, your mind can become engaged in helping to relax the rest of your body.

I first learned the exercise that follows more than twenty years ago and I am still working to perfect it. It is a simple physical exercise that may come to you more or less easily. Twenty minutes spent learning this exercise will be worth your while.

The instructions are purposefully not accompanied by an illustration. It is important that you take the time to work through the process. Ask a friend to talk you through it if you wish. Once you are able to do the exercise a few times, the instructions will seem very clear. It is this clarity that you seek.

ONE STEP, TWO STEPS

Standing with your feet a little more than shoulder width apart, try to balance your weight evenly on both feet and evenly on the balls and heels of both feet. Let this effort take awhile. Explore your whole body in your mind as you do this. Accomplishing only this much may be enough for one session.

Once you learn to be comfortably balanced on both feet, begin shifting your weight back and forth from foot to foot. Be aware of any feeling in your body as you do this.

ONE STEP

- *Keeping one foot in place, step forward then backward again and again with the same foot. Switch feet and do the One Step again on the other side.*

- *Keep one foot in place. Step forward again and again as you pivot around the foot held in place. Switch feet and go in the other direction.*

- *Pivot backward. Switch feet and repeat the movement in the other direction.*

If you feel any dizziness, slow down. Notice whether you feel energy or tension anywhere in your body. You may feel tension in the back of your neck, tightness at the top of your head, or a constriction high in your chest. Breathe as though you are breathing into the location of each of the feelings you notice. Each time you do this you can help that area relax. Getting to this point may be enough work for now. Once you have become comfortable with *One Step, try Two Steps.*

TWO STEPS

Stand with your left foot pointing forward about a foot ahead of your right. Your right foot should be slightly, comfortably turned out, away from the direction in which your left foot is pointed.

- *Keep your left foot in place. Step forward with your right foot.*

- *Slowly turn your hips to the left, letting your feet turn as well, until you are facing the opposite direction. At this point your left foot will be forward.*

- *Then step backward with your left foot, keeping your right foot in place.*

- *You are now standing with your right foot in front of your left and facing the opposite direction from where you started. See that your right toes are pointed forward and your left toes comfortably away to the left.*

- *To complete the movement, reverse the process and go back to where you were to begin with.*

- *Step forward with your left foot.*

- *Without letting your foot stick to the floor, turn your hips to the right until you are facing the opposite direction. At the same time allow your feet to turn so they will face the same direction as your hips.*

- *Step back with your right foot.*

- *When you have successfully moved from the original position and back again, you have completed one whole set of Two Steps.*

- *When finished, you should be standing in your original position, facing the same way as you started, left foot forward. If you are not exactly in this position, take a short break and try the exercise again from the beginning.*

- *Once you have done it successfully, try two stepping for just a few moments to make sure you have the hang of it. Learning to do just this much may be enough for a whole session.*

N O T E

If after some effort you are still having trouble doing this exercise you may contact a local Aikido dojo and ask if you can come in and have someone teach you how to do this. The dojo may know it as the *Two Steps*, or "irimi-tenkan," or "udefuri-undo."[16]

Once you have learned to do *Two Steps* well, giving twenty minutes a day to the exercise can have a positive influence on your physical, emotional, mental, spiritual, and organizational well-being.

16

IF YOU NEED HELP FINDING AN AIKIDO DOJO IN YOUR TOWN, CONTACT THE AIKIDO ASSOCIATION OF AMERICA IN CHICAGO OR THE UNITED STATES AIKIDO FEDERATION IN NEW YORK CITY.

If you are going to teach this exercise to others, it is necessary to practice *advanced two stepping,* as described below. Important in this process is that you consciously observe and consider the manner in which you personally went through it when you first tried. The more difficult it was to accomplish, the more it was an indication that you were not operating through your center of balance. Knowing this about yourself can give you valuable information for working with others doing the exercise.

ADVANCED TWO STEPPING

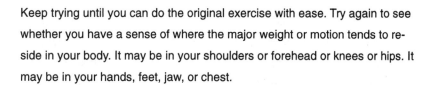

Keep trying until you can do the original exercise with ease. Try again to see whether you have a sense of where the major weight or motion tends to reside in your body. It may be in your shoulders or forehead or knees or hips. It may be in your hands, feet, jaw, or chest.

When you are doing *Two Steps* fairly easily, you can begin to move more quickly. As you move faster, you are liable to find yourself leaning backward as you take the backward step. If you experience this, you can begin to shift your weight forward at exactly the same moment that you step backward. This will compensate for the centrifugal force and the momentum going in the opposite direction. As you begin this compensation movement, you are liable to find yourself tilting to the front. As soon as you become aware of this happening, begin to shift your weight toward your center of balance.

If you have been successful in taking these two steps at a faster and faster pace, you may notice that your hands and arms can have a lot of effect on how the movement works. If your arms are just flying around, they can pull you off balance. The higher the speed, the more this is true. If you are holding your hands and arms stiffly, they will make your body stiffen and will inhibit the speed at which you can turn. Begin to relax and you can gain gentle, supple control of your hands and arms as you turn.

Try to start the turn with your hands directly in front of you, fingers relaxed, arms relaxed and slightly bent. The palms are facing each other a few inches apart. Your hands should be extended a few inches away from your body at about the level of your navel. Starting with your left foot in front of your right, if you are re-laxed, your left hand may be slightly ahead of the right. Take your next *Two Steps.*

As you make the turns, bring your left hand close to the front and center of your body, cupped with the palm upward. Lay your right hand into the cup of your left hand with the fingers pointed in the opposite direction. As you face the opposite direction, extend your hands in front of you again. Now your right foot will be forward and, if you are relaxed, your right hand may be a bit in front of the left.

If, after effort and practice, this does not make sense, then contact an aikido dojo for guidance. It is not unusual for people to need some assistance in ac-complishing the exercise at this level. If you can work it out for yourself, there will be hidden benefits. The more you practice the easier it becomes.

This exercise will bring you into a working relationship with your center of balance. Being in your center of balance will enable you to be much more aware of the balances involved in your work. Working from your center of balance is very helpful for suc-cessful Improv work.

Once you have mastered this movement, you may find that it is an excellent activity to teach to small groups. It has been my experience that vast amounts of development can be accomplished in a minimum amount of time by teaching this simple task. Do it with minimum talk. Do not plan the actual presentation. Lead the presentation.

Spiritual Leading

The use of Improvisation to its fullest brings us again to the invisible aspect to life. Improvisation can entice individuals to look more deeply into internal, invisible as-pects of their lives and personal motivations, which will lead to the extraordinary in-visible powers of laughter. Laughter is a healing mechanism. Laughter brings people together and helps them to overcome differences. Laughter offers perspective. These are the very things of which the spirit is made.

The leadership of the spirit comes not from the way in which we do things, nor from the way in which we talk about things. It comes from the way in which we walk in the world. In The Improv we walk facing the invisible, looking into the realm of spirit. This is also the direction of the source of creativity.

We all must approach and learn of the spiritual world from our own personal perspectives. Improvisation works and has value as merely a methodology and technique. The extraordinary benefits, however, come from this deeper exploration. Much like deciding to investigate the deeper aspect of *Two Steps,* we must decide to seek the depth of the invisible, the realm of the spirit. We must put its lessons into practice, and then perhaps, in a lifetime of joyous pursuit, we may learn to master a spiritual approach to improvisational leading.

Finding your feelings and feeling your way are methods of living "an examined life." Doing this will require you to become aware of the feelings and emotions of others, as well as to become aware of your own feelings and emotions. When you engage The Improv, you will find yourself faced with such realities as the power of love and the depth of blending. You will learn to delight in the responsibilities of physical and emotional leading, and the wonders of the spirit of The Improv.

You can also use Improvisation as a tool without considering any of this. You may use the games, gain the benefits, walk the paths, create the creativity, and benefit from the results without doing anything more than participating and playing according to the rules. The depth and power are part of the process, and if you really work with it your consciousness will be altered. In order to develop the process and take advantage of the power of The Improv, it is good to review and notice the power of language, as seen in the next chapter.

CHAPTER NINE

Language Is a Funny Thing

Language is the means by which we engage in conversation, literature, poetry, information, directions, prayers, curses, invectives, and babble. Language is both "funny ha, ha" and "funny peculiar." Language is the most important of things and the least important of things. Words have many meanings and endless connotations, yet any single word is merely a symbol squiggled on a page or a wave vibrated through the air. At the same time, a wrong word can leave an eternal scar. A right word can help us transcend time itself.

Language is the least meaningful in its verbal form. The messages sent by your body can overshadow the meanings of the words. Body language can modify, enhance, expand, or deny the message of your words. Body language can send messages that are either parallel or at right angles to the original intent. Effective Improv management suggests that you engage in extraordinary attention to the details involved in all aspects of the use of language.

A LOOK AT LANGUAGE

The human vocal system is capable of hundreds of small sounds. Standard American English has forty-seven specific sound units called phonemes that have been cataloged and identified in the International Phonetic Alphabet.[17] The human body is capable of thousands of subtle movements. The small "sounds" of the human body have not been catalogued, although some researchers calculate that as much as 75 percent of our message is carried by our body language.

English language dictionaries define around two million words. There are some definitions of body language on which we agree: a wave, a shrug, a mug, the irritated tapping of a foot. There are definitions of physical signals used in various industries—airplane directors, TV and movie directors, military leaders. There is an agreed-on international sign language for people with hearing difficulties. There is, however, no general dictionary of the language of the body. This language is, so far, too personal and too vast to encompass. A wink of the eye may say nearly anything.

You cannot objectively observe your own body language in action. You never really know exactly what is being said by the language of your own body, if only because the meaning resides in the interpretation.

In spite of this, as an Improv executive, you must become extraordinarily aware of what is being said by the bodies of the individuals and the body of the gathering. This skill develops with awareness of your own body.

Improvisation operates at amazing speeds. It activates deep feelings. Without an understanding of the depth and nature of the language of the body you will often find yourself far behind the curve. Without an understanding of the languages of the body, you may actually create resistance and ill will within the gathering. Being completely present with and aware of body language opens many doors to using Improvisation as a business tool.

PRESENCE

At least 15 percent of your communication will be transmitted by your personal *presence*. One form of presence is what we think of as stage presence—the ability to fill the room with your energy and to make your being felt by all. This has to do with energy and the ability to be completely and passionately involved in what you are doing.

<hr>

17

FOR AN EXCELLENT OVERVIEW OF THE COMPONENTS OF THE HUMAN VOICE AND LANGUAGE, SEE GLENN, E. C., GLENN, P. J., AND FORMAN, S., *YOUR VOICE AND ARTICULATION*. ENGLEWOOD CLIFFS, NJ: PRENTICE HALL, 1989.

Improvisation, Inc.

This form of presence can be most apparent in your relaxed confidence. It is reflected in the brightness in your eyes, the lightness of your step, and the ways in which you reach out to the people around you. Everyone knows someone who commands attention on entering a room without fanfare nor introduction. This is sometimes called "star quality" at higher public levels. When working at a business level, some skill in outgoing presence is a basic requirement.

The other form of presence I have spoken of before. It is being present *in the moment,* that is, the act of being totally and completely in this moment, with these feelings, in these surroundings, doing this thing, focused on these people, thinking about this event and these words, without reference to any other time or place. The most powerful presence comes from being so completely in the present moment that there is simply nowhere else to be.

Let's take a moment to add up the amount of communication "stuff" that is used up before you utter a single word. Seventy five percent body language and 15 percent presence comes to 90 percent. I maintain that an additional 5 percent of available communication energy is wrapped up with the language you speak, the syntax of your language, and the semantics of your meaning.

This leaves 5 percent for cognition, energy, process, or whatever else it takes to carry the message you have in your mind. Remember that the message is the "last, most important" element in our communication, even though we tend to spend more of our energy and focus on this 5 per cent. If you will offer only as little as 50 percent of your attention and energy to the 95 percent of what happens *before* the words begin, the chances of your success in The Improv can be increased a thousandfold.

GENERAL SEMANTICS

A specialty field in the study of communication is called General Semantics. the study of the meaning of meaning. It considers such questions as "How and why do words have meaning?" and "How do we know what the meaning is?" If something means something it has meaning, right? What do I mean by that? "I mean, what does the meaning of meaning mean?"

This academic pursuit has origins in the work of Count Alfred Korzybsky, as articulated in his work entitled *Science and Sanity* published in 1933. An update in the same field is by S. I. Hayakawa entitled *Language in Thought and Action,* published in 1964.

General Semantics searches deeply into the exciting and extraordinary miracle that words and actions can, indeed, communicate thoughts and ideas, that one human being can actually formulate an idea and another can receive that idea through language. The truth is that we do not fully understand how this happens. That a language can be learned and spoken and written is a foundation of civilization. Whales may be able to "speak" with one another. They cannot, we assume, learn the language of humans or dogs. That human language can be reproduced, recorded, broadcast, electronically transferred, and maybe even psychically transmitted surpasses the miraculous.

Stasis

A very important element of the study of General Semantics is the theory of "stasis." The organizing principle of stasis is that all language-based communication deals with abstract thought.

All that language really can do is to provide names or descriptions for things and processes and relationships. The names are abstractions; they are not the things themselves. The word for a chair is not the chair itself. The word for a thought is not the thought itself. Words are only an imaginary and agreed on depiction of the item or the concept. They function as a map that helps us understand the real thing. However, as Count Korzybsky said, "The map is not the territory." Personal abstractions are "maps" attached to words that may make our communication even more complex.

Consider the following levels of abstraction as we explore the word and idea that we call a chair, a simple thing to sit on. The furniture dealer may abstract the chair to the level of representing his personal income. This is certainly some steps away from the original chair. To a craftsperson the chair may represent an abstraction of her self-image. To an engineer the chair may suggest a structural principle or design pattern, and to an atomic physicist the very same chair may be seen as a combination of atoms and subatomic particles. To a son or daughter a chair may be abstracted to the level of a memory of an ancestor—Grandma's heirloom. To a freezing person the chair may be a source of heat. To a person of the spirit the very same chair may be representative of a higher being, a God who is responsible for the existence of the chair.

Each of these "meanings" indicates a different level of abstraction. The meanings assigned are all at different imaginary steps away from the real chair, this specific chair, the particular set of atoms and molecules that make up this real chair at this real time, which is absolutely unique in all the universe.

When both people are speaking of the chair at the same level of abstraction or at a level of abstraction that is close enough for communication to work, it is said that they have achieved "stasis." If people are speaking of the same chair and one of them is talking about a source of heat and the other is talking about a treasured memory, then the levels of abstraction are far apart and there can be significant misunderstanding. The use they may make of the chair can create serious conflict. In this circumstance the participants have not achieved stasis.

If one sees the chair as a four-legged thing on which to sit and the other sees it as a piece of furniture on which to sit, there is still a different level of abstraction, but they are not so far apart that there will be confusion or conflict. It a child leans back in a chair as an exercise in learning balance, it can conflict terribly with a teacher who abstracts the action to the level of disrespect for public property. With an understanding of "stasis," we can hope to manage our differences; we can actively seek the same or similar levels of abstraction in the matters about which we communicate.

Through this brief description of stasis, we can see how complicated things can become when we are sharing about something as simple as a chair. Imagine what happens as we engage in more subtle and complex matters—things such as emotion, time and space, politics, religion, philosophy, and the unknown. Try talking about love, hate, truth, and beauty without achieving stasis and it may turn out to be explosive.

The realities of communication and the theories of Improvisation speak to the need for understanding and arriving at stasis by the simple engagement of Improv games. This engagement operates at pre-verbal levels. We begin with the commitment of *being in time and on time, here and now, in the current moment*. Because we force ourselves into the time frame of the present, many of the problems of stasis failure are never encountered. Because we are actually inventing meaning and agreeing on our levels of abstraction as we work and play together, we automatically either create stasis or we create situation comedy.

Situation comedy is the embodiment of stasis failure. For example, in the television program "I Love Lucy," almost every difficulty arose from the fact that Lucy was working on some fear, jealousy, or insecurity and Ricky was operating on some ruse or at face value. Improv executives will do well to study stasis and to seek stasis.

ON TIME AND IN TIME

Language is so complex that its fine points operate at speeds faster than jet travel. It actually operates at the speed of sound. It takes total concentration and attention to avoid errors, and even total concentration can fail. To engage concentration it is necessary to be on time and in time. The Improv suggests that you make a real commitment to being on time and in time. One of the less abstract meanings of this idea is that you must be on location and in the location of the gathering before your assigned and advertised time.

It is my experience that unless you are present a minimum of fifteen minutes before the beginning of an event, you may be "on time," yet you may not ever quite be "in time." Fifteen minutes may be enough time only if you have worked in that location earlier on the same day. If you have not, my recommendation is that you arrive a minimum of half an hour prior to the time of group activity.

Being in time and on time requires forethought, desire, planning, focus, discipline, and effort. When I am unfamiliar with a location, my practice is to arrive ninety minutes to two hours prior to the start time. When working in a strange city, my preference is to arrive a day before. In Improvisation, though there is no time spent in rehearsal, preparation is still a major part of the formula.

The truth is that we, as professionals, are able to work in any setting. As an accomplished improviser, I adapt immediately to any circumstance. As a professional improviser, I also know that the seating and the setting can change a walk in the park into an uphill battle.

I have had the experience of sending a floor plan to site planners only to arrive to find the setting completely wrong—not just incorrect, but looking as though it were designed specifically to facilitate difficulty and failure. I have also experienced the delight of setting up a room the night before for an early meeting only to find that some kind soul has rearranged it by meeting time.

PROACTIVELY PRESENT

Even if you are actively involved in a specific discipline designed to help keep you in current time, it is important that you actively engage in some activity to bring yourself into the space of the event and the moment of the gathering. Being on time as described above will result in your being *in* time as well. If you are time lagged, it is extremely important that you engage actively in some practice that will help you get into and stay in the present moment. If you are a "morning person" working in the afternoon, you must give yourself some discipline that will bring you to the there and then.

You will find that five to ten minutes of quiet time can do wonders for your presence. Prayer or meditation is an active practice that can bring you into this moment. A quiet walk, a host of breathing exercises, a wide variety of physical exercises, singing a specific song, and clapping your hands to a set rhythm will all provide help in bringing you to this first most important Improv rule. Several exercises in this book can be used to enhance your presence in the moment simply by focusing on being present as you do the exercise.

SURROUNDINGS

This discussion is still really about language. I make certain that I have time to wander around a larger activity location. Some of this helps me be familiar with simple logistics and housekeeping. It is good to know where the restrooms and telephones are. It is even better to know what the restrooms look like and how the water in the building tastes. This is very important in your own business location. It is even more important when your business has multiple locations and you are gathering people in a location where you do not normally work.

It is good to be familiar with some of this particular day's experience that may have an effect on participants. I have been known to walk or drive in a circle around a building and to wander around aimlessly just to see what the participants see as they arrive. In hotels, convention centers, corporate headquarters, and business meeting facilities, I gain early access to the meeting space, ride the elevators, and check out food, water, coffee, and other amenities. If I can find my way into adjacent areas, audiovisual booths, back rooms, and service access areas, it gives me information regarding the secondary surroundings in which I am working. Go in the side door. Take local transportation. Walk around the block. Do anything you can to experience the surroundings that will touch your participants. In your own company, it is good to look over familiar locations periodically with new eyes just to see what you have never seen before.

When working in a strange city, it is always best to be familiar with recent news and weather, with sports events, and with local politics. Listen to the radio, take a look at a local television station, and read the headlines.

If you are aware of the circumstances that can affect your participants' sense of the present, you have a much stronger chance of leading them into and keeping them in the present moment with you. The more you know about where they are at the beginning, the more able you will be to get them to where you all need to be.

Playing with Words

Humans have a natural tendency to play with words. This can be both fun and frustrating. An informal game we all play is to say one thing when we mean another. Inside each of us is a very important place to look at our language. When working with people, and especially when working with Improvisation, what you are saying out loud and what you are feeling inside needs to be the same. If your words to the people with whom you are working are "Hello, I'm glad to be here," and inside, you are asking "What am I doing here?," the inside message will be transmitted.

The people around us usually know how we really are, no matter how good we are at keeping our thoughts and feelings inside. The second Improv principle is that you must strive to become honest with yourself. The third Improv principle is that you must learn to be honest with at least one other person. So, even when you are really good at keeping your internal language to yourself, you are breaking basic rules if your internal language differs from the external.

Avoiding the Pun

My son, since the age of three, has been delighted by the fact that words can have more than one meaning. As he has grown he has both loved and hated the fact that many words can sound the same and have different meanings or sound the same and then have the same or similar meanings and different sounds.

> *To pun:* "To play at using words in such a way as to suggest two or more meanings, or using a word in such a way as to suggest the meaning of another word similar in sound."

The word "pun" first appeared during the 17th Century. Its roots are in the idea of quibbling over a fine point. The pun is a limited form of word play. Except in the game called *Word Montage,* the pun has little value in working with Improvisation and can actually be detrimental to its goals and purposes.

The best way I can explain the detriment of the pun is to have you imagine that there is a "pun gremlin." When people begin to use puns to generate laughter, the pun gremlin appears and encourages an infectious trend whereby one pun results in another and another, often leading to a pun battle.

Pun battles, of themselves, can be fast, fun, and furious. The pun path can lead to duels and to wholesale wars of words. It can also break down into deep silliness and debilitating searching for the next sally. The problem with the pun in an Improv situation is that there is different circuitry involved in the process. The search for the pun requires a survey of old patterns based in verbal language processing.

While the use of the pun can encourage wonderful language creativity, it is not, in and of itself, creative in the sense of creating new things. It is a little like using old Lego® pieces to make new structures, and it can be destructive to the Improv process.

The pun event is also generally based in competition. In learning and business settings, competition is generally counterproductive to Improv processes.[18] Personal, internal competition is something else, but when working with Improvisation it is best that external competition be avoided.

Watching Your Language

Creative word play includes more than the simple use of puns. There are the complexities of semantics and General Semantics to consider, as well as the interplay of cultural and linguistic differences in language.

Semantics refers to the idea that words may have many meanings and a variety of connotations. These meanings can change across regions, cultures, subcultures, and age groups and over time and space. There are many parts of the world in which the English language is spoken, yet can barely be understood by others who speak the "same" language. Other generally recognized issues of language are when we run into words that anger or vilify particular individuals or groups. These may be known as "buzz words," as "politically incorrect" words, or simply as mean, thoughtless words. There are sets of words that cannot be used in polite society without negative consequence

---

18

KEITH JOHNSTONE HAS WORKED WITH COMPETITION FORMS IN IMPROVISATIONAL THEATER. THERE ARE THEATER-SPORTS,® IMPROV OLYMPICS,® AND MANY OTHER FORMS OF COMEDY COMPETITION FOR THE STAGE.

and hosts of words that can mark a person as a member of or as an outsider of a particular social group.

Deeper than this is the fact that individuals associate personal meanings with many words. These meanings may activate memories and emotions and may even generate endocrine system responses. Further, the activation of certain responses in one person can be transmitted to others in the group. Sometimes these reactions are transmitted via body language that may be visible to the observant and prepared executive. Sometimes reactions are transmitted via pheromones even before body language is apparent. A single word can activate human response. The presence of laughter and the forms of improvised creativity can overcome, or at least ameliorate, the effects of the power of words.

Considerations of language and body language and of General Semantics and stasis lead us to the power of being in and on time. To make our language-based communication work for us, we can manage the factors of personal presence and our surroundings. This leads us again to the notion that "information is the last, most important element in a communication."

The mind is like a home; it must be opened in order to be used to its fullest extent. New materials must be introduced slowly and consciously. Old patterns must be changed carefully and with respect. Fear must be allowed to surface and be addressed. The body and its languages must be engaged. Every available element of language must be considered and attended to. Then will come the gifts, joys, long-lasting effects, and miracles of the use of Improvisation as a tool in business and in real life. With a grounding in some of these mechanics, we can begin to use our words, to play with our words, and to discover that wholesome laughter leads the way.

CHAPTER TEN

Wholesome Laughter Leads the Way

Knowing how to use laughter is at least as important as any other single, necessary, business skill. Communication, made safe by the joyful development of wholesome laughter environments, is at the center of creativity. Improvisation is an important subdivision of the study of laughter. Easy and effective use of laughter requires practice. Exercise the skills of laughter to make them strong and to keep them limber. You can train yourself in the ways of laughter and practice the use of laughter. The existence of laughter is a gift; treat it with respect and awe.

"There are three things which are real: God, human folly, and laughter. The first two are beyond our comprehension, so we must do what we can with the third."

ELIZABETH NELD

The laughter that surrounds us provides some true evaluations of the quality of our lives and work. The measurements of laughter are abstract. The precise rules and graphs of laughter's tracks are not perfectly understood, a bit like gravity. Still there are useful things we know about laughter that allow us to see our world under brighter lights.

Using brighter light is a technical matter. The manipulation of light energy, electromagnetic play, is at the foundation of our advanced technology. From the computer to relative quantum biochemical probabilities, we work with light.

If the computer is the box
in which Schroedinger placed his cat,
the computer mouse then
brings us finally 'round the circle
and
Laughter is a Quality of Light.

Laughter energizes relaxation.
Light laughter is a healing thing.
Laughter lightly bears gifts of perspective.
Quality laughter guards against and heals
the roughened edges of stress.
Loving, hearty, laughing, lightly,
guarding, healing colleagues are a bliss.
Natural laughter is a blessing as a business skill.
Hearty laughter has a host of healthy benefits.
Light, real, healing, hearty, quality,
relaxing, energizing, guarding
laughter is a gentle teacher.
Happily laughing students
are easy to learn from.
True and fair laughter
supports living things.
Honest laughter lifts our minds.
Light, real, healing, hearty, quality,
relaxing, energizing, guarding,
teaching, happily learning,
true and fair, supporting, honest
laughter lifts our spirits.

Appropriate and soft laughter among us can make communication easy and productive, especially when the business at hand is both serious and difficult. A basic measure of excellence in organizational development is visible when communication is easy and productive, especially when matters are both serious and difficult. Helping organizational communication to become easy and productive and to stay that way takes practice.

Training and practice in the presence of good, light laughter are more efficient and most pleasant. Training with laughter is a skill and study of its own. It begins with taking notice of some values and disciplines of laughter.

SOME VALUES OF LAUGHTER

It is said that happy, healthy children laugh out loud up to hundreds of times in a day. It has also been calculated that normal adults laugh as few as ten or twenty times in a day. For a creative environment, this is not enough. For some, laughter once a day is as much as can be hoped for. For many, the lack of laughter accompanies loss of vitality and health.

As adults we really do need to practice the art of laughing to keep it alive and well. We can discipline ourselves to make laughter a part of our daily lives. This effort is good for our health, good for our souls, good for our general states of mind. It is good for our children and all our loved ones. It is necessary for our work as Improv leaders.

A FEW SIMPLE DISCIPLINES

A first simple discipline in learning to laugh is to look for things to laugh about and to look for people with whom you can laugh. Perhaps a survey of your life is in order. Over the course of a few days, keep notes to count the frequency of your own laughter. The days you record do not have to be consecutive. Keep a small pad handy to keep a simple tally; it can be very telling. Keep tabs in a number of categories you make up. Do the following:

- Make a mark each time you are aware of hearing laughter in your surroundings. Make one list for home, one for business, another for social settings.

- Make a tally mark each time you hear laughter from your spouse, parent, child, or associate.

- Make a mark each time you notice a silly sign.

- Make a mark each time you smiled at someone and said thanks.

- Make a mark each time someone smiles and says thanks to you.

Set a goal of adding five incidents of laughter to your day. Then set a goal of adding five incidents to each category each day. You can seek out cartoons, jokes, audiotapes, or videotapes, or you may merely look around and find new things that can make you laugh. Once you have started to laugh five more times each day, begin adding five more incidents at random to days or to categories. Then add more categories until you begin to lose count. If you already laugh more often than you can count and if that laughter is wholesome and delightful, then figure out for yourself how you could double your laughter a couple of days out of a week. Perhaps this will be the point at which you can begin to add laughter to the days of others.

A critical mass of daily laughter incidents will manifest itself as an active preference for surroundings that support general laughter. I call the presence of this preference a "wholesome laughter environment." The critical mass of laughter incidents may be as few as fifty or a hundred in a day. It is an attainable and worthy goal.

LAUGHTER WORKOUTS

There are a number of ways of establishing a wholesome laughter environment. One is by simply committing yourself to laughing out loud for no reason other than to generate laughter. Do this ten times per day. If this is uncomfortable for you, then find or manufacture new reasons to laugh ten more times each day.

Laughter Workout Equipment

If you are going to train yourself in laughter awareness, you may want some "workout" equipment. This includes humor books and tapes of all sorts. There are also many cartoon books that deal in really good, clean fun and frivolity. I like some of the larger cartoon books that are available in most bookstores. My personal preferences run to *Calvin and Hobbes, Peanuts, The Far Side,* and *Sylvia.* These works offer a depth and breadth of clean humor that is above the average.

I encourage you to find any available source of wholesome humor. Personal laughter is personal. Laugh at anything that tickles you. Find anything that will help you enter into the realm of habitual, wholesome laughter. I also recommend against material that explores too deeply or too intensely the negative side of laughter. This is no indictment of negative humor, nor of humor about the negative, but negative humor simply does not work as efficiently for the development of a wholesome daily laughter environment.

It is probably also good to avoid strictly topical humor about business, politics, and religion while building a daily laughter environment. Political cartoons fall into this category. These areas are better explored with a firm foundation of daily laughter already in place.

If your taste goes to the macabre, the old *Addams Family* cartoons are worth a look. I also enjoy the *Doonesbury* cartoons, although they tend to a level of seriousness that is, for me, close to borderline. *Garfield* sometimes sits on a negative edge, as *Dilbert* definitely does. Most of the daily newspaper cartoons are not so negative as they are insipid or pointless. They may not make the best laughter equipment.

There are many audiotapes and videotapes filled with great laughter material. Almost any of the tapes, audio or video, are better for your laughing soul than almost any daily newscast. Be aware that many recorded comics are completely based in dirty humor. Again, laugh! Yes, laugh. And note the source of the laughter and go for a high standard. There are a wide variety of books of humor, joke books, and books of humorous stories.

My wonderful friend and fellow humorist, Jeff Justice, recommends that you keep a humor file at home and at work. This file may be a simple manila folder in which you can keep funny pictures, cartoons, and stories that come by you in the course of each day. If you will keep such a file and commit to putting material into the file each day, you will begin seeing sources of laughter that might otherwise pass your notice. These are all training equipment items that can help build a wholesome laughter environment.

The Kindness of Strangers

The practice of engaging strangers in light conversation is more difficult, yet also very effective in the pursuit of a wholesome laughter environment. Random comments made out loud will open conversations or make contact. This practice is not about telling jokes nor "going for laughs."

Engaging others in light conversation is to be done with great kindness, gentleness, and light fun. All comments should be spontaneous and random. It is very easy to make random comments out loud in grocery lines or on elevators. There is very little risk involved, and it can be quite fun.

To make conversational contact with a stranger while standing in a line, look around and notice things going on around you. Then simply make a comment out loud about what you have observed in the direction of someone you do not know who is standing near you. If this is difficult, take a friend along to stand near you who can pretend to be the object of your remarks. Challenge your friend to try doing the same. If there are several people in line or around you, no one will know to whom your comments are made. At first, the comments do not need to be focused on humor or laughter. They do need to be positive and should require no reply. If you keep trying, eventually you will begin to find comments that make you laugh, and then things will appear that get others to laugh. Keep trying, even after you have stumbled onto a few funny lines that you have tried and no one even notices. Keep training. Keep looking at tapes and reading books and looking around yourself for the humor that is natural to life.

Elevator Talk

On elevators it is best to have at least three other people present when you make random comments out loud. A particular business elevator has been in my life for a number of years. The elevator has a voice that says things such as, "First floor, going up" and "Tenth floor, going down." Often, when I am on the elevator with a few others, in response to the elevator I will say, "One day I expect it to say, 'First floor, going sideways.'" I always get a little laughter. Only once in awhile do the people move a little farther away from me.

Elsewhere

When a telephone rings in an office, try a quick imaginary answer out loud to the room just before picking up the receiver. Then get right to business with a smile in your voice. You may have to practice the timing for doing this. Early in your quest to build a wholesome laughter environment, it is OK to practice and to use memorized lines. This is about creating a lifetime of laughter.

During meetings, workshop sessions, or gatherings of any kind, use some of your break time to make a random humorous comment out loud—comments about things you observe in the surroundings. Use the same techniques as you use in grocery store lines. There is a higher level of risk in this exercise because there may be colleagues present. Find anything to say about a painting or make a comment to a coffee pot in imaginary conversation. Do this out loud. It is not necessary to become a "jokester"; it is necessary to practice engaging people in conversational laughter. It is also fun and pays great dividends. A discreet healing laughter-focused comment to a person near you, or merely out loud to no one in particular, can create a mirthful moment and a satisfying human event.

If you are too shy or to nervous to engage in these sorts of activities, you simply need to work more slowly with yourself. Start with tapes or cartoons and build up to it. These small practices will add humor to your life and laughter to your day. They can also help you to build a repertoire of stories of human contact if you will keep a laughter journal.

Active participation in laughter discipline, as a necessary and healthy part of life, is important to the successful use of Improvisation by a business executive. You can lead the way by the manner in which you live, not merely by the words you choose to deliver.

IMPROV HUMOR GUIDELINES

These are my own guidelines for Improv humor. I have found that they apply to Improv work at all levels. They also apply to other humor venues as well. They are especially critical when working with family, business, academia, and community. Following these guidelines will help to create an atmosphere of safety in which Improvisation and creativity can work best. The use of these guidelines helps the mind to seek the highest and most creative expressions. The use of these suggestions will help to keep improvising participants in current time. These guidelines can encourage healthy playfulness.

Laughter Heals

Invoke laughter, but do not seek it. Seeking laughter for its own sake is the work of the comedian. Invoking laughter by developing a receptive environment is the work of the improviser. Laughter is a healing force in the human world. The means by which we create laughter cannot be separated from the laughter itself. If we laugh to the delight and innocence of others, we cause an increase in joy. If we laugh at the expense of others, we cause a decrease in joy. Learning about laughter heals as well.

It Is Good to Poke Fun at Yourself

You have the right, and perhaps the obligation, to make fun of yourself. There is strength and confidence in the ability to make fun of your own errors and unique ways. The practice of seeking humor at your own expense develops your authority as well as your humanity.

Beware of Making Fun of Others

To make fun of others is usually dangerous. If you make fun of others, they must be members of a group easily identified as *your own group* or members of a group that is clearly superior to your own.

If you make fun of another who is in a superior category to our own, you may risk being eaten (figuratively, if not in reality). If you make fun of another who is in some category that is weaker than you are, you risk being seen as a bully or worse. If you cannot make these distinctions, never under any circumstances make fun of anyone other than yourself.

Keep It Clean

"Dirty" humor is adolescent, at best. This includes blue humor, potty humor, sex jokes, innuendo, double entendre, and scatological humor. It also includes racist, sexist, ageist, feminist, masculinist, and anything-else-ist humor.

Keep It Gentle

Avoid humor based on gender, religion, sexuality, catastrophic disease, catastrophic events, aircraft accidents, Nazism, and politics in general. It is probably also good to avoid humor based on the most awful news of any day.

Bodies Are Not All That Funny

Generally avoid humor based on bodies. This includes reference to nose hair, ear wax, fingernail and toenail clippings, belly button lint, body hair, body parts, body size, body shape, body sounds, body odors, and all private body realities.

Use Your Own Stuff

Do not use another person's words as your own. Especially avoid humorous lines from movies, the Internet, television, and radio. Others saw the same shows and they will know the source of your wit.

Sweet and Easy Carries the Day

Be considerate, thoughtful, playful, care-ful, kind, fun, delighted, joyous, filled with light, personal, grateful, interested, other-centered, open, relaxed, sensible, and as sweet and easy as you can be.

Will, Not Wit

The very best humor comes from true observation of the moment, not from wit. The best laughter often comes from honest attempt, regardless of the results.

Laugh, and the World Laughs with You

Seek laughter as a part of life, as a discipline of life. Seek the creation of wholesome laughter environments. Laugh. Laugh some more. Keep laughing.

LAUGHTER AS A MEASUREMENT DEVICE

This is the technical aspect of laughter: If you can gain useful feedback using laughter, you can gain some control over the effectiveness of your communication environments. The measures of laughter are abstract and approximate. Some of the measures of subatomic particle activity are abstract and approximate as well.

First Measure: The Type of Laughter

There are qualities in laughter that you can identify. My search for definitions produced an initial list.

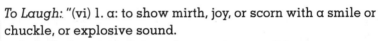

To Laugh: "(vi) 1. a: to show mirth, joy, or scorn with a smile or chuckle, or explosive sound.
    b: to find amusement or pleasure in something.
    c: to become amused or derisive.
    2. a: to produce the sound or appearance of laughter.
    b: to be of a kind that inspires joy."

Laugh: "(n) 1. the act of laughing.
    2. a: a cause for derision or merriment.
    b: an expression of scorn or mockery."

LOL: "Internet chat language meaning to laugh out loud."

Laughter: "A sound of laughing."

Laughing: "See laugh."

I was not satisfied with these definitions. There was nothing in the dictionary that spoke about side-splitting, face-hurting, falling-down, sustained explosions of joy and delight. This kind of laughter had been so much a part of my family experience growing up. I extended my search to a thesaurus and came up with more words.

Snicker: "To laugh in a covert or partly suppressed way."

Chuckle: "To make a continuous gentle sound resembling suppressed mirth."

Titter: "A loud, high-pitched chuckle."

Giggle: "To laugh with repeated short catches of the breath."

Guffaw: "A loud or boisterous burst of laughter."

Something still seemed missing. I was still bothered by all the words like "suppressed," "gentle," "short catches," and "bursts." I think of my fine young eleven-year-old son screaming with *laughter,* "Stop, Daddy! Stop, Daddy! I can't take it any more. My tummy hurts." I remember my mother laughing with me until we both found it hard to breathe, tears streaming down our faces, each word more funny than the last, until any sound or reaction would increase the nearly painful ecstasy. I looked again. Where were the definitions my son would recognize to describe our experience? Where were the words to paint the picture of me and my mom?

Joy: "The emotion evoked by well-being, success, or good fortune or by the prospect of possessing what one desires."

Rejoice: "To feel joy or great delight."

Exultation: "Leaping for joy."

RAWLOF: Internet chat language for "rolling around with laughter, on the floor."

When considering terminology for measurement with laughter, we may also consider and observe other forms and sources of definitions: joke laughter, embarrassed laughter, smut laughter, insider laughter, pun and word play laughter, intellectual laughter, job laughter, ironic and sarcastic laughter, pain laughter, and more.

Enough of dictionary limitations. Let us scale new heights and seek new levels of laughter, delight, glee, light laughter, general merriment, silliness, sympathy, joviality, jocularity, clowning about, and making funny fun. You can find many more distinctions as you observe this wonderful human signaling device called laughter.

For now I dub thee as follows.

Improvisational Laughter: "Uncontrollable and sustained giggling, guffawing, and otherwise exploding with joy in rejoicing exultation until the sides hurt and tears stream and all of existence is filled with the delight of life and light and love."

By knowing such distinctions, we may learn about our humor and laughter. We may use these distinctions as measurements of the level of laughter being generated by our communication and relationship practices. If you are laughing ("becoming amused or derisive") twenty times a day, increase your practice. Try chuckling five times and tittering twice. Maybe you can rejoice at least once. If the laughter in your organization comes from negative or weak sources, it is a sign of problems.

Second Measure: The Frequency of Laughter

Comedians and humorous speakers are seeking laughter each five to seven seconds. If the intervals are longer, there is a chance that the audience is losing interest. If you are doing Improv work and laughter is occurring seldom or only at predictable intervals, it is a measurement signal that your participants are not involved enough. They need to be more physically and mentally active.

During the Improv games, there should be some laughing at important junctures and completions. There should be some chuckling, tittering, and giggling when groups first get together. When people are working in general icebreaking sets, there should be light laughter and general merriment.

At the points of completion, there should be some laughing out loud and maybe a little guffawing. This can be more true when groups are working in circles. There may be some bursts of laughter when whole processes are completed.

There should be periodic laughter mixed with periods of quiet discussion during longer processes. The frequency of the laughter needs to be viewed in terms of the type and the quality of the laughter as well. A good mixture of appropriately timed laughter of the highest possible kind is like the sound of a smoothly working internal combustion engine. You can hear it purr or you can tweak it to make it purr.

Third Measure: The Quality of the Laughter

Deep, resonate rolls of laughter may be the sign of a bonding in the gathering. The very power of the sound breaks down barriers that are unseen. This kind of laughter really means that everyone is working and the source is all who are present.

Hearty general laughter usually indicates that some common core of understanding has been touched or has been brought to the surface. This is one of the reasons that the guidelines of humor are so important. The things that are common to our core are both positive and negative. When we build laughter bridges, we can explore problems and we can leverage our resources.

Light, clear, general laughter usually means that you have said a funny thing and have touched the fancy of the crowd. It is a sign that wit is noted by the gathering. You are being appreciated.

Innocent laughter is a symptom of health and wholeness in any human activity.

Thin, high-pitched, disjointed laughter generally indicates nervousness or stress. It can be a sign that people are not connected somehow. It may be possible to detect the location of the disconnection by listening carefully.

Missed laughter, laughter with bad timing, or laughter at items that are not funny often means that something or someone is out of time and space. It may mean that there is an unnoticed imbalance in the event or the gathering.

Private laughter by a small or isolated group means they may not be in tune with the larger purpose.

No laughter at all is often not a good sign.

General Measure: Where and When

Be especially aware when the negative qualities of laughter are present and when the quality of laughter changes. It may be related to the introduction of new material or activities. Is it related to the nature of the information? Is it related to the makeup of the gathering? Are you wearing socks of two different colors?

Note the locations of the laughter in the gathering. Negative qualities of laughter are rarely general. Negative laughter among a small set of participants may indicate unfamiliarity with members of a subset. Negative laughter quality can indicate an insular subset.

The quality of laughter as a measurement device is unique to every group. You will have to listen and identify clues each time you are present or together. Careful study can make this a useful tool.

Getting Laughs Is Not the Object

Generating laughs is not the object of Improv tools. Going for laughs can inhibit the creative spirit of Improvisation. Building a wholesome environment of laughter is a complex process that requires self-analysis, group analysis, organization, training, and measurement in order to work. There is a distinction between "getting laughs" and "generating laughter" in a laughing environment. The first are events; the latter is a process.

LAUGHTER FEEDBACK

We have learned that things happen when we take small, successful, incremental steps toward our visions. We are lead to flashes of insight, to understanding, and to cognitive leaps. This also works when using laughter as feedback for the Improv trainer.

As you use Improv techniques in your work, you will become more and more sensitive to the details of your communication and relationships with your participants.

- If your steps are the right size, if they are successful, and if they are incremental, there will be various kinds of positive laughter.

- If your goals and processes are driven by relationships, there will be good laughter.

- If the examples and setups of your work are wholesome, thoughtful, and clear, there will be wholesome laughter.

- When people learn from their errors, there will be bittersweet laughter.

- When we laugh at ourselves, it is knowing laughter.

- When people have flashes of insight, it creates inspiring laughter.

- When understanding occurs, it's amazing laughter.

- When a human makes a cognitive leap and the lights come on, that's successful laughter.

If we are strong and clear and disciplined, even in agonizing reappraisal, we can find laughter. The Improv leads the way and shines the light of laughter on the path of laughter.

LAUGHING AT YOURSELF

The ability to laugh at yourself is a gift—to yourself and to others. In Improvisation it is a gift to all who work or play with you. Laughing at yourself is also essential to making great connections with people.

A STORY

I once spoke to the professional development organization of a very large utility company. The evening dinner setting was outdoors by the pool at a fine hotel. I was to motivate and inspire the gathering. The crowd was finishing dinner as I began to speak. As I noticed that there were some people not yet with me, I searched for the words that would make the connection complete.

Suddenly, I felt something drop onto the top of my head. The people became silent and perfectly attendant. There was neither branch nor tree anywhere near, and the deep blue summer sky was cloudless. On my pant leg was the remains of the bird poop that had bounced off the top of my head. The gathering had become wonderfully focused.

It would have been quite easy to have become flustered by this rude interruption. Being in The Improv state, I took a napkin and wiped the remains from my head and said that I hoped this was not a comment on my message. I got a gentle, respectful laugh. They knew I was a professional. Later in the speech a jet airliner flew over. When I ducked and covered my head, the crowd cheered. To this day I thank that bird. It demonstrated that I could laugh at myself. It brought us closer together. It made my serious message more real, more human, more memorable.

YOU LEAD BY ENCOURAGING LAUGHTER

The power of laughter begins with you. You are the leader. You need to learn to laugh out loud for no reason at all. Your example of laughter can lead your participants to their own laughter. Your own laughter can lead you to the most effective tempos, rhythms, and incremental steps in arriving at your vision.

A TEST

Can you laugh out loud for no reason at all?

Can you sustain laughter for one minute with no reason at all?

Can you sustain laughter for five minutes?

Can you sustain laughter for ten minutes?

Can you laugh and laugh until your eyes water and your sides hurt and you want to yell, "Stop, stop, I can't take it any more. My sides hurt"?

If the answer is "no" to any of the above, you can decide that this approach is just too silly or you can work on learning to say "yes" to all the questions. You may even use Improv work to do this.

Wholesome laughter leads the way to a lifetime study. Laughter is an art and craft, and it can open the doors to your own creativity. The basic principles of Improvisation need to be approached with laughter; when you enter the realm of feelings and emotions, laughter will bring the healing and perspective necessary to search more deeply. Everyone knows that wholesome laughter is infectious, that it brings people to us and creates connections. Laughter will lead us through our patterns and the difficulties we encounter as we challenge the patterns that do not work. Although laughter can be caused by a memory, by the vision of a future event, or by the imagination, *the laughter itself is an event of the current moment.* Learning the use of laughter is a discipline of its own that will lead you to the most creative application of Improv management, beginning with the size and design of creativity.

PART THREE

Applied Improv Methods

 CHAPTER ELEVEN

The Size and Design of Creativity

The numbers of people with whom you work and the ways you gather people into sets within your gatherings are very important. How you gather people and how you assign people to sets will have a great impact on your use of Improvisation in all settings. The information presented here is based on professional observation. The ideas apply to general realities of most gatherings of human beings. The realities of the size and design of the gatherings of an organization can be studied as factors within Improv activities. Understanding the kinds of things that can happen when there are changes in group size can give you terrific tools for "tweaking" your organizational development in the search for excellence and efficiency.

Size refers to the overall numbers participating in a group, as well as to subdivisions used to manage larger groups. *Shape* refers to the spatial configurations of the places your work is taking place. It also refers to the physical proxemics among the participants, including such things as the crowding of the space, the setup of the chairs and tables, whether people are sitting, standing, or moving, or whether they can gather in circles or move their chairs around.

Size and design also encompass the general physical location and environment in which you are working. This includes the building and facilities, traffic and parking, weather and weather portents, the city or town, and the major local, business, sports, and news events of the day.

In business and training settings, you must take care not to place participants in physical situations that are too far beyond their levels of comfort and ability. At the same time, challenging comfort and ability is good and necessary in order to promote creativity.

HUMAN SET DESIGN

I call the way we put people together as we work and play, especially in creative settings, "human set design." My observations come from many years' experience with organizations and gatherings. About one third of the observation has been in Improv work. The remainder has occurred in businesses, schools, day care centers, universities, government offices, the military, hospitals, volunteer and non-profit organizations, teams, clubs, crowds, mobs, parties, and martial arts classes.

This chapter contains a lot of numbers. Prepare yourself for this. If you need to, take a break before proceeding. If you need to, get a pencil and paper and perhaps a calculator.

Nearly Natural Sets

In general, there are *nearly natural* sets of gatherings among people. These sets include the following numbers: One, two, three, four, seven, fourteen, twenty-one, twenty-eight, thirty-five, forty-two, forty-nine, ninety-eight, 245, and 499. These numbers build toward seven and then are multiples of seven. Seven has natural factors of four and three.

Certain communication changes and changes in group dynamics can be observed when sets of people go from one of these numbers to another. When such changes are noticed and planned for, they can be managed and used to your advantage. Failure to notice these changes can result in many problems.

Primary Human Sets

The more sensitive you become to these ideas, the more observant you will become with your groups. The more you observe, the more you can become sensitive to dynamics that can and do shift with each change in the *primary human sets:* one, two, three, four through six, seven through thirteen, fourteen through twenty, twenty-one through twenty-seven, twenty-eight through thirty-four, thirty-five through forty-one, forty-two through forty-eight, forty-nine through ninety-seven, ninety-eight through 244, and 245 through 496. Four hundred and ninety seven is like a gathering of 500 to 993. A congregation of 994 is really like a gathering of a thousand plus.

At each of the junctures listed above, changes may be seen in group dynamics, in learning efficiencies, in learning deficiencies, in interpersonal relationships, in personnel management, in environmental imperatives, in personal development, in quality of training, and in Improv results. The larger the numbers, the more the changes have to do with logistics rather than with dynamics.

Small Sets

Set shifts are more easily noticed when there are fewer people involved. The differences between a set of one and a set of two are pretty clear. Our reactions may vary, yet the fact that there is a difference is obvious. A change from two to three is equally clear. Add a fourth person and the differences may still be fairly easy to observe, yet at this point the compound complexity of communication factors become more subtle and more difficult to see. Sets of four, five, or six are very similar to one another.

Larger Sets

In terms of communication, group dynamics, interpersonal complexities, and Improv management, the sets of seven, eight, nine, ten, eleven, twelve, or thirteen function much the same. This means that working with seven is very much like working with thirteen. Adding another person changes the set to fourteen, which is more like working with twenty. There are clear differences between working with nine or with twenty, but I maintain that similar differences occur between working with thirteen and working with fourteen, although this shift is much harder to see. Always remember that a small difference in numbers can find you working with a change in the environment that does not make sense until you remember this theory.

HUMAN DESIGN MIND-SETS

Certain stages of learning and development are normal to human beings. My work with people has led me to be aware that developmental events often take place at ages that match the "human design set" numbers. At seven we usually make the final transition from toddler to child. At fourteen we enter full-blown adolescence. (Unusual life experience and the onset of puberty may skew these numbers.) At twenty-one we become adults, whether or not we are grown up. I think the ages of twenty-eight, thirty-five, forty-two, and forty-nine also provide benchmark events in normal human development.

It is interesting to note that a business, gathering, or organization can go through the same stages of development. An organization can go through the changes in minutes, hours, days, weeks, or months as well as years. The organization, like an individual, can skip around, miss steps, and double back as well.

It is also interesting to note that the creative experience, Improvisation, the factors of group dynamics, and the nature of organizations in general can make people re-create, re-enact, or finally complete various stages of personal development. When we are with people in creative and active settings, we can actually find ourselves working with adults who exhibit the attributes of children or of adolescents going through various stages of development and learning. By the way, human set design numbers are extremely important when working with toddlers or adolescents.

The Toddler

One toddler is a job, two is a stretch, three is a task, four to six is a trial. Eight to thirteen requires professional management skills and, in most civilized locations, education and licensing. Fourteen to twenty toddlers requires a team and a system, twenty-one to twenty-seven toddlers require an organization, and twenty-eight or more toddlers—or children of almost any age—may require an entire school.

The Adolescent

My opinion, based on experience, is that with a fourteenth adolescent in a set, a herd-like consciousness appears and must be dealt with. This is a generalization and, as with many stereotypes, is worthy of note. If the change from thirteen to fourteen is not noticed, a group can become a single unit capable of extraordinary resistance, ignorance, stupor, or hostility. If recognized and managed, this same unit can be capable of the most extraordinary growth and creativity. One adult with good skills, maturity, patience, and luck can keep up with and manage thirteen adolescents. Add one more adolescent and there must either be more adults available or extraordinary methods must be used to maintain positive control. Often this control method becomes military style or "X" style management. Normally, when a single adult is faced with fourteen or more adolescents, he or she recruits one or more of the adolescents to act as a pseudo adult in order to manage the problem. Understanding human set design numbers can give you insight to the changes taking place when adults or gatherings go through normal stages of learning.

The Resistant Mind-Set

When people do not wish to be together, when they do not understand what is going on or disagree with the purposes of the gathering, or when there are hostilities, inanities, or insanities afoot, careful set design becomes very important. Under such conditions, manipulating set design is sometimes one of the few things we can do to create change.

You can tell if there is a need for set design management by listening, feeling, and observing very carefully. When using Improv techniques, one can always tell that set design management (or set serendipity) is working. There will be a great deal of animation and laughter as various groups find themselves completing steps and processes. If things are not working as you would have them, try changing your set design to gather people together in terms of the numbers discussed above.

Issues of sets and set design do not always surface. When people are truly comfortable and have been together a long time, the problems of group size have sometimes been handled. More often they have been adjusted to, settled into, bypassed, or suppressed. If this is the case, you may see attendant limitations to the creativity and effectiveness of your organization and efforts.

How to Use This Information

The first thing to do with this information is to think about it and observe the sets that are active in your organization or gathering. A survey of the numbers can be very important. How many people are there in the company, the division, the location, on the factory floor, in the office, at the gathering, in the breakouts, in the subsets? I have seen many small businesses and groups that simply could not grow past a certain point. This point is usually at or around a natural set number. The next consideration is size of subsets.

Size of Subsets

When using Improv games, you may find that two-person activities, when there are observers, tend to be more risky and require a higher degree of ability or self-confidence on the part of the participants. If you divide the gathering into smaller groups, where pairs may work together and there are fewer observers, it may reduce risk. Subdividing the whole gathering into sets of two will also relieve pressure of having "watchers" and can reduce the sense of risk. However, reducing the set to two in intimate settings, where there is no feeling of others present, can *increase* the sense of risk.

Working with people in circles may reduce some of the risk factors and can help to create a space of safety for many participants. For other groups and purposes, a circle may lead to too much intimacy or confrontation. The number of people who may be accommodated in a circle varies. Circles with six or fewer people often seem too intimate to work well. I have worked successfully in circles with up to forty-eight people. At forty-nine the dynamics change and circles become difficult or inefficient.

How Big Is Small?

Some of us are more comfortable and most interactive in a small group. Many prefer medium-size groups, and others find the most personal comfort in larger groups. The expectations of a gathering may also influence our comfort levels. A prepared public speech may be comfortably presented to a "small" group. Yet, just how big is small? Having to make impromptu remarks before an influential group of ten may make ten seem like a very large number.

A particularly shy speech student of mine was convinced that three was a large audience. I once spoke to a very small gathering with only one hundred people present. The definition of small, medium, and large is in the eyes of the beholder.

Traditionally, the number in a "small" group has been defined as somewhere between four and twelve, maybe fifteen, depending on the author, the time, and the location. Two is defined as a dyad, three as a triad, and one as a lonely number.

Among those who know, or claim to know, a "medium-sized" group may have as few as seven and as many as thirty. Some experts insist that a group is "large" when it reaches twenty, or thirty, or fifty, or whatever makes their personal perception of "lots of people." Often, "large" is defined as more than one hundred. There are cultures whose system of numbers counts: "One, two, three, and many."

The nature of an event has an effect as well. Perhaps three *is* a crowd. A group waiting for a store to open may be considered small or large with twenty or thirty, depending on the size of the store. In a big theater, fifty to one hundred may be a small group. A concert attendance of 250 to 500 may be small.

Size and design of a space may have a dramatic effect on perception of size. An elevator can make ten people quite a large crowd. In high school our team made it to the regional football finals. We played in the Rose Bowl in Pasadena, California. There were more than three thousand people from the two schools attending the game, the

Improvisation, Inc.

largest gathering in the history of both schools. However, almost everyone had a seat near the fifty-yard line and the rest of the stadium was empty.

We each have preferences, perceptions, comforts, and definitions in regard to the size of gatherings. As Improv executives, our personal feelings, perceptions, and definitions need to be managed in favor of functional realities of the group.

Group Size and Behavioral Change

If a human being does not feel "safe" in terms of the size and design of the set in which he or she is working, it is unlikely that behavioral change will take place or that information will be retained. Feelings of safety may not reach one's consciousness. They may stay at the emotional level. Panic is a standard feature of human reaction when certain numbers in a crowd or certain numbers in a confined space are perceived.

Just remember that a set of three or four can be intimidating to some and a set of fifty can be safe to another. A set of seven may be liberating to one, in the same way that a set of twenty-one may be confining to another.

SELF-EVALUATION

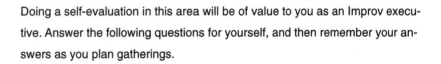

Doing a self-evaluation in this area will be of value to you as an Improv executive. Answer the following questions for yourself, and then remember your answers as you plan gatherings.

- *What is your most comfortable set?*

- *How do you define small, medium, or large in a gathering?*

- *Do you prefer small, medium, or large gatherings?*

- *What types of circumstances or situations make you change your feelings?*

- *What size group best allows you to make changes in your behavior?*

- *Does the size of the group affect your learning retention?*

TAKE CONTROL OF SET SIZE

When we are consulted about overall group size, there is a tendency to make generalizations. If you have control of the numbers of people you will be working with, try to gather participants into natural sets.

Set and size design can be a powerful tool for creating structure and safety or for generating disturbance and the need for change. Sometimes merely breaking patterns precipitates change. Just as a certain degree of safety is necessary to promote change and learning, a certain amount of disruption or disturbance may also be necessary.

If random, haphazard, unconscious, or thought-less set design happens to work, there was an element of luck. Perhaps set design was not an issue, or perhaps the success may have been a result of what I call *design chaos* or *design serendipity*. It is also possible that nothing really happened at all.

If you do not have influence over the number of participants, it is imperative that you be aware of set dynamics and influences. It is always best to take control of the subsets that you use in working with Improvisation. Real success is built on our awareness of these factors.

Set Gatherings

When there are ninety-seven or fewer participants, the most efficient sets are the primal sets noted above. When there are ninety-eight or more people involved, as noted previously, the dynamics tend to have more to do with logistics and setting than with the mechanisms of this discussion. However, even with larger sets, the subsets will follow some of the patterns noted here. People will "settle" and gather into sets that are most comfortable for their personal feelings of "how big is really small."

The most powerful and healthy set is a *unity of the whole*. If you are working with six people, a set of six is the most powerful and dynamic. A set of six is, however, extremely complex. It can be six sets of one, two sets of three, three sets of two, sets of one and five, or sets of two and four, Moreover, it can change with fluidity between these various sets, at will, and as a result of reaction to change and challenge, learning, and creativity. You do not have to micromanage the numbers. You must, however, be aware of the process that is going on and how it can affect you and your participants.

Odd Sets

When we have a gathering that is not consistent with the realities of human set dynamics and with primal numbers, very interesting things can happen.

Remainders

Unless the number in the general gathering or the subsets is evenly divided by smaller primal numbers (two, three, four, and seven), there will be remainders. Remainders can greatly affect the workings of a group, creating disconnected individuals. Disconnected individuals can operate in the same fashion as free radicals in a living organism. They can cause general breakdown and deterioration of the greater system. If you can identify people who are remainders, you may pull them from the groups and have them work as "observers" who may wander from group to group without participating. They can also help you manage the set design, and the position of the observer can be used for learning and developing creativity.

Set Breakdown

When there are ten people present, a group may, by luck or magic, operate as a unity of the whole. They may also be managed as sets of seven and three. When ten turns into three sets of three with one left out, there is often a set breakdown. The unmanaged set of ten may shift into sets of four and four and two, which can be very difficult to deal with if you are trying to reach a group goal. This same breakdown can be good to gather ideas to bring back to the gathering of the whole. Another example of an unmanageable ten is five and five, which can also be two sets of three and two, which can result in cliques, conflict, dissonance, and inefficiency.

Shifting Individuals

Specific individuals are not *necessarily* hard-wired members of a particular set. Rather, individuals can move and shift among various sets as circumstances change and responses vary. Sometimes, individuals or groups will roam about trying to find or create a comfortable natural set. This can result in a loss of focus and energy. Sometimes two or more people may function as a single unit in a set. The process is a little like the action of atoms and electrons, which attract and attach and detach from one another in the processes of molecular change and development. *This process often looks like chaos or resistance.*

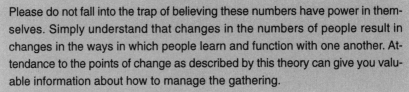

N O T E

Please do not fall into the trap of believing these numbers have power in themselves. Simply understand that changes in the numbers of people result in changes in the ways in which people learn and function with one another. Attendance to the points of change as described by this theory can give you valuable information about how to manage the gathering.

MEMBER OR MODERATOR?

If you do not establish or understand whether you are a member of the group, a facilitator, a moderator, or an observer who stands outside the group, you may be the cause of a set change and perhaps the cause of confusion and resistance.

A set of seven you are facilitating is a set a seven, plus a facilitator. This can be a very strong group as a unity of the whole set of seven. If you unconsciously become a member of the set, then there are eight in the set. I do not like to work with sets of eight. Eight is a number that is hard to bring to a unity of the whole, and it breaks down into too many sets of small, insular units.

There are actually fourteen combinations of the primal sets when there are eight humans together, and the only combinations that have natural strengths are the whole set of eight, which is difficult to maintain, the set of 2 + 2 + 2 + 2, which is not particularly functional as a team, and the set of 4 + 4, which can function fairly well. Yet if you are one of the eight, it keeps you effectively absent from more than half of your group.

It can be necessary for you to become a set member to keep the numbers in line as you go through some group progressions. It may be necessary for you to identify and utilize people who are knowledgeable about these theories as roaming units whose function is to adjust and change sets to more functional numbers.

Set Progressions

As an Improv facilitator you should be in charge of set progressions. You need to make the decisions about how the group will be gathered and what numbers will be included in the subsets. You are in charge of the progressions, including the pace of change and the way in which numbers are added to or subtracted from sets at any given time. You may decide to let the group make its own sets, but this should be a conscious decision. If you do this, one of your goals should be observation and analysis of the group in this process.

Critical Situations

An evaluation of whether there is a "critical situation" is always good when considering set design management. Generally, in critical situations it is best to start small and grow slowly. Begin with sets of two or three and gather the people together in increments related to the primal numbers.

Making changes in the subjects under consideration is critical when hard new information or change is coming, when you do not know the group well, if there are a lot of people who are strangers to one another, if there is tension or fear in the organization, if there is hostility in the setting, if people do not want to be there, or if previous programs have been seen as a waste of time. Add to this list as you will.

When making major shifts in matters being explored, small set changes are generally better than large set changes. When new material is being introduced, unconscious set changes can disrupt the process. I have seen a group of twenty-eight, making extraordinary progress, that was destroyed by breaking the group into sets of seven at the wrong time. A necessary interim step may have been two sets of fourteen.

SOME THOUGHTS ABOUT SUBSETS

- The unity of the whole is an ideal, most efficient set.

- Subsets should be created with the objective of achieving the unity of the whole.

- While building it is generally best to grow a group upward toward the largest sets.

- When experiencing successful participation, it is usually good to build upward.

- When introducing chaos, it is generally good to move to smaller sets.

- When experiencing chaos or resistance, it is generally good to move toward smaller sets.

- Sets of three are stable.

- Sets of three are good for mixing strangers.

- Sets of three can create cliques.

- Sets of two are good for creating bonds or building safety.

- Sets of one can create alienation.

- A mob is composed of sets of one.

- Sets of seven are very powerful and flexible structures.

- Sets of eight are unstable, as they shift into even numbered subsets.

- Sets of eleven, thirteen, seventeen, and nineteen are often unstable or unruly, as they do not factor into strong primal sets.

- Add or subtract people to create primal sets and subsets.

- It is often better to disassemble sets and reassemble them at higher numbers rather than to simply add sets together.

- Groups of twelve are natural to our culture and our minds, yet if they break into subsets of four there can be good flexibility with little stability. If they break into subsets of three, there can be great stability but little flexibility.

- When sets are added together, the existing internal subsets can tend to maintain their integrity. Thus, unless you are doing something to make it work otherwise, a set of seven operating as 3 + 4, when added to another set of 3 + 4 will very often end up as a two sets of three and two sets of four, rather than two sets of seven or one set of fourteen.

SUMMARY OF HUMAN SET DESIGN THEORY

Once you become aware of the patterns and dynamics of human set design, you will begin to gain a natural feeling for the changes that occur. The numbers and benchmarks described so far are useful for preplanning and excellent for post-analysis. It is complicated and sometimes a bit difficult to work and manipulate set design factors as you are in the process of working with people. It is also very easy to get caught up in them and to put the theory between yourself and those with whom you work.

Sociologists and mathematicians may quarrel with the numbers used. Others may argue about the numbers identified as "primal." Your interpretation and use of these numbers will be greatly influenced by your personal background. You may wish to change the numbers to fit your unique system. What does not work for you does not work. Re-

       Improvisation, Inc.

gardless of the exact numbers used, the basic truths of human set design can be of value when you must help people to learn and to change their behavior as a response to the information that you have to impart. Use your experience and imagination. Notice what happens.

Try not to get caught up in the numbers. Do study the ideas and watch for the signs of "set design breakdown." Try not to manipulate or work your groups according to any formula. Your work needs to be in the direction of management. Do consider a re-evaluation of the set design before you give up on a gathering, give up on yourself, or give up on the ideas you are working with. Do use these sets when gathering people together for Improv games.

While working with Improvisation, it is good to be very sensitive to set design factors. Any time there is a change in the set numbers, the next activity is best kept simple or stable and nonthreatening. Sufficient time must be allowed for the individuals to settle into new set patterns. When the process is working well, it is a sign that the set design is working. When this happens it is time to reinforce and verify the success by making the next activity slightly more relevant or serious.

If you learn to become aware of the sets in which people function best, you will achieve success and you will learn an incredible amount about the group, the individuals, the organization, and the next steps to take. This is a truth that operates beyond the specific focus of the gathering.

The larger the group, the more carefully and consciously you need to create and manage the set design. Excellent and creative set design can lead to extraordinary success with gatherings of "many" in your company or your event.

Careful human set design can create useful management controls when working with hundreds or even with thousands of people. Creative set design is an important element of working with Improvisation.

PARTS OF THE WHOLE

One of the most powerful, effective, loving, loved, and satisfied people I have ever known is Vernon S. Cox, director of The Marin Center for Independent Living, who was made quadriplegic by polio at the age of eleven. With a partial set of physical tools, this man gives more and experiences more than most people. With his heart and mind and the partial use of one hand, he exhibits exceptional human ability and creativity. His work and life have influenced my thinking at every turn.

Ability to function with parts missing or not working is also an attribute of groups of people. A remarkable amount of good work and good product can be created by small numbers, even within a dysfunctional or debilitated organization. We sometimes become satisfied by the work generated by small groups within the whole. Unfortunately, as smaller and smaller numbers take command, greater and greater numbers can become isolated and disenfranchised.

If we do not move in the direction of creating a unity of the whole, we can be in danger of creating its opposite, the mob, an extreme case of "critical mass" in a human group. A mob occurs when the entire gathering breaks down into separate individuals. The gathering resembles a unity of the whole, yet is actually its exact opposite, a large group that has deteriorated into sets of one. Someone may yell, "Break down the doors!" or there may be some other inflammatory call to arms, but the people do not turn to one another and discuss the process.

A SHORT PLAY ABOUT SOMETHING THAT NEVER HAPPENED

[Shout from off stage]: "Break down the doors!"
First Mob Participant (Yells): "We got it about the doors, shall we break the windows as well?"
Second Mob Participant (Confused): "I don't know. We'll look into it and get back to you."
First Mob Participant (Shouting above the crowd): "Hey, you people! Yes! You over there!"
Member of Second Mob Group (Irritated): "Yeah, what?"
First Mob Participant: "Are we breaking windows too?"
Member of Second Mob Group: "I don't know. Wait a minute."
First Mob Participant: "OK, but please hurry. There's a mob to run here."
Member of Second Mob Group (To member of third mob group): "Say, are we breaking furniture or just doors and windows?"
Member of Third Mob Group (Surprised at the naivete): "Sure! Why not?"
Member of Second Mob Group (To second mob participant): "Yeah! Furniture too."
Second Mob Participant (Gratefully): "Thanks. Say, do we use rocks or are bricks all right as well?"

A mob comes from the breakdown of the sets. The gathering of the whole group becomes disconnected, frightened, lonely, hurting, sad, mad individuals, each and every one of whom is out of control. When you have been a leader or a trainer for a long time, you will have had to deal with a mob in one way or another. Usually they do not break down the doors and lynch the innocent. They merely refuse to change behavior or to learn. Any one person who is not part of the process at hand is a potential member of a mob.

REPAIR PROCEDURES

Much of the work in Improvisation and communication requires making and keeping connections. When connections are weak or not working, it is usually necessary to make repairs. Many of these repairs are a matter of size and design of the gathering. You do not have to understand all the reasons why repair is needed. You may never know exactly what happened. In the early stages of working with an organization or a gathering, the participants do not even need to know that a repair is being done. In the early stages it is usually not very effective to stop the process, analyze the situation, and conduct repairs in public.

Small Changes

The first procedure in bringing about repairs is to make small physical or structural changes. In a group something as simple as a stand-and-stretch break may restore the balance, timing, or comprehension level and thus allow for willingness to move forward. It may also restore connections among the people. An extra long break may be too much for this process. Many groups of people express their need for a break in the form of set shifting, resistance, confusion, noise, distraction, fear, and similar mechanics. A proactive change in the set design may be needed.

> ### N O T E
> If one set design change does not make a difference, it is likely that there is some deeper problem and a second set design change will not work either. It is just as easy to get caught up in our repair design as in our original organizational or information design. It can compound errors and create complex troubles.

A shift in the physical location of the executive or manager, presenter or trainer may be needed. A simple shift to the side of a room may do. A change in the physical distances between individuals or particular groups of participants may be a clear enough structural change to repair small problems. It is possible to repair a group by working from the back of the room or by having the participants rearrange their chairs.

In a business setting, this sort of repair procedure may be accomplished by small changes in the locations of extraneous furniture and *space focus elements* where people are working. Simple space focus elements may be pictures, water coolers, copy machines, or free-standing tables or chairs. If making such a change is complicated or time-consuming, it no longer qualifies as a *simple* structural change.

A change in the format of the work being done may work as well. In presentational style, changing from lecture to interaction, to feedback, to a game, to a physical activity, or to some sort of information processing can start repair processes. In the organization, similar repair may be brought about by small changes in patterns of communication, such as changing the times of or the locations of regular meetings or changing the memo format or locations of bulletin boards. Try to find small changes that can be made in Internet or local network communication systems. Use your imagination and creativity to come up with small structural changes that can help shift the organization at times of need.

You may discuss this idea with the participants and use Improv games to encourage the organization to come up with creative, simple structural changes that may repair problems.

LEVELS OF OPERATION

Levels of operation refers to the complex interplay of the following elements:

- Complexity or intensity of the material

- The seriousness of the matters at hand

- The degree of participation by the participants

- The pace of change

- Competence of the leadership

- Confidence of the leadership

- Confidence in the leadership

- The sense of safety among the participants

- The set design factors of the gathering

Many more elements can be added to this list, depending on your unique situation.

Change in any of these elements results in a step up in the level of operation. Such changes can be increases or decreases in intensity or additions or subtraction of elements. Changes in set design or small changes is structure should accompany a changes in the levels of operation.

Share the Problems

Another repair element may require sharing with the gathering that there is a problem. Sometimes simply noting that there seems to be a lack of connection will make connections. Similarly, telling the organization or group that you are observing resistance may actually release the resistance and things will work well from then on. Keep in mind that the fourth Improv principle is that one must put work out for public view. Be careful not to present this information as criticism or blame, merely as an observation. You may need to accept responsibility for the problem noted. Also remember to acknowledge that resistance in an organization indicates resistance in every individual at some level.

Sometimes just asking the people what they are feeling or thinking about the process will clarify something that was confusing or allow for release of fears so that balance can be restored and connections re-established. If asking such a question produces general open discussion, there is probably a processing problem in need of work.

Sometimes simply sharing with the gathering that you, the leader, executive, or presenter, are feeling disconnected or experiencing your own resistance or lack of balance or confusion (or whatever you are really feeling at that point) accomplishes repair.

The Pit Stop

If you are experiencing a serious problem related to connectedness, it may be time to stop the whole thing and go into what I call a "pit stop." This may take the form of a general group discussion of the work being done or of the feelings being brought up. If this is necessary, you should work in facilitation mode and operate from a different perspective than the one used for repair procedures. Your primary goal will be to create "ownership of the process" by the participants. (This is always a good goal.)

Often participants simply do not see the purpose of working with the program or game at hand. There may be fear surrounding the way people are thinking and reacting in relation to their working or learning environment. There may be difficulties between cohorts. There may have been changes in levels of operation that have not been noted or attended to. If any of these is true, it is probably time for a pit stop.

Another use for a pit stop may involve the creative use of set design. Breaking into small groups for facilitated discussion or for mini "self-help" teaching breakouts may accomplish the repair. Sometimes a pit stop is a longer break. Sometimes it may be accomplished by having the participants do a written process, by two-person debriefing, or by a discussion process.

Letting Go Again

Another repair procedure calls for letting go. Sometimes the Improv work operates at extraordinary speed. You may have accomplished more than you think. It is possible that the deep work has been completed before the process is complete. It is at this juncture that you must let go of the goal or the plan as originally conceived.

Occasionally the Improv process itself has been used at an inefficient time and the original goal of accomplishing that process must be released. Another possibility is that a weak process was selected to begin with. In any of these instances, it may be necessary to "abandon ship" and to go on to another process. Let The Improv determine the next process. Go back to a basic game.

Letting go is sometimes difficult. We must first admit that there is some problem we did not anticipate or a plan that did not work out. We must then present ourselves and the problem to our organization in our most weak and vulnerable state. We must then release in public our plans, our goals, and our thought processes.

The only thing that is more difficult than admitting an error is dealing with the consequences when we have made errors and we do not admit and repair them. If we have seen the error and do not correct it, it is worse than if we did not notice the error at its inception or in development.

The size and design of creativity is a discussion of critical detail. Details really count in all we do. Paying real attention to people is very much a matter of attention to detail. Creativity itself requires close attention to detail. In formal research settings, the perception of your relationship and role in the search for truth is called *reflexivity*. The role you play and your knowledge of that role in relationship to your working sets of people, to your gatherings, and to your business can be the determining factors of success. Active participation in making repairs will serve your purposes. Giving full consideration and awareness to these details will reap nice results. With the explorations to this point in mind, you can now begin the fascinating Improv adventure of working with others as you consider the opening exercises in the next chapter.

CHAPTER TWELVE

Opening Exercises

The great Chinese philosophical work known as the *I Ching* or *Book of Changes* cautions us, saying: "Difficulty at the beginning works supreme success." It tells us further that "Times of growth are beset with difficulties. They resemble first birth. But these difficulties arise from the very profusion of all that is struggling to attain form."[19] Working with Improv techniques requires great care at the beginning, because of the profusion of all that will be struggling to attain form. Preliminary steps are needed to bring the organization or the gathering into The Improv or up to optimum Improv participation levels.

Your own confidence in the process will make a great deal of difference. Plan to start slowly and with easily accomplished work. Attend to set design. You have done work and study to get yourself into the present moment and now you must help those participating with you to get into the present moment. You need to help them attain the desire to participate.

There are many ways to begin. You may have them do some simple, physical, and active things. You may, as suggested in Chapter Six, request that they stand up and turn around twice in one direction and three times in the other. Another good and simple action is to

19

I CHING OR *BOOK OF CHANGES*, THE RICHARD WILHELM TRANSLATION, RENDERED INTO ENGLISH BY CARY F. BAYNES. NEW YORK: PRINCETON UNIVERSITY PRESS, 1950, PAGE 16.

ask the people with whom you are working to all shake hands with someone who is two or three people away. Easy, simply demonstrated action, which generates 100 percent participation, can create great stirs of activity and begin to build desire to play.

If the whole assemblage is not moving easily and quickly, it may help if you tell the gathering what you are doing. It is also good to demonstrate the actions you are going to ask people to take. Do not simply describe the action. If it cannot be simply demonstrated, the action is probably too complex for beginnings.

Games designed to analyze the gathering as well as to engage people in physical activity are particularly useful. Such exercises can help you learn how readily your participants may accept Improv games.

PAPER CHASE

The exercise that follows requires a supply of loose 8" x 11" sheets of paper. Plan on three to five sheets for each participant. You may use the distribution of paper as an exercise itself. The exercise may take ten to twenty minutes, depending on the amount of detail you engage in. Distribute the paper.

STARTING THE EXERCISE

- *Wad a single sheet of paper into a ball, throw it into the air, and let it drop at your feet in front of you.*

- *To the participants say exactly, "Take a piece of paper and do the same thing." Note how many of them follow your lead exactly. Note how many do something else (catch the paper, toss it to someone else, let it land behind themselves or to one side).*

- *Ask them to pick up the paper balls. Notice how they do this. If you need to, have them redistribute the paper balls so that everyone has one again.*

- *Without saying anything, begin to toss the ball into the air, catching it with one hand.*

- *Switch the paper ball to the other hand, toss it and catch it with that hand. Be silent and keep doing this until everyone, or nearly everyone, is doing the same thing. This step may take some time and patience.*

- *Toss the paper ball from one hand to the other until everyone follows along. Prompt only if necessary and note if you have to do so.*

- *Toss the ball to another participant.*

- *Begin to increase the number of paper balls being handled by the group. Do not give instructions regarding the increase. Let the participants figure it out.*

- *Make and juggle two, then three paper balls. It is fine if you cannot juggle three at once. This is not about juggling nor accomplishment; it is about opening doors to creativity with simple activity, participation analysis, audience bonding, having fun, playing, and taking small, successful, incremental steps toward a goal.*

- *Invent other things you may do with the paper balls. Let The Improv inspire other things to do with them. Help the participants become inspired to invent other things that can be done with them.*

- *By the time you reach the juggling phase, you may note those who are beginning to "drop out" of the activity. Some may quit participating because they are not willing to go any faster or any further, others because they have reached some internal limit. You will learn a great deal about how quickly you can move the group. Others may begin to "over-participate" or fixate on accomplishing the task as they currently understand it. Others may enter into competition (either as winners or as losers). Notice who is doing what as you go through this exercise.*

- *At the end of the game have the gathering clean up the paper as quickly as possible. Tell them you will time the clean-up activity. You may tell them that if they deposit all the paper into a container within sixty seconds there will be a twenty-minute break following the activity. If it takes longer, there will be a ten-minute break. Ask if anyone is willing to recycle the used paper. Let The Improv spirit invoke new ways to deal with the paper.*

If you play this game with simplicity and gusto, you will have fun and your participants will have fun. You will gain a wealth of information about the people with whom you are working and you will have established a sense of play and of activating the cooperative process.

SCAVENGER HUNT

Here is another model of a simple active, mind-opening exercise. You will need a list of fourteen to twenty-one items that this group should be able to find easily in the immediate location in which you are working, for example, a paper clip, a pencil, a quarter, and a notebook.

- *Very quickly ask the gathering to form in groups of three, four, seven, or fourteen, depending on the overall size of the group and the imperatives of the location.*

- *Tell everyone that each "team" will start by finding seven items. The first group to find all seven is to yell out, as a group, "We have them." Then a spokesperson must name the collected items out loud.*

- *Stop the process when the first group finds the items. Ask the winning group to select and join another group, doubling the size of that group.*

- *Ask all the groups to join with other groups and then call out three more items to be found for a total of ten.*

- *When a group yells out that they have found ten, call out four more items, until a team calls out that all fourteen have been found. Then name four more items.*

- *When a group has called out that they have found the eighteen items, name three more. At this point twenty-one items are being searched for.*

- *Depending on the number of people with whom you are working, you may ask the groups to team up with other groups at each increase in the number of items to be found. With skill you will achieve a great degree of controlled chaos.*

- *It is not necessary for all groups to be successful. It is only necessary to observe carefully and consciously the dynamics of the participant groups. As Yogi Berra said, "You can observe a lot by watching."*

An important skill of working with Improvisation has to do with moving at exactly the pace of change that the gathering can handle. Moving too slowly can be as problematic as moving too quickly. If you have moved at the pace that works well for this organization, there will be a flurry of activity, participation, self-organization, reorganization, and production. Also, a number of small, incremental, successful, steps toward following directions and altering behavior will have been taken.

AN INVITATION TO BABBLE

Babble will be discussed at length in Chapter Fourteen, but I wish to introduce the idea here. I have found *Babble* to be valuable and applicable with virtually every group and every level of mastery. I have used this precise methodology early in organizations and gathering with a success rate nearing 100 percent.

I use the following script or template for introducing *Babble* into the minds of the people in a gathering or an organization.

INSTRUCTIONS

This exercise will take a small amount of time. You may spend about five minutes with it to get an insight. You may easily give yourself ten or fifteen minutes to do this exercise yourself, alone. If you do it with another person, it may take twice as long. With a larger group you can present this exercise successfully as up to a thirty-minute period of real exercise.

BEGIN HERE

"I shall ask you to take some action. I will ask that you follow some easy instructions and do some simple things. I am going to ask you to do some things you may not have done recently or before. Is that OK with you? If it is not, then we may need to play some preparatory games before we go on.

"Will you do a favor with me? I want you to make real, out-loud sounds with me." (If I were with you, the reader, I would make the sounds as well.)

[Pause]

"Babble a sound that comes from you at this moment. Make a couple of nonsense sounds, something such as, 'Bla, bla bla. Bla! Bla! Bla bla, bla. Bla. Bla!' Make some more sounds of your own." [You can extend the time you spend here. You can also explore this process many times with many groups and gain new insight each time.]

"Next try making some nonsense sounds that you might make if you were angry. Try to do more than just growling. Make the noises sound like words: 'COLOSIL GOP DAGIBIL WAT!!!'" [You can extend the time you spend here. You can revisit this exercise many times.]

"Can you can make babble that sounds like language? Can you communicate in that language? Can you place emotion into your communication? Take some time and play, out loud, with your new languages."

[Read the following sentence out loud.] "Ble-galing profo-dalop mandel fluflu-flu." [Try it again with more volume. Say it with determination. With humility, with delight, with grave understanding, with comfort.]

"Use your *Babble* language to talk about your sadness. Then tell about being happy, confused, delighted."

It may be a good idea to do this exercise for yourself a few times and to read Chapter Fourteen, *Babble,* before you demonstrate and ask others to do this work. You may encounter some resistance the first time you ask others to make sounds of babble in public. If you encounter resistance, you will find that it probably is a reflection of your own resistance, and if you relax and move at a pace appropriate to the gathering and Improv principles, the resistance can be turned into creative energy. It takes personal trust and self-confidence to make this game work as an introduction. The more love you can include in the process, the better. The game itself, if done playfully, helps create the trust and confidence needed.

You should start the next procedures after you have been successful in leading the group of participants in making fairly loud and enthusiastic *Babble* responses.

Another quick *Babble* game asks you and the people with whom you are working to mingle with one another and to introduce themselves to three or four different people using only "babble" sounds. Closely monitor the reactions and responses of the participants. You may be able to identify resistant individuals or pockets of resistance at this point. You can do this, with variations, for up to five minutes.

You may also want to lead others through the exercise called *Exercise in the Present Moment,* which was detailed in Chapter Two. Learn to conduct that exercise in your own words and with your own timing. The exercise works best without the use of notes. Conducting the exercise to maximum effect may require practice with a tape recorder until you have the sequences in your control.

META-DYNAMICS: THE LIFE OF THE GROUP

Just as there are group dynamics, there are group perceptions of realities, which may override your purposes in organizing, leading, motivating, or training any specific set of people. There can be feelings that "the more things change, the more they stay the same." There can be perceptions that "the decision makers do not really want to change." There may be expectations that "they" are at it again. There may be a legend that "this change or reorganization system will go the way of all things." There may be perception that "learning new resources is a form of disloyalty to the older ways." There may be the presence of a sense of malarkey. These are a few of what I call "meta-dynamics." If these feelings are present in the group at large and you are not aware of them or you do not deal with them, your program may be in danger.

In organizations it is necessary to be aware of the absence or intermittent attendance of leaders, decision makers, executives, managers, supervisors, or others who are key players. In professional and academic settings, corporate or organizational culture identifies and creates many "meta-dynamic" behaviors. The Improv is operating at multiple levels and the meta-dynamics of the participants can become visible by the manner in which the people engage in the activities.

Note any who are not participating in the program even if they are present. Note whether the absence is due to distractions or to state of mind. Willingness to allow such distractions may tell you a great deal about the "meta-dynamics" of the organization with which you are dealing. It may give you clues to glitches in your organizational communication.

The Improv process is so powerful that people find it very difficult to resist—if it is done in the right spirit, using the guidelines and rules intelligently. People will see changes in themselves and in others. For some it will be proof that change is possible. For others it will reinforce their natural desire to learn and grow. For some it will generate a kind of meta-dynamic distraction syndrome. For a few it may bring up strong struggles. For some it can reveal a deep and great resistance. For these and other reasons, it must be engaged in with love and respect for all.

RESISTANCE IS NOT ALL BAD

Resistance on the part of some individuals some of the time is not a bad thing. Resistance by all the people some of the time is not a bad thing. Electricity does not work well without appropriate and intermittent resistors.

Some resistance often precedes "breakthrough" experiences. I have heard it said that some metals become extremely hard prior to the onset of metal fatigue. They become harder than normal. Such metals then become brittle and can shatter with a light impact. People can exhibit similar behavior in creative developmental and learning environments.

Watch for the hardening effect within yourself and among the people around you. Whether resistance and hardening appear in the group as a whole or in only one individual, become very patient. The individual may be expressing the group mind. There may be human fatigue and the need for tender love and care. This is a core Improv event. The Improv is, after all, an agent of change.

Opening exercises prepare the path for the people in your organization. The path of Improvisation will lead them through all the learning, self-analysis, discovery and challenge of patterns, and feelings and emotions that you have experienced to this point. Going through these things together will increase their effect. The beginnings are the most critical times. You will want to move both as slowly as and as quickly as the gathering needs. You will want to adhere very closely to Improv principles and pay close attention to keeping to the fundamentals. How you lead creates how others will follow. You will wish to make creative use of human set design factors. Carefully listen to the people with whom you are working so that you can be aware of the meta-dynamics of the organization. This will serve you and those who are important to you.

We have discussed getting started. We have explored Improv fundamentals and opening exercises. With this information we can now explore the basic Improv games.

PART FOUR

Basic Games

CHAPTER THIRTEEN

Word for Word

You first encountered this game as a method for opening the mind in Chapter One. *Word for Word* is a classic Improv form that is nothing less than a miraculous communication tool. In over twenty years of exploration, I have yet to find the limits of the use of this game.

This game was originally developed as a performance piece and is easily converted to presentational purposes. Three participants stand shoulder to shoulder facing the rest of the gathering. You ask the others to help you come up with a name of a personality from the past or from fiction. Playful people may ask for Christopher Columbus, Elvis, or The Road Runner. More serious people may ask for the "CEO" or the "auditor."

The goal is for the group of participants to make a complete sentence. The participants answer questions as though they are a single person, each limited to a single word at a time.

> **NOTE**
> As your skill and practice advance, you may play this game with sets of up to twenty-seven people. I have played this game with sets of two to ninety people at a time in groups of from ninety to five hundred people.

Another goal is to see whether the teams can make sentences quickly and smoothly, so that it sounds like the normal speech of a single person. Humor comes from the mere accomplishment of the task. There is a bonus is the fact that the cooperative effort usually results in funny and insightful responses.

The benefits include cooperation, creating and being in relationships, being true to the process, going for broke without hope nor fear of the goal, and putting it out there. Seeking laughter is not necessary. The game brings the laughter with it when it is played in the spirit of Improvisation. Here's an example:

"Mr. Columbus, what was the greatest challenge you faced in reaching the New World?"

> One person: "There"
> Next person: "were"
> Third person: "too"
> First: "many"
> Second: "waves"
> Third: "in"
> First: "the"
> Second: "ocean"
> Third: "period!"

The next person in line begins the answer to the next question, and the process continues. This can go on very successfully for two to three minutes for each set of people who try it. This game works best in gatherings up to 270. This is ninety sets of three, each with no observers.

If sentences are not working or people are stuck or breaking down into conversation and discussion, or sentences are going on forever, you may intercede. You may make coaching comments out loud to the whole group or you may make side comments to sets or individuals. It is often good to make coaching comments in the direction of someone who was doing very well in order to have maximum effect on others who may not be doing as well. Give credit to this person for good work.

In a typical circumstance seven questions for each "character" is about the maximum that this process can support before it loses some charm.

BEFORE YOU BEGIN

People learn best by doing. It is usually an error to spend too much time talking through the processes. Too many instructions at the beginning of an event can be lost on us. How many people read the entire manual before opening the new computer or a new software program? Imagine a new car buyer:

> "No, I don't want to take my new car with me today. I'd like a few days to read the manual thoroughly first. Here is my down payment. Please call me a cab and I'll be back next week."

Too many instructions, steps that are too big, and big chunks of information can spawn resistance. As you work with small steps, there is much to be gained in careful observation and analysis of the responses to your instructions. Observing people who have received short, quick instructions that are not too detailed can give you large amounts of feedback. You can then use the feedback to guide everyone into the next steps.

A lot of people, because of their training, their individual personalities, their public personas, or their public and private responsibilities, do not wish to take action until they are assured of success. Sometimes they must be convinced that they know what they are supposed to do before they take action.

INTRODUCING THE GAME

Word for Word begins as a tool for analysis of the participants and participation dynamics. It is also an introduction mechanism useful for taking people through small, *successful,* incremental steps toward a goal.

For some adults a thing called a "game" is not to be taken seriously. With some gatherings you may wish to name the exercise in terms your particular group can best accept. "Communication exercise" is good. "Interactive process" may work. "Communication simulation" might be all right.

N O T E

It is important that you do not call this "role play." Role play is a practice of its own. Improvisation is not role play, and the use of the term can cause assumptions and confusion.

If there is concern on the part of the participants, talk with them about sensitivity to the word "game." You may need to refer to the game as an "overt, intentional, interactive, intra/inter-human, interpersonal, introspective, co-developmental, programmable analog, analytic, virtual communication matrix for future needs fulfillment." You may diffuse resistance and get a laugh by then saying something such as, "A game is still a game."

FORMING SETS TO PLAY

Word for Word is excellent for working in small circles. It is good with sets of two. Primal sets are good grouping sizes. Smaller sets can sometimes help people to be more comfortable. Building to larger sets can help develop interaction as well as confidence and communication skills among the participants. I prefer standing circles for this game, although they are not necessary. Sitting around a table can work, but a table can also become a barrier that inhibits movement of the body, mind, and spirit.

Tell the participants that the goal is for the group to answer a question by making a simple complete sentence with each participant contributing a single word at a time. It is not unusual for some people not to understand this instruction. You may need to repeat the instruction and to do some demonstration work with a single group as an example.

Sometimes, however, you may decide to observe whether the group will try to make a sentence without being told to do so. If they make a sentence on their own, you may compliment them on how quickly they are moving. If they do not, you may congratulate them on their participation and *then* tell them that next they are to try to make a complete simple sentence.

You may demonstrate with something like "What do you think of the weather today?" then point to each person around the circle as you say, "I . . . think . . .

it . . . is . . . very . . . hot . . . today." Laugh and point and say, "Of course you may get 'The . . . day . . . cold . . . what . . . beautiful . . . huh.'"

- *Formulate a simple question about something that has absolutely no risk to it. You may use the season or the current surroundings ("How do you like the meeting facility?"). Keep the subject matter neutral. It is sometimes even best to avoid questions about sports.*

- *Select the person to start the process, with a group in a circle, in a line, or in small sets. You may merely point to someone and indicate whether the answer will move to the right or to the left. You may ask for a volunteer, select a "volunteer," or have a volunteer select a volunteer. Do not spend much time getting started.*

- *Ask each question clearly and loudly, "What do you think of the weather today?" and repeat the question at least once or twice.*

- *Say "go!"*

- *Say things like, "OK, that is a perfect example of the next step; we all must [speak up, speak clearly, try not to think too hard, etc.]. Now, let's try it again."*

- *Let the process unfold itself.*

- *Success should be rewarded by great encouragement.*

- *Difficulty or failure should be praised for participation and effort. Laughter should be encouraged.*

If Any Game Is Not Working

- *If your "level of operation" is simple and the process is not working, make a quick personal evaluation and continue playing.*

- *Attend to problems regarding connections.*

- *Make small changes in the structure of your work—have participants answer going in the opposite direction, have participants change places, have small groups re-mix.*

- *Investigate and help the release of patterns.*

- *Explore changes in the elements affecting the levels of operation.*

- *Seek the management of fear.*

- *Make sure instructions are being given at a pace selected by the people involved.*

- *Encourage exploration into more serious matters followed by things less serious, followed by things more serious.*

- *Promote and manage emotional responses in the work.*

- *Identify and help people who are blocking the process. A typical blocking response is resistance followed by confusion or nonparticipation, or the reverse.*

- *Identify and help people who are helping too much.*

- *Give instructions quickly and prompt quick action and a lot of it.*

- *Encourage more playfulness.*

- *Attend to language quirks.*

- *Encourage more laughter.*

- *Check for set design problems, including dropouts and position shifters.*

- *Do more. Play more.*

If Someone Is Blocking

If someone appears to be stuck, unable to utter a word, or holding his or her breath, simply say "breathe." Have everyone take a breath and try again. You may need to have someone repeat the group's words up to that person's turn. If others in the group try to provide words, say things such as, "Thank you, but let's let her come up with her own word." Say, "Breathe." Repeat the words to that point again. Start over if you must. You may have to prompt the blocked participant, saying things such as, "Make any sound; a sound has some sort of, uh, sound to it" or "Say any word. Say 'word.'" Be light and in laughter as you do this.

If an individual simply cannot or will not participate at this level, reorganize that set or all the sets and begin again. There is no such thing as failure in this process. The process itself is filled with feedback. Listen to the feedback and try something new until there is forward movement. The only way you can make this game not work is to ignore the feedback.

I watched a group of teenagers in a theater arts program handle *Word for Word* the very first time with minimum instruction. I started them out as a group of eighteen. (I know, I said that this is too many adolescents. Exceptions prove rules.) I gave them a complex and serious question on the first try. (I know, I said to start small and simple.) They came up with a compound complex sentence that not only made sense, but had a great deal of wisdom in it as well.

There was another group of mature businessmen in an oak paneled board-room. These were men of substance, experience, creativity, and training. They were embarking on a two-year multi-million-dollar project. There was no one who was shy. There were clear and simple instructions for *Word for Word*. It took nearly half an hour before they were able to come up with their first clear, simple sentence.

This game, with continued practice, and use of solid Improv principles, can help address many hard questions easily and creatively.

GUIDING DISCUSSION

After the group has had success in answering a reasonably difficult question, it is good to have a guided discussion about the *Word for Word* process. First, ask the people involved what they think made the exercise work. You may hear answers such as "teamwork," "cooperation," "listening," "participating." Encourage a lot of responses. This is my list.

Behaviors That Make *Word for Word* Work

- *Everyone participates. If anyone does not add a word, the whole process stops.*

- *No one overparticipates. (You know the overparticipators. They never stop talking.)*

- *Everyone listens to every word being said.*

- *Everyone remembers the words that have been spoken.*

- *Everyone considers what has been said before his or her own turn.*

- *Everyone thinks about where the sentence is going.*

- *Everyone works as a member of the team.*

- *Everyone also expresses his or her own individual power. It is your word.*

If any one of these elements is missing, the game will not really work. The list you share with the participants may be different.

I find it helpful to present a serious moment at this point. I shall share my serious moment with you. What would your world be like if you were assured at all times that these behaviors would be present whenever you spoke to another person: equal participation, listening, remembering, consideration of what has gone before, consideration of what can follow, working as a team and as an individual responsibility at the same time?

Look at your own communication habits and think about how often you engage in all these behaviors when others are speaking with you. What would your world be like if the people you live with and love and work with could always be assured that you would engage in these behaviors all the time?

VARIATIONS OF WORD FOR WORD

The basic game is played with each player supplying one word at a time, speaking in order in a pattern. A variation is to have the players use *two words each*. After doing two words successfully, have the players use three words each. *Do not use more than three words.* It changes the dynamics of the process and turns it into another game, *Group Storytelling*.

Another variation is to change the order in which the players contribute their words: *Have each player point to the next person to speak.* In a circle or in a crowd, encourage the participants to point to others randomly. Help them avoid pointing to the person next to them so that the game does not turn into going around in a circle again. Encourage the players not to pick the same person each time they point to the next speaker.

Another variation allows each player the discretion to *choose either one, or two, or three words at each turn*. Encourage the individuals to avoid the tendency to fall into a pattern of using a particular number of words.

Working with Pairs

Many applications of this game can be engaged by having people play *Word for Word* in sets of two. When working with pairs it is a good idea to have the two face one another. You may also prompt them into saying their words faster and faster each time. This game is especially powerful for bridging gaps and forging bonds between individuals. When people are in conflict, this process can also be used to get them to communicate at a basic level. It can allow them to say things that they could not say to one another otherwise. It may allow people to speak cooperatively who could not or would not under other circumstances.

Working with Large Groups

Working with this game in larger groups requires making the demonstrations bigger and less complex. Also, the use of a public address system is usually required. In a large group you are working more for energy than for achieving specific results. The amount of interaction and laughter that can be generated with this game in a large group is immense.

Building Sets

This game is wonderful for creating a set of the whole. Start with sets of two and progress through the prime sets. Get group answers from sets of two, then three, then four, seven, fourteen, twenty-one, and so on. A very connected set of the whole can be achieved very quickly. Your goal is a quick and smooth transition for a large number of people.

DEBRIEFING

It is good to facilitate a group through a debriefing whenever there has been a significant event or a completion of an Improv game. Instruct the participants to talk among themselves about what they have been experiencing. You may engineer the groups along human set design lines or you may let the group gather as they will. Walk around and listen to some of the conversations. If the talk is general and social, you may need to attend to more of the social needs of the group prior to continuing. If the conversation is more about the process of the game, you are on the right track and you can go on to more complex work.

You may decide that you have accomplished as much as you can with the gathering at hand. If you can get this far, you will at least have a good number of things to say to the group about the game and its use and effect in creating a group mind. Conclude with a summary of the benefits of listening and cooperating with the game.

APPLICATIONS

Celebrations of Beginnings and Endings

Word for Word can be a good opener for gatherings, seminars, presentations, and projects. It can be used to open a demonstration or for entertainment at the culmination of a gathering.

In business, training, and educational settings, you may try using personalities from the organization rather than historical or fictional figures. Used this way, the game is a good focusing device, attention getter, and icebreaker. Historical figures from the participants' field of business are also good choices. Other examples include founders, inventors, lecturers, researchers, discoverers, innovators, and retired persons in the field.

Inanimate and abstract things can be made more real, less formidable, and more human with this game. The new computer, the new filing system, the new desks, and the latest reorganization, for example, can all be made animate and asked to "speak."

The competition, the other department, the outside consultant, the new kid on the block—all can be subjects of spontaneous creativity while helping the gathering or organization come to terms with sensitive issues. A special feature of the game used this way is that the answers are not the product of any one mind.

Discovery of Direction and Focus

Use *Word for Word* to answer the simple questions, "What is our purpose here today?" and "What would we like to accomplish here today?" The game is a good tool for directing a meeting, class, or training session. To use *Word for Word* in this fashion requires that the gathering be grounded in the use and rules of the game.

A good question to ask to help focus a workshop or new program is "What would I like to learn or receive from this event?" This use of *Word for Word* requires the question to be considered by the individuals while calling on the group mind for an answer.

A common business complaint is that many meetings have no clear focus or direction. These types of questions, answered by the group with *Word for Word,* can give a meeting a focus and direction that could otherwise take a long time to achieve.

Review of Accomplishment

Word for Word is also useful for finding out what has been accomplished. Such questions may be framed in the following forms: "Today we have come to the conclusion that. . .," "With today's work we can now. . .," "Our next step is to. . .," or "This work tells us that. . . ." If meaningful answers do not arise in this process, or if the process breaks down into silliness or silence, it may be a good idea to take a really good look at the event to see whether anything actually was accomplished.

Problem Solving

Frame the questions in the form of the problem to be solved and play the game. For this to work the participants must be grounded in the use and rules of the game. You may have to play with the game a little before applying it to the serious aspects of problem solving. The first lighthearted or even silly dis-jointed answers will clear people's minds and help to pave the way to the group's more committed and serious work.

The more times the group is willing to go around the circle with new attempts at answers, the deeper and more real the answers can become. Given enough time and commitment to the process, the group can often find serious solutions and serious action steps. Allow for instances of silliness and confu-sion interspersed with good sense and wisdom.

When a problem-solving group or a strategic planning meeting comes to a plateau or other minor problems, *Word for Word* can re-energize the group and refocus the work at hand. When side issues come up, the game can be used to resolve them and get the group back on track.

Simple Learning and Reinforcement

Word for Word is a good game for helping people work with information learned from other explorations. Imagine any topic. Begin the process by framing a content question such as: "The merger was undertaken because. . .," "Windows requires the operator to. . .," "The new compensation system will allow us to. . .," "OSHA requires new employees to. . .," "The marketing func-tion is characterized primarily by. . . ."

There may be silly answers and even individuals who have no clue. However, if the process is adhered to, the results can be considerable as the players begin to develop creative answers as a group.

Word for Word is a game with unlimited possibilities and variations. It is easy to begin and can be developed into complex forms very quickly. It has fun and creative elements that can be used to teach Improv principles. The game can help develop awareness of Improv fundamentals and can provide a forum for valuable practice in working together.

CHAPTER FOURTEEN

Babble

You first encountered this game in Chapter Twelve as an opening exercise. *Babble* is a challenging game capable of deep impact when applied to real-time situations. It is a primary developer of pre-verbal human communication skills. Some people consider this to be an advanced game. If used in basic form with reasonable goals, it works very well as a starter game. I have used it as a basic game hundreds of times with extraordinary success.

In traditional Improvisation the use of meaningless language is called *gibberish*. The classic game is called *Poet Interpretation*. One participant makes gibberish noises in such a manner as to suggest a poem. Another player "translates" the poem into English (or whatever is the common language of the gathering).

In non-theatrical crowds I prefer to use the term "babble." It is easier to convince people to "babble" than it is to convince them to "gibber." At a deeper level, Western culture has an ancient interest in the city of Babel and an archetypal relationship with Babel and its meaning in reference to the search for heaven.

BABBLE

This "game" sometimes seems innocent and silly on the surface. Do not be fooled by the simplicity. The work being accomplished goes to an extraordinarily deep level in the human psyche. There are elements of meaning and connectedness that are not visible while the game and process are being explored. However, they do become apparent over time.

It is necessary to approach this game with great care and exceptional sensitivity. Special care must also be focused on management of the set design in order to work with the elements of risk.

The elements of risk and the challenges to our sense of meaning and purpose can shake an individual or the gathering to the point of distress or disorientation. In these instances most people shut down rather than act out. If this happens, you may experience it as resistance or perhaps as a negative evaluation at the end of a program.

The specific structure of the teaching depends entirely on the nature of the gathering. In some cases it may be necessary to use more explanation in the introduction to this game. In other cases it is necessary to weave the explanations into the activity.

You may need to use demonstrations more in one case and less in another. You may need to call on allies in the audience in order to move the group along. You may need to move very slowly in one case and very quickly in another.

> **NOTE**
> This game can work as an introduction to Improvisation at a business level. *Babble* can give you a deep evaluation of the people and your organization. If you are not sure of the creative capacity of the audience, it may be best to use *Word for Word* as your primary introduction to Improvisation. *Word for Word* followed by *Babble* can accomplish a great deal.

INTRODUCING THE GAME

If you are truly on time and in time, introducing and using *Babble* will go quickly. If you are not on time and in time, there is a very good chance that the audience will resist or block the process.

This game has an extraordinary range of uses. As an icebreaker it can be taught and used in a few minutes with yourself and one other willing participant. If your purpose is to illustrate a principle of communication, it may be introduced and demonstrated in as little as twenty minutes. As a team-building exercise, it may take an hour. As a deep form of group dynamics development, it can cover a three-hour block of time. You can play this game many times with the same group. There is always a deeper level to which this game can take a group.

It is possible to introduce this game as an icebreaker by a simple demonstration with neither conversation nor explanation. Working with an audience member as a partner in the introduction can lead others into the necessary connections. With a larger audience or where there is little commonality among the participants, it may be necessary to work with a prepared co-presenter.

LET THE GAME BEGIN

- *First, introduce the crowd to the basics by proposing the idea that we often tend to speak in "babble." This idea will be discussed in detail below.*

- *Demonstrate the most basic "babble" by saying, "Bla, bla bla. Bla! Bla! Bla bla, bla. Bla. Bla." Ask the participants to do the same.*

- *Each step requires that you be aware of the real participation level of the group. If they do not respond at the highest and most enthusiastic level possible, then you must play with them more, encourage them more, demonstrate some more. You may say such things as, "This usually requires that your lips move" or "'Babble' is often accompanied by sound."*

- *Ask them, as a group, to "babble" as though they are angry. Encourage and wait for a response. Demonstrate as needed. You must become a measuring device, a sort of sound meter. If the meter does not go into the red zone, you may need to cheerlead and encourage them even more.*

- *Babble your own anger more energetically, more loudly. Bring them to a high pitch. A high pitch, not a fevered pitch. (Small, incremental steps.)*

- *Ask the crowd to babble as though they are sad. If you developed the anger response to full advantage, you should not need to encourage anything here.*

- *Ask them to babble as though they are confused. Asking them to sound out their confusion is necessary.*

Interpretation Formats

If you are familiar and comfortable with poetry forms, you may use the poem interpretation format. Prompt the gathering to call out possible poem topics or titles. Then have one participant speak babble sounds to convey the feeling and cadence. The other player translates it into a poem. A translation may be done in free verse, which does not have to rhyme.

If you or the audience is not comfortable with poetry, it is possible to substitute a variety of topics for the interpretation. You might try "supervisor interpretation," "politician interpretation," "boss interpretation," "regulatory agency interpretation," or "computer programmer interpretation." Also, virtually any process or system can be used as the material for the interpretation: "executive management," "quality control," "atomic theory," or "math 101."

A Communication Lesson: Part One

You may introduce and use this game as a communication lesson. This process can take half an hour. This step is not necessary to the introductory use of *Babble,* but it is a powerful lesson in creativity and can be used to take the game to deeper levels.

- *Begin by asking the audience the following questions about languages. The precise words in these instructions have been developed in response to a lot of feedback. You may feel free to adapt this process to your own style and words, but be careful to keep the idea very clear and simple.*

- *Ask, "What is the language spoken by the largest number of people on earth?" Depending on the crowd, people will usually say Chinese, English, Spanish, French, and German. Depending on the gathering, you may get blank stares.*

- *Prompt people to answer out loud. Continue prompting even if someone gets the right answer immediately.*

- *Often an audience will hear someone say "Chinese" and everyone will stop giving responses, assuming that the answer is correct. If this happens, compliment them with some comment such as, "I like a knowledgeable group. Someone got the answer so no one else needs to say anything." Continue to prompt them anyway. You will get some more answers.*

- *If someone gives the precisely correct answer, which is Mandarin Chinese, ask what language is next on the list.*

- *Prompt with gestures—hands open, arms out, palms turned upward, fingers motioning toward you as though you are beckoning them.*

- *As you receive responses, give the crowd positive feedback, saying "Good," "Yes," and "More."*

- *After you have received three or four answers, compliment interesting and unexpected responses.*

- *If you have not received any particularly interesting answers, you may note that some creative individuals in other groups have answered "body language" and "Esperanto." I had one particularly sweet person say, "The language of love."*

- *Whether it is called out or not, mention that "body language" is a good answer and note that body language can be as specific to a particular culture or country as is verbal language. Notice whether heads are nodding at this point.*

- *Now give a short talk about the answer in your own words.*

This is the outline I use: The language spoken by the largest number of people as their first or primary language is Mandarin Chinese. At the end of the 1900s there were approximately 1.3 billion who spoke this language. The vast majority of the people who speak it are residents of China.

The next language on the list is an object of debate among linguists. Many count Hindi and Urdu as the same language. Hindi is spoken in India by 476 million, and Urdu is written in Pakistan by 104 million. Combined, the Hindi/Urdu language is used by 580 million.

The next most widely used language on the planet is English. Approximately 497 million use English as a primary language, and it can be heard nearly anywhere on earth. As much as 80 percent of the language used in computers is English. Most of the mail in the world is addressed in English. Spanish follows at 425 million.

In many crowds it is good to know the numbers of the next languages in line. In millions they are Russian (279), Arabic (235), Bengali (207), Portuguese (187), Malay/Indonesian (170), French (127), German (126), and Japanese (126).

There are approximately 165 million Jewish people on the earth, so Hebrew could be listed (probably between Malay and French) and may actually be the most widely distributed language of all. This brief discussion may be necessary to create focus, answer questions, and to bring the group into the present moment.

- *Following your discussion of languages say, "I believe, however, that there is a language that everyone uses at some time or another. That language is 'babble.'" There is often a laugh at this point.*

- *"How many of you have had someone babble at you recently?" You will normally get some hands in the air.*

- *Prompt for more with, "You know how this happens. You are watching their lips move and sounds come out and you have no idea what they are saying."*

- *Then you may say, "How about being really honest. How many here have spoken babble to someone else in the last couple of weeks?" I have noticed that this question almost always elicits general agreement and enthusiasm. Encourage this.*

- *As you explore these issues with the group, move back and forth between humor and seriousness. Encourage participants to go into details and to tell stories.*

Communication Lesson: Part Two

To go more deeply into the communication lesson, you may ask the participants to consider situations in which people in the same organization, department, or household have been at odds with one another.

- *Ask them to remember whether there were heated discussions about some issue.*

- *Encourage them to share their own stories with the general group.*

- *Ask if anyone has ever seen two people standing "toe-to-toe" in a major disagreement and noticed that the two were really saying the same thing.*

- *At this point I tell a story about communication without the use of language. You are free to share this story if you are willing to give credit to the source. It will be much more powerful, however, if you can find a story of your own to share.*

- *Better still will be to search your current world for some similar revelation about the ways in which people communicate with one another beyond the bounds of language.*

Once, in a large city, in a great plaza, it was my privilege to be present for a very sweet human event. It was springtime and there were blooming trees scattered about the plaza. I watched as two people were witnessing an event in nature. A mother bird swooped to a branch and pushed a fledgling back into a nest. It was a simple thing made notable by the surrounding metropolis.

The two I was watching then turned toward one another and each noticed that the other had seen the same event. They both turned to look again at the tree, then back at each other, and then together they laughed and laughed.

The important thing was that he was a man, perhaps eighty or eighty-five years old. He was Asian and the location made it probable that he did not speak English. She was seven or eight, European, Caucasian, and almost certainly did not speak his language.

They had little in common, neither age, nor culture, nor nationality, nor gender, nor language, nor family, nor anything except their humanity. Yet, without connections they communicated quite eloquently.

A truth is that we are all, always, speaking babble. Whatever I say, you must translate in order to arrive at understanding. You must decide that I have something of value to say. You must decide whether my truth has meaning to you. You must decide whether I know what I am talking about. You must translate everything to come to common meaning.

I will sometimes do a demonstration by acting out babbling as a toddler who needs something and does not have the words for it. I then turn away from the imaginary child and look at the audience and then back at the child as though I am an adult responding to the child and say, in a disgusted voice, "I'm sorry! You just come back when you can express yourself more clearly." Use this and notice the audience response.

Make the point that we should respond to our co-workers and our loved ones, indeed to everyone, in the same way we need to respond to children and to those who do not speak our language clearly, that is, with the understanding that *we must participate in the translation.* Reinforce the idea that we must take the time to allow for translation. We need to understand that what we *mean* and what we *say* are often very different. We can understand that what we say and what others hear are often not the same. This is not because we are inattentive, nor stubborn, nor bad listeners. *It is simply because we are all always speaking babble and we must translate in order to make sense.*

Striving for 100 Percent Participation

If you are working with three or six or thirteen, strive for 100 percent participation. If you are working with twenty-seven people, strive for 100 percent participation. If you are working with any number between one and 1,500, strive for 100 percent participation. If you cannot strive for 100 percent participation, then limit your goals and revise your horizons.

You may introduce the idea of *Babble* and you may take the first step, or even finish the game, with less than 100 percent participation; however, you cannot progress to higher levels without achieving 100 percent participation periodically during the process.

Please keep in mind that achieving 100 percent participation is possible. This does not mean that you can maintain 100 percent focus and attention all the time. As a matter of fact, if you are actually influencing people they will wander away and into their own thoughts when you reach inside them deeply enough to have an effect. Your goals and purposes need to be deeply involved with gaining and regaining, and regaining and regaining, 100 percent participation. *Babble* is uniquely suited for obtaining 100 percent participation.

Generating Genuine Emotions

This work touches on deep levels of human experience and communication. If you demonstrate angry babble only from your mind and not from your soul, it will not be real to the audience and they will follow your lead. They will be just as unreal as you want. If you babble it from your heart, they will follow as well.

If you do not have some understanding of your own internal anger, it may come out too strongly in your own demonstration. The effect will be that you may back away from the reality and the audience will follow your lead.

Holding *Babble* Conversations

To develop confidence in the use of *Babble* you may help the participants to babble with one another at the level of conversation. This works best with larger gatherings.

- *Start by demonstrating a babble conversation with one person. Make eye contact with an audience member and babble noises that sound like a question. Expect and encourage an answer in babble.*

- *Repeat the babble sounds until you get an answer in babble. Answer in babble and engage the willing member in a conversation.*

- *After this you may ask the general gathering of participants to move about and babble with one another. The best forum for this process is open seating, where the participants can stand up and move around.*

- *Ask the audience members to find someone they do not know well and engage in a babble conversation.*

This exercise can be extended into a general workplace to create a break and a shift in the day's energy. In this phase it is not necessary to have 100 percent participation. It is, however, a very good time to evaluate the connections between you, your audience, and the process. If people are not moving about or if there is less than a great deal of noise and energy, you may need to backtrack and repair before moving on. You may increase the energy and participation by asking your participants to engage in communicating a frustrating or serious, touchy or difficult, reality or fact with their babble partners.

Translating Introductions

This is a babble translation process. You will need to demonstrate this step. It works best with sets of seven to thirteen. It is good to identify volunteer group leaders in the gathering.

- *Tell the participants that a volunteer, or a person selected by the volunteer, will start the process.*

- *The person who begins will introduce himself or herself to the audience in babble. The babble can be so basic as "Bla, bla, bla, bla," or it can be as sophisticated as to sound like a real language. (Make sure that the participants do not use a real language.)*

- *The person to the beginner's left must translate the introduction into English for the rest of the group.*

- *Then the first translator introduces himself or herself in babble and the person to the left will translate, and so on around the circle.*

- *Show the people how to babble in short phrases and show the translators how to translate in short phrases.*

> **N O T E**
> A problem you may encounter with this game is that one group may move more quickly than another. Adjust your instructions to help people who have finished to keep them engaged in the event. You may have quick sets play *Word for Word* or discuss some of their thoughts or feelings while others are completing the task.

Whenever you finish using an Improv game, it is good to ask the gathering for feedback about how the process worked and about their feelings. You may start by asking whether people found meaning in what they heard. Ask for examples. Prompt with such questions as, "What happened in your group?" "Did anyone experience feeling silly when you were babbling?" Share your own experience of this exercise.

A STORY

When I first began using this form I was "the comedy teacher" and I thought that the people expected me to be funny. It was pretty easy to get laughter with the babble. I could act a little foolish and put a lot of energy into it and people would laugh. When I became good at making my babble sound like real languages the audiences and participants loved it.

When I had to translate, however, it was often not funny. I think this was true because I was trying to make it funny, breaking the first Improv rule, working outside the present moment by trying to achieve a particular end. To make things worse, the participants who were not trying to make something happen would say whatever came to their minds and the results were most often very funny.

I became convinced that it was more difficult to translate than to babble. As I used the form more with business and professional audiences, I began to notice that a lot of people were uncomfortable with the babble part. It became apparent when a participant came up to me and said, "If you make me babble again I am leaving."

I have surveyed many audiences and it turns out that about 45 percent of us find the babble tougher and about 45 percent find the translation more difficult. Without exploring feedback, I would never have known about the discomfort of the persons babbling.

APPLICATIONS

Babble can be used as a simple basic introduction to Improv forms, principles, fundamentals, and structures. It can also be used as an advanced tool for deep exploration of ideas or emotions, problems, systems, and relationships. The variations have not been fully explored. As you work with this game, you will become more familiar and more comfortable. You will find that you can combine or include *Babble* with *Word for Word, Four-Square Matrix, Storytelling,* and with many of the advanced games described in Chapter Seventeen. The more you use the game, the more you will discover applications of your own.

CHAPTER FIFTEEN

Four-Square Matrix

In organizational development and teaching situations, this game can be adapted to almost any setting and circumstance. Attention needs to be focused on area labels, the relationships, the setup, and logistics. Interspersed will be consideration of the subject matter being explored. Except for area labels, the other elements of this game have applications in most of the games discussed in the *Grab Bag of Advanced Games,* Chapter Seventeen.

FOUR-SQUARE MATRIX

BEFORE YOU BEGIN

Divide the playing space into four distinct areas by making a large plus sign (+) on the floor. This can be done with the imagination or with masking tape. Select one to four participants to stand on the squares. Ask the participants who are not on any squares to call out contrasting emotions; then you assign one of the emotions called out to each of the four squares. Call these emotions the "area labels."

INTRODUCING THE GAME

Give titles or relationships to the players to provide a focus. For example, you could use a business focus (executive, finance officer, sales manager, line worker) or family focus (father, son, sister, brother). You may use unrelated professions (computer analyst, graphics artist, web master, architect). Imaginative pairings can also focus energy and thoughts in a group. As their skills increase, label people with their own actual positions in relationships at work or in the family.

SETTING UP THE GAME

The game can be presented as (1) a problem to be solved (new system will be a week late, desk-top computers have arrived before the new desks); (2) a conflict to resolve (two employees and only one vacation date, conflicting areas of responsibility); or (3) things to do (prepare for a meeting, plan a future event). As an introduction or to teach people how to play, the situation can be unusual or bizarre (lost on an ice cream cone, captured by army ants).

LET THE GAME BEGIN

Tell the players that they are to talk through an interchange based on the relationships as described. They are to move around the playing squares, through the spaces with area labels. As they move into each different area, they must immediately change their emotions to match the label in that area.

You may decide the manner in which the participants will move through the squares. A simple way to use the matrix is to have people talk about a challenge as they move between the squares, changing emotions as they move. Encourage the participants to keep moving from area to area. They may walk in a circle or move randomly from area to area. The simple necessity of speaking from four different viewpoints often brings enlightenment and understanding.

You may have individuals discuss an issue as they move through the squares together. Try one person in each square. Have each one talk about an issue or problem from the viewpoint of the area label where they are standing. Then have the group shift one space clockwise until each person has spoken a few times from each position. Keep the subject the same. After people are familiar with the game, have them create their own area labels, setups, and issues.

Playing with Larger Groups

It is possible to have a fairly large number of sets of four operating at once. It is not difficult to have five hundred people in 125 sets in a ballroom.

Participants may be seated at small, square tables, standing, grouped in the corners of a room, or gathered into more general areas that you have designated. In each area ask the people to talk among themselves from the perspective of the area label. After a reasonable period, ask them to rotate to another area and to continue conversations from the perspective of the new area label. Everyone must have a chance to be in each of the four squares at least once. It is best to have the people move rather than to move the area labels.

More than six changes will tend to exhaust the range of conversation of most large groups. The wrap-up can be done in smaller discussion groups, through large-group discussion, or as part of the process following the game. The logistics, as with all Improv parameters, are subject to change and invention.

Investigating Area Labels in Depth

Great creativity can come from the thoughtful use of area labels. Emotions work well as area labels for entertaining, icebreaking, teaching the basic game, and for playing before beginning to discuss serious business matters.

When using emotions as area labels, it is good to let the participants call out the emotions. You pick out a strong, clear, simple, direct emotion, then repeat the process asking for a contrasting emotion. Do this twice more, each time asking for an emotion that is in contrast with the last one. This can take just a few minutes.

If participants are not comfortable with their own emotions, they may have difficulty calling out emotions. In this case it may be a good idea to have a set of emotions in mind when you begin. Such basic emotions as happy, sad, angry, and confused can be used early in the process. As competence, creativity, and enthusiasm set in, be prepared to use emotions of heightened intensity, such as ecstatic, mournful, enraged, or disoriented.

If you feel you must provide the emotions for the participants, it is important to understand why you believe the participants cannot do this without your help.

Assigning Relationships to Participants

You may also assign relationships to the people who are working in the exercise. The relationships among the people who wander through the labeled areas can create a great deal of fun and can lead to much insight by the participants.

If you wish to explore a particular relationship that exists in the organization, you may place two people with a real relationship into the four-square matrix with area labels attached. Have the participants talk about a selected topic as they move through the squares. Remember the rules of complexity and simplicity when you try this.

If a relationship is strained, it may be good to have two alternate strong people play the roles while those in the real relationship observe. If there is a particularly strained or difficult relationship, it may be necessary to set up an allegorical or symbolic relationship. In this fashion relationships may be described as "big and small," "strong and weak," "tall and short," "plus and minus," "old and new," and "true and false."

When using this game to work through relationships, the area labels need to be carefully considered. Emotions are effective. Environmental conditions provide an excellent working grid. Such names as hot, cold, dry, moist, heavy gravity, light gravity, windy, and rainy are effective. Qualities of light, sight, and sound can provide effective changes. Area label names may include bright, dim, grainy, high-contrast, invisible, fuzzy, loud, low-volume, and unclear. The rule of complexity and simplicity is at work again. The more complex and sensitive the relationships, the more simple and less serious must be the area labels. Conversely, the more complex the area labels, the simpler or safer must be the relationships.

Using the Setup to Advantage

You can also use the setup as a problem that helps participants move toward a solution. Seeking a solution is more powerful as a process than as a thing. If solution seeking is viewed as a thing, we may find ourselves creating solution after solution without really addressing underlying problems.

It is usually best to lead participants to the ability to develop the setup. This provides an opportunity for them to frame their own concerns and to analyze their situation in Improv terms of "Our problem—Our solution."

The Form of the Setup

- *The setup may be business. It may be based on the ways in which we work with one another.*

- *The setup may be about communication, the ways we talk with one another. It may be organizational, based on the rules, formats, and forms we use.*

- *The setup may be educational, analytical, playful, directive, free-form, focused, or specifically not focused.*

- *It may be social. If the setup is based on the way we act with one another, a good problem choice would be a social problem—something that has to do with getting to know and to trust one another. Examples include adjusting to new members of a group, dealing with differing perceptions, or differences in emotional commitment to ideas and organization.*

- *The setup may focus the group's ability to receive and respond to directions. Here the setup is organizational and goal-oriented. It might be good to use resource difficulties. Examples might include a problem of having more deserving people than there are bonus days available or perhaps only one person can go to a conference.*

- *The setup itself is designed also to be a tool for learning the game.*

- *The setup should be simple, non-threatening, seasonal or environmental, constructed in fun, and dedicated to two ideas.*

The *first* idea is that our old friends "small, successful, incremental steps toward change," at the beginning, will lead to wonderful leaps toward behavioral change.

The *second* idea is that a purpose of Improv exercises is also to give the executive or facilitator feedback about the group as it is functioning here and now.

Selecting Subject Matters for the Matrix

You may use any subject matter in this game. The deeper and more thoughtful the discussion and subject matter, the deeper and more meaningful will be the Improv experience. It must only have to do with the truth and with reality.

Truth in Improvisation

There is a stage in life and during Improvisation in which people must learn to say true things among peers, superiors, and others. This can be a very subtle event and process that must be practiced before entering into deeper, more serious business matters.

When dealing at the level of truth, it can be good to pose classical human problems. You may use the game to explore such things as angels on the head of a pin. Your organization and communication can benefit from some well-spent time dealing with higher human issues. Consider some interesting human questions: "Which did come first, the chicken or the egg?" "If I hurry I can't get it right; if I go slowly I can't get it done." "What is the smallest particle of matter?" "How do I balance work and family?"

Hybrids of the Matrix

It is valuable to learn to mix area labels *creatively* with the setup and then mix these together with the relationships and subject matter. This can lead to extraordinary results.

An entrepreneur, an arbitrageur, an impressionist painter, and "a sincere sense of wonder" move through areas labeled "the investor," "accelerated time," "solutions," and "contradictions."

A blue sky, a graphics program, an ad campaign, and time discuss a problem of inventory control while wandering though areas labeled "why not?" "been there," "yes, and. . .," and "windswept."

A cow, an ear of corn, a dietary supplement, and a fine Swiss chocolate argue through areas labeled "food," "hunger," "starvation," and "eating disorder."

Business Matters and the Matrix

You can use terms to express current issues in your business. Start slowly, build processes, and create relationships of trust and safety. Start with general issues, move through regional to local issues to specific organizational issues, as described below:

- *If the issue is creativity, you may practice active creativity by playing with area labels such as "clarity," "tools," "permission," or "denial." The participants could be "right" and "wrong." The discussion could be about "possibility."*

- *If the issue is quality of communication among the people in the communication loop, play with area labels such as "appreciation," "honesty," "good sense," and "kindness." The participants could be "internal" and "external." The discussion could be about "courtesy."*

- *If you are dealing with issues about groups, networks, and individuals, the area labels may be "groups," "networks," "individuals," and "observers." The participants can be the same. The discussion can be "complexity," "emotion," or "technique."*

- *You may use this game to help discover new and creative ways to use this game.*

- *In training and academic settings, begin your deeper explorations with philosophical issues, move to general considerations, then specific details, then the problem at hand.*

- *In organizational development events, start with positive elements and matters of small initial risk. This will allow the participants to establish safe communication links within the problem areas.*

- *Listen carefully for feedback so you may help the group leadership to develop on its own.*

- *Listen for and engage in laughter. Be willing to interpret, facilitate, and to give up power when exploring at these levels.*

THOUGHTS ABOUT USING THE GAME

With this game you are creating a real, programmable, living matrix, which is an emotional, virtually logical, interactive, analog human computer. It takes a good list of details, with all the elements addressed and a strong integration of the various possibilities, and it takes a lot of playfulness, yet it can be done.

Take this game where you will. You may have different area labels among different sets of "four squares." You can have overlapping squares of four. You might have them spin together as pinwheels to create a virtual communication dance around a real issue. It is possible to have the results of interactions turn into new discreet squares. You can use more than four squares. You may use colors or work tools as area labels; you may add music to the process.

ADVANCED APPLICATIONS

Deeper exploration can be achieved by using communication postures for area labels, such as "must always say no," "must always be right," "must always block new ideas," "must always praise every idea," "must always see the bright side," "must always see the dark side," "must always be unsure," or "must always say yes." You may wish to make up this list based on what you know about the people with whom you are working. It can be good to include postures that exist as well as postures *to be desired* within the group.

You may want to use real people from the participants' business, organization, or industry. It is usually safest to start with general titles and positions, however. If you are strong and centered, you may use the names of real people, if they are also strong and centered.

Area labels can describe areas of responsibility, such as management, accounting, line workers, and investors. Try consumers, developers, R&D, sales staff, and marketers. In an educational setting, area labels such as teachers, students, parents, and administrators can work well.

Use your imagination and your creativity in developing area labels and follow the rules of complexity and simplicity: The more complex the area labels, the more simple must be the goals. The more complex the relationships, the more simple must be the labels.

When this game has been learned and the communication needs of the gathering are being cared for, it can be used to explore deeper levels of real problems in business and learning.

For example, identify the areas as "strategic," "tactical," "logistical," and "personal." Identify the relationships of the participants. Create a list of participants who may have an interest in the organization or the problem (such as engineer, cost accountant, executive, foreman, lead worker, competitor, consumer, government agency or bureau). Play with people moving through these labels while discussing serious and specific questions of business.

Sometimes you will need to act as a facilitator and direct the gathering or organization through a whole exercise. Sometimes you will need only to prime the pump. There will always be more power if the group can take its own lead. The Improv works better when the leadership and the participants are operating from a perspective of "Our Problem—Our Solution."

Playing in general and playing with the *Four-Square Matrix* specifically can help you deal with other, perhaps more common perspectives such as:

- *"Your problem, you fix it!"*

- *"Your problem, I'll fix it!"*

- *"What problem? I see no problem!"*

- *"I am the problem; there is no solution."*

- *"Life is the problem, and what would we do with a solution anyway?"*

- *"This is my shop, and we have no problems in my shop!"*

- *"Oh, that problem. Are we going to solve that problem again?"*

- *"We do not discuss family problems outside the family."*

- *"This is his or her problem. Why should I have to fix it?"*

- *"Our problem is as old as earth. Solving this problem could mean our end."*

- *"The problem's solution is more money, time, energy. . . ."*

- *"Life is hard. Get over it."*

This list could be a good source of *Four-Square Matrix* area labels.

Development of Insight

Some people are moved in this game by the simple fact that they have trouble changing their viewpoints. Others gain insight by watching people express themselves from unexpected viewpoints. Interacting with others from different perspectives often brings clarity to one's own views.

Most people are willing to consider opinions and positions of others as they wend their way through the problem of business. Many people who are further up the ladder will share the experience of having been in positions down the ladder. Doing this in a semi-public forum adds a large amount of power to the process. When done in the spirit and form of Improvisation, the exercise rises to a level very much like reality.

When you need to analyze programs, you need to know most about the people in the programs. The *Four-Square Matrix* process will allow you to observe the people in relationships in valuable interactions. You can see communication weaknesses, conflicts in style, and aspects of blocking. You will also see how smooth the people can be, how creative they are, and what potential is there.

This structure can be used as a building block, as a feedback tool, as an exploration of group dynamics, as a problem-solving technique, as an analysis tool, and in many more ways your creativity will invent.

Training Values of the *Four-Square Matrix*

Students of any curriculum can benefit from the *Four-Square Matrix*. The areas may be labeled as eras of history, the most important individuals, the most important rules, the first steps, the laws of physics. Have the 1920s, the 1930s, the 1940s, and the 1950s become the locus of discussion and feedback about hiring practices or employee benefits. Answer questions about the new computer program while moving through time perspectives. Use Microsoft, Intel, Macintosh, and AT&T as platforms to discuss the Internet.

Try having a rotating discussion of the computer system. The participants or the area labels can be "the hard disc," "the monitor," "the keyboard/mouse," and "the operating system." Try a look at the stock market, rotating people through the perspectives of "the Securities and Exchange Commission," "the investment banker," "the CEO," and "shareholder."

This game provides a review of what people do know, or don't know, at a given point in time. The evaluation for the participants can be established quickly enough, safely enough, and with enough laughter to provide a high level of motivation for further study and learning. Having to publicly present the facts, issues, or events moves information out of the realm of thought alone.

Four-Square Matrix is another good basic introduction to The Improv, and yet it has very complex forms that are as yet unexplored. Use the game to teach the game; use the game to explore the depths of your organizational development needs or to work at deep levels of relationships among the people who are important to you.

PART FIVE

Advanced Improv Techniques

CHAPTER SIXTEEN

Storytelling with Improvisation

Storytelling is a basic skill of professional and public speaking. It would be great if we all had the craft to charm others merely by telling a story. Most people actually do have some of this craft. All it really takes is a comfortable moment in a safe atmosphere, someone to listen, and a person who is willing to talk about something interesting that has happened to or been witnessed by him or her.

The craft of the classic storyteller is taught in other books. Improv storytelling is a different kind of thing. There are, however, common principles. Helping people to tell their stories is an important skill of the Improv executive. Stories teach us about one another. Helping people tell their stories easily and clearly takes the creation of an atmosphere of safety, openness, laughter, and playfulness.

People like to tell stories when it works. Even the most shy person can enjoy the attention of being a storyteller when a gathering is huddled around and listening intently. A problem occurs when the storyteller forgets about the story and begins to think about himself or herself or becomes too aware of an audience. This is an example of being out of time—and not centered in the moment.

The tricks in general storytelling are in selecting and saving good, applicable stories, learning to tell the stories well, and staying in the present moment while telling them. The most loved stories are personal stories told with fire or longing in the eyes.

Early in my consulting career as *Improvisation Incorporated*, I was seeking participants for a program called "Team Building with Improvisation." The idea was new and a little radical. It was my great good luck to come upon Dr. Ed Metcalf, then of IBM Corporation. Dr. Ed, as everyone calls him, is an innovator and trainer who continues to captivate people around the world as a speaker, writer, and consultant.

I pitched my pitch with deep belief that Improvisation works. I launched into the virtues of Improvisation and its wonders in the field of team building and asked Dr. Ed if he would attend my workshop. He immediately said he would send two people. I had lots more to say before he was supposed to say yes. I caught my breath, put on the brakes, gave him time and place, and said thanks.

Before I could hang up, he said, "Do you know why I agreed so quickly to send people to your program?"

"Uh, no. No, um, not really."

Dr. Ed said, "Do you know the etymology of the word 'enthusiasm'?"

"No, I don't."

"It's from the French," he said. "It is formed by *en*: within, and *Theos*: God. Nicely translated it means the expression of the God within. I don't know anything about you nor your program. I just felt your enthusiasm."

If your stories are told with enthusiasm, they will be well-received and they can be valuable in creating connections as well as in advancing the practices of improvisational communication.

STORIES BY AN INDIVIDUAL

Part of creating a space of safety requires sharing our own experiences. Charlie Rose, the National Public Radio interview host, says, "We are all always telling our stories." Sharing is a vital part of the leadership process that encourages people to move toward the openness needed to promote action and learning. A story that is *personal* and *relevant* and *well-told* will do extraordinary things to open the doors between the Improv manager, the project at hand, and the people gathered.

Personal Benefits to Storytelling

Sharing stories from our own lives is a practice that gives depth and clarity to our own experience. The effort of reaching into our own lives and seeking the things that teach us about our truths—and about truth itself—is its own rich discipline.

Sharing our stories forces our perceptions into the public light. This is also the embodiment of the fourth Improv principle. Sharing is extraordinarily important to our participants, our families, and our children. As we practice finding and sharing our own stories, we become more aware of the most important events that shape our thinking and that lead us to who we are in the present moment.

Developing Your Own Stories

You can begin by starting a list of important times in your life. This should be an effort of the mind and memory, not a research project. Then make a list of people who are important to you, another list of places you have been, and another list of things you have seen. Review the lists and, over time, begin to make up possible "titles" that could describe each of the items on your lists.

Keep the lists so you can add to them as you remember things and as new experiences occur. Find a time when you can work without disruption, pick one of the items on the list, and tell a little story that is suggested by the title. You may speak out loud using a recorder. You may write the story. You may find a helpful person to listen. It is not necessary to complete the first story the first time around. It is good to work on different stories over time. Allow the titles to guide you. Capture the stories with notes or outlines.

As you build on the details of stories and add more stories of your own, you can begin to understand how the best stories relate to your sense of yourself and your needs.

Once you have a set of your own stories, you may wish to collect stories from other sources. A simple collection of old, simple stories that make quick points will serve your development. Give credit to the sources.

Telling Your Stories Well

Learn to tell your stories well. Practice telling them at the highest level your time and ability will allow. To do this you may need to study some and to practice. Find a storytelling class. Join a storytelling club. Listen to storytellers. Listen for the stories others are telling. Read about storytelling in Keith Johnstone's book. Read any book about storytelling. Volunteer to read stories to children or elders. Tell a story to your family twice a week. No, make that three times a week. That's right! Three times a week. Tell the same story three times. Tell yourself a story twice a week. Keep working on your list of events with their titles. Tell a stranger a story once a month. OK, once every three months. OK, once this year. OK? Begin to make storytelling a part of your presentation style.

Here are a few basic guidelines to use in telling a story in a business setting.

SOME GUIDELINES FOR TELLING STORIES

- Always have a clear and relevant point to make.

- Use the "rule of the sandwich," taught by my friend, the humor teacher, Jeff Justice. The sandwich suggests that you introduce the point you wish to make, tell the story that illustrates the point, and then make your point again.

- Practice telling your stories. Practice out loud. Do this more than once. Do this more than twice.

- Keep a story as short as possible. Cut out all unneeded words. Add details only when absolutely necessary.

- Develop a very clear and inviting opening to the story.

- Make the conclusion simple and easy. Do not add new information once you start the conclusion of your story.

- If you are telling a story from another source, tell it in your own words and give credit to the source.

- Practice it often so that it sounds as seamless as your own experience.

- Remember, the point of the story is not really the point of the story. You are the point of the story. The audience is the point of the story. The relationships in the gathering are the point of the story. Communication is the point of the story.

Telling Funny Stories

A funny story or one told just for laughs is a very different instrument than what was discussed above. Telling funny stories should be approached as its own specialized form. If you do not study and practice the skill of seeking laughter for its own sake, you can encounter serious problems. If you attempt a humorous story and do it well by accident, you may risk being typecast as a humorist or entertainer, and it can be a very hard act to re-create.

STORYTELLING AND IMPROVISATION

It takes a great deal of preparation to make Improv techniques work well, even if you are telling memorized stories. The best guidance I can give is to be sure you know as much as you can about the people for whom you will be telling the story.

First you must make the effort to understand your organization and its participants. This is true whether the organization is a huge corporation, a small business, an academic department, a non-profit group, volunteer group, study group, association, leadership training group, continuing adult education class, business education class, or professional development group.

The more completely you understand the people in the group you will be working with, the more relevant your stories. The more relevant your stories, the more they will connect you to the people who are there. The more connected you are, the more people will learn, and change, and remember. This is the point of storytelling.

IMPROVISATIONAL STORYTELLING FORMS

Group Storytelling

Group storytelling can generate a great deal of energy and insight. As a training and learning program, it can help participants become more adept at telling their own individual stories. It can also serve as a bonding exercise. The activity itself will help fulfill the need for playfulness. As with all the Improv forms, there are many variations, including those yet to be invented.

The basic Improv storytelling form begins with a small group in a circle. All the participants take part in the telling of the story. More complex is a small group seated in front of and facing observers. The larger the audience the more fearless and experienced the group of storytellers must be.

A title or the theme for the story is selected. If there are no observers, it is best for the facilitator to make this selection. If there are observers, it is good to ask them for the theme or title.

The first person begins telling the story with a very short sentence or a phrase. The next person takes over where the first left off, and then the third takes over, and so on through the group until a story is told. The story line may go through the group a number of times. It is good to encourage people to stop before a sentence is finished: "Then the bear walked into a . . .," leaving the next participant to complete the sentence and perhaps to start another.

This game can be played with a large number of sets. Each circle can tell the same story or a story of their own. Story titles can be drawn from a hat. This process can be accomplished in as few as fifteen minutes as an introduction and icebreaking process or can be extended to about two hours as a full exercise. Extending the exercise consists of storytelling followed by debriefing, followed by deeper levels of storytelling, and by having various groups present stories to the whole gathering between telling stories in the separated sets.

This is a very effective analytical tool. By watching the participants and noting the length of their story segments, the inventiveness of their ideas, and the manner and confidence of their presentations, a great deal can be learned about each individual.

Deep insight into the group dynamics can also be obtained. It can be particularly helpful with groups in which there are mixed levels of authority working together. This exercise also helps build group participation. Many people will come forward with small bits who would not or could not contribute if they were required to speak at length by themselves. Listening and memory skills are encouraged and sharpened.

This exercise can be used to bring executive-level participants to a more accessible level in the eyes of others. It is never embarrassing if the facilitator is careful, yet the process reveals the players as "normal" people. Group storytelling can also enhance the stature of people who are not regularly included in decision making and planning by giving them the limelight for awhile.

As with all Improv exercises, early practice with light topics should be followed by stories of substance and consequence. It can be very interesting to have storytellers relate a "history" of the company, the larger organization, the industry, or some event they have all experienced. It is possible to personify an issue or conflict. The history of a particular individual, department, product, or organizational initiative is a little more risky, yet often quite revealing and good fun.

The story may be focused on the future. Have the group tell the story of the expected outcome of the current meeting. Another good future focus can be elements of your strategic planning. A group tale of the future history of the organization can be very powerful as a starting place for team building, as can large-scale change initiatives. Storytelling can also serve as a brainstorming mechanism.

Group Story Writing

This is a simple exercise that begins with the facilitator announcing a story title that is written at the top of a page of lined paper on a pad or clipboard. The story title may be functional or fanciful. The title may be decided by the gathering or assigned by the leader. An interesting way to come up with a story title is to use the game *Word for Word*. This method can be used in the basic game as well.

Each participant is to write a single line of the story. With a small group, the story may come around more than once. It is important that subsequent entries by the same individual not be consecutive. Designated "teams" may be each assigned to a story or a story pad may be sent around one group and then traded with another group.

Ask the participants to read no more than two or three lines before their own entry as part of the Improv discipline. They need to write only enough to keep the flow of a sentence, not to make "sense" of the larger story.

Make sure to tell the gathering that the story or selected stories will be read out loud at the end of the process. The pad can be passed around the room over any length of time. It may take the length of a meeting, a work week, a business quarter, a workshop, a seminar, or a conference. Reading the group's story to the general session can make an excellent closing or transition activity. The process can actually carry over a long period of time. For teachers and trainers conducting courses of a monthly, quarterly, or semester basis, a rather long story can be developed.

This exercise is good for changing the energy of a group. The writing process calls on a different set of senses and mental processes than does oral storytelling. The form is more private and personal than most group activities. The exercise can be very effective in developing community. At the least, group story writing can provide a fun closing activity. At its best it can bring the group together as they gain interesting or powerful insights.

This activity can be an excellent precursor for planning practices. Use titles such as "The future of . . ." or "When the change was made, we. . . ." Start the story a few days before the planning event and read some stories as an opening to the actual exercise.

Story, Story

Another form of group Improv storytelling is a little more risky for the participants. It is also more energetic. It can be done in front of the audience by a brave group or by sets of participants arranged in circles. Either way, the process requires a volunteer to facilitate the telling of the story.

A facilitator points to a person who must speak continuously until the facilitator suddenly starts pointing at another participant. The faster the pointing moves from person to person, the more frantic and the more fun the game. Each person must pick up the story where it left off. It is possible to catch people in mid-sentence and mid-word so the next person must take off from a place completely outside his or her own mind. The people may be in a line or a circle.

If there are individuals who are not yet comfortable in the group or if group unity is not sufficiently developed, the process will be slow and perhaps labored. A goal of the game is to make it go quickly, but there is nothing wrong in it being slow or labored if people are learning.

Story, Story for a Show Game

This game can be used as a performance event at the end of a meeting, using a line of storytellers facing an audience. It is best to elicit a story theme from the audience. You may present this game as a competition by giving the audience a way to judge its merits. You could have them watch for errors, for example, "the pause." If you point to someone and she takes a long pause before speaking, the audience can remove that participant from the game by yelling out, "Gone" or "No! No! No!" or "You're outta here!" It is a good idea to practice with the audience yelling as a group a few times. Urge them to yell loudly and enthusiastically. The audience adds wonderful energy to the play.

The types of mistakes that can take a player out are not really important, but you may wish to give the audience some guidelines. For example, "errors" may be grammatical errors, errors in the logic of the story, or lack of enthusiasm. Pausing may be called an error; so can repeating the words of a previous player. Three or four errors are enough for the audience to look for at one time.

When a player makes an error, he or she must quit the game immediately. It is important that players who are "gone" not question nor struggle with the decision. The process continues until there is one player left to finish the story. Sometimes it is good to have the last remaining player provide a moral or conclusion to the story.

As the facilitator, you may point to more than one person at a time. You may point at each person for as long as you wish, or move around the group as quickly as you wish. The more playful you are, the more playful the game. The more playful the game, the more powerful it will be.

To challenge the players further have them tell the story in a style of their choice. The styles may be such things as "headline news," "mystery story," "wildlife documentary," "adventure story," or "sportscast."

As with all games, you can eventually have the group make up relevant and serious stories. At this level you can elicit interesting insights with this game.

The Metaphor

Almost all stories are either based on a metaphor or can function as one. We naturally search for comparisons to give meaning to objects and events. We say things such as, "This is like my . . . " or "This is like the time I . . ." or "This is like the problem with. . . ." The metaphor is a *simile* if the word "like" is used to compare the original object with something else. Each person we know can provide a simile. We say things such as, "This person is like me!" We may say, "This person is like the person I wish to be." Perhaps we say, "This person is not like me; I don't want to be like this person."

It is very human to compare like and unlike things in order to search for connections and understanding. The case can be made that every action or interaction we are engaged in is a metaphor of some sort. The metaphor is a way to learn about life and the universe in which we live.

Here we are exploring the storytelling quality of *The Simile Game,* described in more detail with applications in Chapter Seventeen, *Grab Bag of Advanced Games.*

THE SIMILE GAME FOR IMPROV STORYTELLING

Ask the participants to write down a number of short similes. It is good to prompt about fourteen of these. Begin with basic statements such as: "My work is like [fill in the blank] because. . .," "The world is like [fill in the blank] because. . .," "Life is like [fill in the blank] because. . .," "Love is like [fill in the blank] because. . .," "Fear is like [fill in the blank] because. . . ." The participant must fill in the blank with the first thing that comes to mind and then fill in the answer to the "because" statement.

Archtypical Stories

It is possible to invoke deep human thought in the process of telling stories. This can be done by having a story start with an ancient or historical reference using forms such as these:

- "The year 2000 is like the time of the Ancient Egyptians because. . . ."

- "Our reorganization is like the time the Cherokee people first became a nation because there was a wise woman who. . . ."

- "Our new telecommunications system is like the story of Paul Bunyan because. . . ."

- "The new client program is like humans emerging from the African Continent because. . . ."

Combine a simile for the basic premise, an invocation of a deeper idea, and the use of *group improv storytelling* and you can produce a wonderful story and a delightful effect, and you may gain valuable insight into the deeper nature of your business.

Feed a Story

For this technique, a storyteller is given a story title. As he or she is telling the story, the storyteller pauses at key places and points directly at another participant. The person indicated speaks up with a noun or an adjective that does not relate to the story. The more creative the word the better, as this example shows.

> "The agency director had . . ." [Storyteller pauses and points to another who says, "The Great Pyramid at Giza."].

The storyteller continues, "Yes, uh, the agency director had The Great Pyramid at Giza on his desk as he contemplated . . ." [pauses, points to another person who says, "Pizza receipts."]

The storyteller integrates each new word into the story. The teller must use the story to justify each new word or idea. It is good to have four or more people feeding the storyteller.

Variations include using words that are on slips of paper pulled from a hat. This game can be done starting with pairs of a storyteller and a word giver and adding people until four or five word givers are working with one storyteller. You may also work in a circle with the added option of rotating the role of storyteller.

A nice variations is to focus the *story title* to fit specific training or educational goals and subject matter, the subject matter of your presentation, your training course, or business matters at hand. Using titles that are descriptive of real world events and problems provides a broad platform from which to create applications. These types of focus may be added to any of the Improv storytelling forms. Here are some possible story starters:

TELL THE STORIES

* "The Day PC Met Macintosh";

* "The Subatomic Particle That Would Not Stay Put";

* "The Retreat of the Butterfly from Singapore."

GO DEEPER

* Tell a story about yourself.

* Tell about your own developmental path.

* Tell about the paths of others.

Beyond its value as an interpersonal communication tool, the telling of our stories enhances the quality of our communication at all levels by giving us insight into the paths of people and our processes.

These games are useful for focus on specific business matters, for problem solving, for thinking on your feet, for team building, for competition, for public speaking, and for language skills at all levels.

SUMMING UP

Just plain storytelling by the facilitator is a peripheral Improv activity. Effective use of single person stories requires practice and rehearsal and research into the stories as well as into group with whom you are working. Storytelling is a valuable skill for executives, managers, presenters, and teachers. Learning about storytelling will enhance your work with Improvisation as well.

Storytelling with Improvisation is a doorway to a wonderful world all its own. A lifetime can be spent understanding that it is our stories that make us human. If you can tell stories, your leadership can take you and your organization wherever your imagination can go. You can explain your vision and goals in plain, understandable, human, realizable terms.

CHAPTER SEVENTEEN

Grab Bag of
Advanced Games

In formal situations you might wish to call Improv games by the formal name that you may remember as "overt, intentional, interactive, intra/inter-human, interpersonal, introspective, co-developmental, programmable, analog, analytic, virtual, communication matrices for future needs fulfillment."

Effective use of advanced Improv games requires good understanding of at least three or four game forms. The basic games of *Word for Word, Babble,* and *Four-Square Matrix* are easy to understand. You will fare better if you have worked with these basic games before using any of the advanced Improv games in public. It is possible to use any set of Improv games to teach Improv principles, yet I recommend that you use the suggested basic games before trying any of the advanced games presented here. Advanced games are usually more complex and often more daunting.

My long list of Improv performance games includes over 350 forms. Some games are better suited for creativity development, some for the purpose of teaching Improv basics. Some are better for developing interpersonal communication and for the creation of workplace unity. Most of the games help with public and professional speaking skills.[20] Many are excellent for teaching and testing specific topic material.[21] Some games are better for creating a sense of safety by addressing planning practices and training and learning needs. Some games help us approach our groups, networks, and other individuals with a spirit of cooperation and exploration. Some help us define and develop "community." Some games help us to practice spontaneity among ourselves, help us to release creative impulses, allow us to develop our personal selves and our organizations. Most of the games give us clear and consistent feedback that gives us "pretty good" measurement ability and analysis tools that allow us to develop the quality of our communication and thereby the quality of our working. All the games can be focused on Improv principles for performance. All the games work best in the spirit of playfulness. All the games have not yet been invented.

About fifty classic games are known and have been played by virtually every Improv player in the world. Probably another one hundred games are well-known and have been played at one time or another by most serious performance players. Virtually every Improv team, teacher, and director has a few specialty games or variations that are their signature or trademark pieces. All Improv games have variations in form or structure, which brings the total named Improv games to somewhere around one thousand. Only about seventeen games are described in this chapter, depending on how you count them.

The number of available forms expands enormously when you consider the elements of theme, focus, purpose, specific topics, explorations, research, and creative playfulness. The games noted here and the applications discussed are not intended to be exhaustive. The Bibliography will lead you to a host of other games, sources of games, and sources of playful thinking. Your own exploration and inventiveness will lead you to many others. The serious playfulness of your participants will lead you to ones no one has yet seen.

Many of the games mentioned in this chapter have suggestions for their applications. These are meant only as suggestions to prompt your own thoughts on how to use them.

20

ANDREW HAIG AT THE UNIVERSITY OF NAGOYA HAS PROPOSED AND WRITTEN ON THE USE OF IMPROVISATION AS A TOOL FOR ENHANCING LANGUAGE TEACHING SKILLS.

21

DR. LEONARD TEEL OF GEORGIA STATE UNIVERSITY HAS BEEN AWARDED AN OUTSTANDING TEACHING INNOVATION AWARD FOR THE USE OF IMPROVISATION AS A FINAL EXAMINATION FORMAT.

All the Improv games may be used to teach and reinforce the skills of improvisation, spontaneity, creativity, and playfulness, as well as the gift of laughter and human connectedness.

A TO Z

This is a nice game for playing with information and ideas. If we are able to play with information we can remember it more efficiently. When we play with information it becomes our own; when it is our own it can change our behavior.

BASICS

A to Z is easily played with two people. A setup is established. The first player begins a dialogue with a statement that must begin with a word starting with the letter "A." The second player responds and continues the dialogue with a statement beginning with a word that starts with the letter "B." The players go back and forth in this fashion, one statement at a time, until they have gone through the entire alphabet.

COMPETITION

A to Z can generate a very positive competition level with other participants replacing those who may falter. (I know, I said to avoid competition.) The replacement can be done in a "tag-team" fashion. If a player falters, uses the wrong letter, or pauses too long, he or she is replaced by a new player who must pick up at the point of the error and continue. One way to handle the transition is to have someone who caught the error call out, "Freeze!," stop the action, and replace the player who has faltered. It is important that the person who is "frozen out" not dispute the freeze. The game can be made increasingly complex by starting in the middle of the alphabet, by going backward through the alphabet, or by assigning one player to progress forward two letters while the other goes in the opposite direction. Switch to other language alphabets or mix them. This works particularly well in multilingual settings.

By assigning a topic, you can focus the players on specific business matters. With a given topic as the focus, you begin to see the power of Improvisation as a learning tool. It is possible to use this game with competition switchout, so that those who do not use correct responses or stay on topic are "switched out." As you use *A to Z* in a conversation with co-workers about material being learned, you can gain great insight into what has been learned and retained.

ADVERTISEMENT

This game can produce a lot of fun and energy. Any focused topic can make this game very useful. The players create a spontaneous commercial of fifteen to sixty seconds in length. An extended project may be created by improvising a fifteen- to thirty-minute infomercial focused on the business matter at hand. This game can be used by creative presentation teams to polish skills. In order to improvise advertisements for a departmental change or OSHA regulation, participants will have to have a very good basic understanding of the information. If they cannot create such advertisements, they may not have that understanding.

DURING, BEFORE, AFTER

This game can be used to review historical patterns and explorations of cause and effect. The basic game can be played by three sets of two players each.

You set up a business problem. It may be fictional or real. It may be an historical event or a possible one, for example, "moving to new business quarters." Another possible historical event could be a story of what might have happened the day of the invention of your most important tool—electricity, plastic, the personal computer, or your most important product.

The first set of players talk out—and maybe even act out—the story of the event as though it is happening in current time (during). The players may pretend to be participants in the story or observers of the event. It is good for the players to give each presentation of the story a beginning, a middle, and an end.

The next players listen very carefully to what has been said. They must then "play out" what went on "before," and most logically led to, the "during" part.

The next players bring the whole thing together by presenting what must have happened "after" the "during" event. With imagination and cooperation, the possibilities are endless.

EMOTION SYMPHONY

This is a good game for exploring cooperation, expressing emotions, learning listening skills, working together, and committing to a process. It is a good feedback device for discovering the level of participation that has been achieved. It's also a good game for ending a program or workshop event.

Seven or so participants stand next to one another in a line facing the larger group. Each player selects an emotion and a noise that could possibly sound like the emotion selected. (The sound does not really have to match the emotion.) You may learn a lot about your group if they become stuck in the effort to find a match between the emotion and the sound.

Once the players have selected their emotions and the sounds, tell them, in these exact words, "Say the name of the emotion, loudly, and then make the sound." This step will let you see how closely your participants are following instructions. Often people will make the sound while saying the name of the emotion. This is not according to the instructions and is an indication that the participant is not with you completely and may be lost in personal thoughts.

If more than one of the participants is not following directions, you may need to go over the process again using the exact words, "Say the name of the emotion, loudly, and then make the sound that goes with it." Repeat the process until you have the level of participation you need to proceed. You may not need perfect cooperation to proceed, depending on your goals. If you are doing this to generate energy and have fun, then the rules are not so important. If you are trying to develop listening skills or a sense of community, the ways in which the participants respond becomes more important.

Once the group is in synchronization and has established the sounds, you will conduct the group like an orchestra. As you point to a player he or she must make his or her sound and continue to make the sound until you point to another player. You may also point to more than one player at a time.

If you lift your hand the player or players should become louder. Lowering your hand directs the players to become quieter. If you can watch a symphony director in action, you will gain information about how to direct an *Emotion Symphony*.

Levels of participation can be analyzed by watching how attentive people are to the needs of the process or how self-concerned they are in their discomfort. The participants' ability to make clearly audible sounds and to increase and decrease the intensity of the sounds is an indicator of their ability to engage in behavior modification and to express emotions.

Interesting realities may be used in place of the emotions. You may try "board meeting symphony," "historical symphony," "training meeting symphony," "client meeting symphony," or "Windows® 98 symphony."

EMOTIONAL BLOWUP

This game is a good workshop exercise. You should introduce the game and play the first segment. Stand before the group or gathering and makes a simple remark that has little emotional content such as, "The sky is blue." Begin to say the phrase over and over while slowly engaging emotional energy as you speak. It is good for you to select a particular emotion on which to build. It is also powerful if you can let the "Impro" present an emotion as you develop your energy, confidence, and commitment to the process.

Continue to build on the emotional content by talking about the initial statement and finding more and more reasons to become emotionally involved. Take the event to as high a level of the emotional content as possible. Demonstrate a slow build. The tempo of the emotional build is important; many people will rush through this process in order to avoid dealing with the feelings that may come up.

Once you have reached the highest possible level of emotional expression, abruptly bring yourself to neutral and then make a neutral statement such as, "Dinner is ready."

The next player starts with the phrase "Dinner is ready" and then builds the emotional content with a new emotion in the same fashion you demonstrated. In smaller groups all the participants play, one after the other in what is called a "roll-through" style.

This exercise will help people learn to engage in emotional content in their play, their work, and their communication. By requesting that the neutral statement focus on a particular business matter, you can use this game to encourage emotional involvement with real time information. If there is emotional involvement in real time information, personal development, and life surroundings, there tends to be a good chance of behavioral change.

This exercise is also very helpful in developing creativity, professional and public speaking, interpersonal communication, and quality of communication in general.

FIRST LINE, LAST LINE

This game can be very effective in a general exploration of your presentation information, course materials, or particular business matters at hand.

Two players are selected and a setup is established. Either you or the participants in the gathering select a phrase that must be used to start a conversation between the people working with the game, a "first line." Then select a phrase that must be used to end the scene, a "last line."

To begin the game, lines from the general culture work best, such as "Stop, look, and listen" or "Frankly, my dear, I don't give a damn." As the players become more skilled and confident, lines may come from a specific culture, as in "What's the bottom line?," "Publish or perish," or "An actor's first job is to be seen and heard." As the game progresses, a line from a current business matter will work, such as "The ideal pressure is 150 PSI," "Always back up your work," or "Seek to understand and then to be understood." The purpose of the exercise is to move the scene as logically as possible to the point at which the second player is compelled to speak the "last line."

The game can be made more complex. It is possible to insert a third person who must bring in another line somewhere in the middle of the exercise. Individuals may be given their "lines" with instructions to use them whenever possible in the general conversation or the "conversation" may be carried on over the length of the workshop or conference.

Applications of this game may include the study, analysis, and understanding of specific topics, progressions, and relationships. Improved goal setting and enhanced achievement are some benefits of using this game.

FREEZE TAG

This is a classic game used to warm up participants and observers. Two people come to the playing area and begin moving freely about, swinging their arms, twisting and turning, bending at the waist, touching their shoulders and knees and heads until you yell, "Freeze!"

The participants literally freeze immediately, in position. They must then construct a conversation based on the positions in which they find themselves. It is important that they attempt to justify or explain the positions as they talk. They can describe directly or suggest more subtly why they are in such positions and doing what they are doing. It is important that they continue moving as they conduct the conversation. When a conclusion to this conversation is reached, you yell "freeze" again and new players take the places of one or more of the "frozen" players.

Notice whether the players freeze their entire bodies exactly at the moment you call out. Note whether the replacement players take the exact positions of the persons they replace. If the participants are not doing this, consider it as feedback and think of the possible need to alter your pace or to reconsider your next steps or goals.

You may increase the level of seriousness if you direct the participants to base the scenes on the business matters of the day. They must associate with and focus their conversation on the business matter at hand while paying attention to making unusual movements and functioning in an unusual relationship. You may encourage participation and develop ownership of the material being explored and the process itself by teaching the players who are watching to take responsibility for the freezing of the scenes.

This process can help people use new mind connections while dealing with serious material. It can help in the development of groups, networks, and individuals. It can be used for community development, as well as for training and learning needs.

HEADLINES

This is a good game for familiarizing participants with subject matter in business as well as in popular periodicals. Among the things you can use are policy manuals, in-house newsletters, product brochures, newspapers, magazines, annual reports, or instruction manuals. You may use management training books or computer instruction manuals.

You simply read a headline from the selected periodical and have the participants act out a representation of the main idea. The players may create a "thought storm" or a visual image. The representation may be done by any number of people or by the whole set of people working together. The representations, at first, do not need to be accurate to obtain good results. You end one scene by saying "black out," clapping your hands loudly, and saying "freeze," or by dimming the lights and then reading another headline. The first attempts may only last a few seconds. This exercise primarily requires commitment and energy.

As the participants develop and become more confidant, they will move from simple conversation to more elaborate presentations. If you play this game a number of times over a period of time, you will be able to chart the progress of the group's creativity and cooperation.

THE HERALD AND VARIATIONS

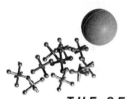

The Herald and its variations are advanced Improv game forms that have two or more people playing together with a "setup."

THE SETUP

The full *Herald* setup establishes three elements for the players to work with "who" (Who are the characters playing?), "what" (What are these characters doing?), and "where" (Where is the action taking place?). The players interact with one another as limited and developed by these elements.

You may provide a predetermined setup to get the people started and comfortable with the game. However, if the setups are provided by the nonplaying participants it engages more of the Improv process.

The situations created by the Improv process can lead you and your organization into a wide variety of creative activities. The emphasis of these games should be on problem-solving efforts, rather than on "playing a part." If the participants are trying to "act" correctly, they will have entered into the realm of acting and its special requirements.

VARIATIONS

As skills develop it is possible to use any one of the setup elements (who, what, or where) to generate the games. The setup may be designed to facilitate any goal. You may take one of the parts yourself in order to develop or teach the process. Participants may play in a tag-team format. If a player gets stuck, he or she may call on another team member to take his or her place and to continue the scene. You may signal a change of players to include others in the process. The following variations add levels of complexity to the design.

Improvisation, Inc.

EMOTIONAL SPOT

To change *The Herald* into *Emotional Spot,* call out "Freeze! Continue in . . .," then name an emotion. The players continue to work with the problem using the emotions as directed. The simple form is to name one emotion that both players must use. More complex is to give each player a different and contrasting emotion. It is a good idea be very well prepared with a long list of emotions and speak very clearly and crisply. To develop such a list, see *A Survey of Feelings,* in Chapter Eight.

It is usually best for you to be prepared to provide the emotions. It is also a good idea to encourage the others who may become engaged in this exercise to call out the names of various emotions as a warmup for getting into the game.

Emotional Spot can be very effective in discharging stressful or tense situations in an organization or gathering. This can be accomplished by calling for odd and unexpected emotions in familiar situations. This game is particularly effective in helping to overcome emotional resistance to learning and change, in connecting emotions to the human development process, and in conflict resolution.

STYLE SPOT

The Herald becomes *Style Spot* when you call out: "Freeze! Continue in the style of . . .," and fill in the blank. The participants must immediately try to continue playing in the new style as directed. Both players can be given the same style, or each can be given a different style. Creative contrasts of style can lead to some very interesting events.

"Style" can describe different types of business settings (corporate headquarters, sales and promotion, accounting, engineering, annual reports), scientific disciplines (civil engineering, biochemistry, mathematics), academia (history, business communication, English literature), theater (Shakespeare, musical comedy, avant-garde), movies (action, comedy, film noir), literature (Steinbeck, Faulkner, Stephen King), cartoons, computer programs, architecture, paintings, and TV shows. You may name styles from any source you can think of.

Another group of styles can come from situations that are typical to your organization—stockholder meetings, board meetings, customer service encounters, job interviews, or team meetings.

Style Spot may be used to explore organizational and operational contrasts. "Continue in the style of:" Windows 98, then UNIX, the 20th Century, the 21st Century, management, or labor; "Continue in the style of:" one who cannot learn, one who learns with ease, one who knows, one who does not know, one who learns visually, one who learns by sound. The game has been used to examine business style contrasts, aesthetic contrasts, philosophical contrasts, theoretical contrasts, political contrasts, and regional, national, or historical contrasts. The variations are endless.

PLAYBOOK

Playbook is a good game for familiarizing participants with new materials in written form. It also works well in building the individual skill of scanning written material.

The game starts with two players and a "Who, What, and Where" setup. One player engages in a conversation in which he or she can say anything, while the other player is limited to a book for all his or her lines and must scan the book looking for short phrases with which to respond. The responses selected from the book need not be whole sentences.

The book may be a new training text or product manual. To learn the game and build confidence, a work of popular literature works well. Children's books provide for wonderful expansions in perspective. Consider a setup with a marketing vice president and a chief financial officer encouraged to discuss a real problem of development versus costs with one of them limited to responses from *The Little Prince*.[22]

When working with larger groups, it is easy to organize many sets of two, each with its own book. Sets of two in a group of six to twelve provides a good forum for this exploration. This game is also a nice way to introduce your organization's new written material. Applications of this game include: text familiarization, analysis, perspective training, eye/speech coordination, confidence building, and text analysis.

POEMS

You or the general gathering provides the topic of the poem. You may prompt for a particular focus, depending on your overall business focus or purpose. The players make up lines of a poem. Each person's line needs to be short and about the same length. Rhyming is not required.

If rhyming is desired, it adds a level of difficulty, fun, and wonder. Rhymes can be created using the rhyming form of AA'BB'(where the line by player A' must rhyme with the line made up by player A and B' with B). You may also rearrange the players so that every other player must rhyme in the sequence ABA'B'.

This is a risky game. For the sake of pure fun, failure at making a poem work is fine and acceptable. In order to succeed at the task of making a poem with Improvisation, the players need an understanding of the cadence, scansion, and forms of poetry. Without such understanding this Improv game may cause loss of face and embarrassment. Use it cautiously. However, do note that this form can be a very effective tool for teaching the subject of poetry itself.

22

ANTOINE DE SAINT-EXUPERY, *THE LITTLE PRINCE*. NEW YORK: HARCOURT, BRACE & WORLD, 1943.

Variations include having sets of people write single lines of a poem on a single sheet of paper passed around the group—to be rhymed or not as is appropriate or feels correct. A single group of four or five may work on a poem in a circle.

Placing mundane events and concerns into poetry form can change the emotional foundation of the business matter you are exploring. The poem may serve to diffuse tensions, to alter perspective, and to generate laughter and joyfulness. It can also reinforce the learning of any subject of interest to your business.

Applications of this game may include team building, linguistic development, broadening of a reference base, and the interrelationships of topics.

PROP MONTAGE

Besides its obvious power for developing creativity and imagination, *Prop Montage* can be an effective form to use in helping trainees become familiar with tools and equipment.

Prop Montage was originally a line game, but it can also be done in a circle. A set of six to thirteen works best. Players make a simple item (a "prop") become many things (but not what it really is) with words and imagination.

In a circle it is good to pass a single item around and have each person either describe it or pantomime it as something it is not. Encourage the use of words as well as action. The person may name the item as something that is suggested by its shape or physical attributes, yet any response is really acceptable. The object of the game is to practice offering any response, and sometimes the only thing that comes to mind has nothing to do with the object at hand.

A second time around the circle with the same object can create interesting new results. A third time around can open new channels of the creative spirit. It may be necessary to go around more times than is comfortable for the participants in order to elevate the group to the next higher level of creativity.

You can prompt the participants by having each participant fill in the blank after using the words, "I see this as a. . . ."

An entire exercise may last up to half an hour, depending on the number of people involved. The game can be developed by going through each of the senses, one at a time: "I *hear* this as. . .," "I *smell* this as. . .," "I *taste* this as. . .," "I *feel* this as a. . . ." You may wish to attempt another level altogether by having the participants finally say, "In my heart I know this to be . . . ."

Another complete exercise can be developed by taking a single item and having the participants pass it around a circle many times until the participants get bored, fed up, tired, and break through to new peaks of imagination and creativity.

My favorite group doing this exercise was a set of five-year-olds in a Montessori school. We spent over half an hour taking a stick around the circle and never ran out of new things for it to be.

If you wish to really enter the world of human creativity, spend a long time working with a single prop. I once spent three hours with a set of excited Improv players. Our prop was a blank piece of paper. It became more than a thousand different things.

PROP MONTAGE EXERCISE

Look around the room where you are right now. Look for something you can touch, touch it, and call it something it is not. Say, "I am touching this. . . ." If you are touching a doorknob, for example, call it a book, or a pen, or a light bulb—anything but a doorknob or a synonym for a doorknob. Do the same thing with another object, then another, and another. Keep doing this until it gets hard, and then keep doing it with everything you can touch until it gets easy again.

Do this exercise with a group at the beginning of any process in which you need an open and clear mind. You can do it many times without repeating yourself. The more you do it, the better it works and the more creative you will become.

There is nothing wrong if you are having trouble with this exercise. It is only an indication that your mind is not clear at the moment. Your mind is stuck on the names of things as they are supposed to be, the names we have agreed on in our culture and language. If you will spend time doing this practice until it becomes easy, your mind will open to many wonders.

RADIO TALK SHOW

One participant plays the host of an imaginary radio talk show. The remaining players, standing behind or out of sight, "call in" to speak on a topic designated by the "host." "Callers" may ask questions or give opinions. Variations include working in a circle, in which case the "host" may work with eyes closed. Once again subject matter should be of the broadest possible variety.

Beyond a focus on business matters, applications could include exploration of specific topics, solving problems, developing the ability to think on one's feet, learning to be spontaneous, and resolving conflicts.

THE SIMILE GAME

This game can be used to explore any topic or business you wish. The use of the simile is a powerful tool in all human communication. In telling stories and creating understanding, few tools are as effective for opening a person to a new viewpoint.

A simile is a metaphor created by the language format with which we say: "A is like B because. . . ." Understanding that one thing is "like" another can build bridges of understanding and perspective. Making the connections with a simile is a deep value of The Improv.

One person takes the focus. Other participants provide the two elements of the simile. You can prompt this by asking first for a noun or a verb. If the first word selected is a noun, you can say, "OK, an 'orange' is like what? Someone give me a verb." When a verb is selected first, say, "OK, 'flying' is like what?

Someone give me a noun." This needs to happen very quickly or people will tend to give words that they have already thought through.

You then say, "An 'orange' is like 'running' because . . . " and the player must repeat the simile and fill in the blank very quickly three times. "An orange is like running because it goes around and around," "An orange is like running because it is the pits," and "An orange is like running because it is appealing."

The next player starts with the same line and gives three new responses. The response does not need to make sense nor need to be correct in any way: "An orange is like running because it is blue, it has spots, and it is named George." The next player uses the same simile and gives three new responses. Then a new simile is created and the process is repeated.

There are deep archetypal processes involved when the human mind creates a simile. The use of the game will develop creativity, enhance professional and public speaking skills, bring insight into interpersonal communication, and help develop the quality of communication. The more serious and specific your topics, the deeper will be the effects.

SPACE JUMP

This game can be used to explore particular business problems and various progressions of events in your business and organizational development. This game helps build skills of listening and memory. It can be used to enhance awareness of the perspectives of others.

A player takes the center of the circle and starts a monologue based on a word or idea suggested by you. Once the opening monologue has been established, you "freeze" the player with a loud clap and the words "Space Jump!" The participant must freeze in the physical position in which she finds herself. She must remember this exact position. A new player then takes the stage. As soon as the new player enters, the first player drops the "freeze" and comes to a neutral position. Then the two players begin an entirely new conversation, not connected to the first scene.

Once the second conversation is going well, you "freeze" the two players, clapping and saying "*Space Jump!*" The two must freeze in position and re-member their positions and what they were doing. A third player enters to start an entirely new conversation with three people. The process is repeated until there is a conversation with up to five players.

When the fifth scene is essentially complete, you call, "Freeze! *Space Jump*! Backward!," at which point the fifth participant leaves the game. The remaining four must return immediately to the positions and activity and conversation in which they were engaged when the scene was frozen to bring in the fifth player. This process continues back through the numbers, three, two, and one. Each time the players must re-create, as closely as they can, the physi-cal position from the earlier freeze, and they must continue and complete the conversation they left behind.

If you develop this game with a large number of people, all working in smaller sets, the simple act of calling out of a number referring to the *Space Jump* scenes that were previously done can cause a great flurry of activity.

By limiting the conversations to specific business concerns or subject matter, this game can be used to review or explore any topic in depth.

TELEPHONE TAG-ANSWERING MACHINE

Telephone Tag is a conversation game in which the participants do not look at one another. The topic may be assigned by you or the participants may decide the role they will play when they "answer" the ringing phone. This is a valuable game for teaching interpersonal communication skills and for enhancing lis-tening skills.

The first player pretends to be a caller and says "Ring, ring."

The person "answering" says, "Hello," and the "caller" identifies the recipient and the purpose of the call ("Tom, I have been waiting for my copy of the annual report. What is the problem there?" or "Hi, Sheila, we've been expecting you in the Building B conference room. Are you coming over?").

The player answering the call must respond and interact with the questions and demands of the caller. The recipient may also answer as he or she wishes ("Hello, this is John's whimsical house of cards"). In either case the "caller" must accept whatever is given. One should not say things such as, "I'm not Sheila" or "I don't have anything to do with the annual reports" or "Sorry, wrong number." The players must go along with the premise offered.

For the sake of complication, the answering player may choose to be an answering machine, immediately coming up with a "recording" that ends with "beep." Then the caller must leave a message.

You, as the leader or facilitator, end the scene by clapping and calling out, "Freeze." Following the freeze, the one who answered becomes the next caller and a new player answers the phone.

This game can easily be applied to real circumstances by limiting the calls to a specific business topic or by incorporating real people or real departments and organizations into the calls.

Applications of this game include training in telephone skills, including listening, clear and articulate speaking, responsiveness, and thinking on your feet. It is very useful for teaching sales skills such as prospecting and closing.

THE TONIGHT SHOW

This game is played in the format of a David Letterman late night talk show. The person playing the host identifies and introduces a guest. The host also describes the nature of the program. For learning and early development, the nature of the program may be light or silly. As the participants gain skill and confidence, make the program nature more serious and real. The host asks questions and the guest answers. The answers may be frivolous or real, however you develop the game. It is good to get the players to end the interview at a high point with applause and some cheering. At this point the host leaves the scene and the guest becomes the next host and introduces a new show and a new guest. The players roll through until all have played. You may also indicate the end of each segment by saying, "Blackout," or by dimming lights.

A learning focus can be achieved by having the players introduce a particular business topic, a new product, new training program, a new manual, or a training book and then identifying the next participant as the author or developer of the material. The shift from guest to host advances The Improv and develops skills in change management.

WORD MONTAGE

This game is the same as *Prop Montage* except that a word is used rather than a physical object. It is best to use a word with many syllables. This variation takes the process out of the physical and into the mental realm.

WORD MONTAGE EXERCISE

Say, "A perfect day at the beach would include . . ." (insert something entirely ridiculous such as "a thumb tack"). Then say, "A great meal should have . . ." (insert another absurdity such as "the king of hearts"). Now begin to make up your own openings ("A birthday really needs . . .," "A fine movie must have . . .) and fill in the blanks with things that simply do not match. These exercises need to be done at a very quick pace. Any time spent "pondering" defeats the purpose.

This exercise is valuable for the development of creativity, of skills needed in professional and public communication, and of interpersonal communication.

This short list of advanced games represents a grab bag full of opportunities for you as an Improv leader. Each exercise can be used to teach the basics of Improvisation, and every one of them can be used to focus on, explore, or teach any particular topic. Grounding in the basic games of *Babble, Word for Word,* or *Four-Square Matrix* will still serve you in making the jump to advanced Improv games. The Bibliography will refer you to sources of many, many more games. Applications of these games and inventions of new games will be your responsibility. In order to use the games noted here, in order to develop the ability to invent new games, and in order to receive the most value from this work, you will have to make The Improv your own. In doing this you will begin creating your own creativity.

PART SIX

Make Improvisation
Your Own

CHAPTER EIGHTEEN

Create Your Own Creativity

Whoopi Goldberg was apparently once asked if she would rather have a "starship" or a "holodeck." She said that she would rather have a big box of crayons, for with them she could create a holodeck, a starship, or anything else she could imagine. The most wonderful thing about Improvisation is that it is a multifunctional tool chest. As with a box of crayons, you may do with it whatever you wish. You are not limited to coloring with the correct colors, coloring inside the lines, or even coloring within the pictures in a coloring book. With Improvisation you can *Create Your Own Creativity.*

The first thing you must do is to play the games and use the exercises. So long as you attend to the basic principles and practices, The Improv works, and it works every time. So long as you stay true to its spirit, the process and value will reveal themselves with more and more interesting applications. So long as you approach Improvisation as "one who learns," The Improv will continue to teach ever-increasing depths of creativity.

With creative Improvisation you can address issues of professional and public communication, interpersonal communication, the quality of communication, many processes and levels of organizational development, as well as developmental and interdependency needs of groups, networks, and individuals. Improvisation, when applied to specific subject matter and business concerns, will enhance community development, planning practices, training and learning needs, measuring procedures, and the analysis of people and programs. The Improv, practiced as a discipline, will enhance the quality of work and bring out the need for playfulness in the world of real concerns and real business problems.

Every Improv game and exercise embodies all of The Improv. Each game begins as a source of learning, human interaction, laughter, and fun and extends infinitely into learning, analysis, and changes in behavior. The process itself will lead to new combinations, permutations, applications, and depth of insight . Each game can reward its players with all the pleasures of the creative mind. In order to do the most with The Improv you need to make it your own.

BEYOND THE PRESENT MOMENT

Primitive humans and most animals live only in the present moment, with both positive and negative effect. Living only in the present moment creates problems for most of us. When facing the future we must do some serious planning or it can be very difficult to deal with whims, crises, and the unexpected.

When we do not learn from our mistakes, we are likely to repeat them. Without a sense of the past and a plan for the future, it may also be very difficult for us to accomplish a large, or complex, or detailed, or long-term goal. Yet, even when we're working on large, long-term, complex, detailed matters, the actual work must be done in the present moment, day by day, moment by moment.

Mixed Time and Present Time Consciousness

One of the ways in which we learn to make The Improv our own is to learn to use consciousness of present time to deal with the past, present, and the future.

Without training we tend to do almost everything in what I call "mixed time." Reflections about the past are usually conducted in the midst of the day's activities, with interruptions from the present moment as well as hopes and fears of the future. Evaluations often are conducted in the context of future hopes and expectations, mixed with impressions of other past experiences. We tend to review our experiences and lessons in "mixed time" as well. Even when managers and executives are doing excellent work in review, adjustment, reinvention, and reinforcement, these events done in mixed time can produce less than the best possible results.

Using the Present to Capture the Past and Future

The Improv suggests that we identify a time frame in the past and then review it within a dedicated present time—set aside time and space to do nothing but review the chosen event or time frame from the past. Focus your attention with the same dedication and passion with which Margaret Mead focused herself while listening to a stranger. Use your present time focus to re-create the event with your mind, your heart, your spirit, and your emotions.

You can handle evaluations in the same fashion. Set time aside for doing nothing but comparing predicted results with actual results. Use your Improv discipline to keep yourself in the present time as you conduct the evaluation. What was really done and what was really produced? If you spend time comparing actual results with imagined possible results, you will take yourself out of present time and muddle your conclusions. If you wish to get the most from a comparison of actual results with possible results, do this as an analysis exercise of its own in present time consciousness.

Previews are very often conducted in mixed time, clouded by comparisons with past successes or failures and the successes and failures of others at other times and places. Again, you will gain the most clear results if you set aside a time just to look at the future and then conduct the preview in present time consciousness when nothing else is going on.

It is a good idea to set aside the time for planning and conducting the act of planning in present time consciousness. If you must evaluate the plan while you are making the plan, you can use the general Improv skills and principles to help you be the most effective.

You may plan in the present for awhile, then shift gears to evaluate for awhile, and then go back to the plan again. If you do not have disciplined and explicit transitions and time parameters, your time consciousness will mix and probably dilute your results.

As you learn the use of Improvisation, you will gain skills in the use of current time—both to learn from your efforts and to develop yourself as a leader who is operating in the present moment, an Improv executive who is creating your own creativity.

Taking Delight in the Present

Another step in creating your own creativity and making Improvisation your own requires special disciplines. With focused effort, Improv disciplines become a daily delight as you seek the ability to find and to stay in the present moment. If we spend our days in the "busy-ness" of being busy, without this discipline, it can be difficult to come to the present moment.

CREATIVITY IN DAILY DISCIPLINES

A number of games are helpful for creating your own personal discipline. My son, Jonathan Michael Mawle Lowe, helped to develop the disciplines described below. In sharing the explanations below, I am sharing some information about the most important person in my life. I hope the sharing is not a breech of something personal.

"Let's See What We Have Never Seen Before"

Jonathan is eleven and our favorite ice cream parlor looks out over a shopping center parking lot. While we sit with our double scoops in sugar cones, we play "Let's see what we have never seen before."

We begin to gaze through the windows at the familiar shopping center parking lot. One of us must find something in the panorama that we have never noticed before. It cannot be a living or temporary thing like a bird or a person or a car or a leaf. We must find something that clearly has been there a long time, yet we have not noticed it until that moment. It takes a great honesty with one another to do this fairly.

If he finds two things, then I must do the same. If he finds three, I must find three. As I write, we have done this about once a week for five years. After all that time, every time, there is always some new detail that reveals itself. Some days we will both find three or four new things. Some days are more lean and we can see only one or two. Some days are a real challenge and we must look, and look, and look, and look; then a breakthrough occurs and we see each other differently. We see everything differently. Some miraculous days I actually accomplish a positive change in my behavior. Most days, he breezes through massive changes in his behavior, growing as he plays with this discipline.

No matter what else is going on, the game enables us to relax into the reality of a perfect, real measurement. We have the gift of a perfect moment that has never existed before and will never exist again except in its influence on how we think and how we act.

We delight in the game and in the presence of one another. I take my clues from him. He has taught me to watch the people with whom I work and live very carefully, very openly, very honestly, and very playfully. I watch his face and eyes relax. I look for this kind of relaxation in the eyes and faces of the people who are engaged in Improvisation as an exercise. As Jonathan loses his need to "do things right," his excitement increases and his mind and body show that he knows there is always something new to see, even in an old familiar place.

He clears his mind. He knows that he has searched this horizon time and time again. Delight surrounds him and his knowledge of play takes over. When people are working with Improvisation as a vision generator, I look for these same things in them.

Jonathan becomes so excited that his speech is quick; he is in a rush to share the moment. He seeks challenge. Now I am on the spot. I must be prepared to play. When I work with people using Improvisation as a personal development tool or an organizational development tool, I am seeking this excitement in the participants.

Wherever you are at this moment is not any old familiar place. Your spot on our small planet, spinning through the universe, is really thousands of miles away from where it was even a few minutes ago.

I recommend the use of this exercise as a discipline. Better yet would be to invent an exercise like this of your own. I suggest that you do this exercise with someone who is important to you. If you are a young executive, I recommend that you find one person who is much younger than you and another person much older, find a place where you may share a cup of coffee or an ice cream cone, and play this game with him or her. I think that doing it during a meal may be too disruptive to the game.

> **N O T E**
> You may use The Improv itself as a way to generate excitement, playfulness, relaxation, honesty, playfulness with focus, hunger for the new, discipline of change, and a rush to share and be challenged.

"Let's See What There Is to See"

Another game I play with Jonathan is: "Let's see what there is to see." You may begin this adventure with an active event—a "setup"—such as walking around the lake, walking around the building in which you work, building a model airplane, exploring a creek, going to dinner, exploring a new store, walking through the plant or offices, or going shopping. Going to a zoo or a circus may be too complex to serve this game well.

Whatever you choose, transform it into an exercise for your creative mind. As you engage in your task, take time to name new things that you see. At the lake it may be a bird; around the office building it may be the pattern of the windows. In the office you could institute a "Let's see what there is to see" moment at some fun length and interval. Interesting things or the strange juxtaposition of objects can seem to appear out of nowhere. You may become aware of patterns and shapes, smells and sounds that can make the familiar appear bright and new. I suggest that you do this game in important places.

Sounds and Rhythms

There are many ways to exercise your creativity in a daily practice. In the movie *Tap,* Gregory Hines plays the son of an old-time tap dancer. His father was famous for finding new beats and tempos in the sounds of the city, the clatter of the people and machines, and their daily tasks. The cacophony became drum phrases for him, producing foot-tapping harmonies in a surreal swirl of creativity. This was his daily creativity discipline. The intent or this exercise is to overcome noise and distraction and to practice being in the current moment by listening to it carefully.

I have heard of an Improv player who became expert at making sounds for the stage—doors opening, people walking, phones ringing. He apparently works on a factory assembly line. As he makes each movement of the assembly process, he practices making a noise until he gets it perfectly. He brings these to The Improv.

Whether you focus on sight or sound—or any other sense—make an exercise of creativity a daily practice. A conscious effort to see and know new things is part of the path to owning The Improv and developing the leadership necessary to bring it to others.

New Names for Old Things

A different way to stretch our creative muscles is to give new names to the familiar things we handle each day. A basic form of this process has been discussed. The game can help you make unexpected mental connections that help free our Improv process.

Whether or not you notice it, each time you interact with physical things your mind names them and names the action. "My 'hand' 'reaches' into my 'pocket' to get my 'keys.'" "'I' 'grab' the 'doorknob' to 'open' the 'door.'"

Try replacing a single word at first: "My 'windmill' reaches into my pocket to get my keys." Then try replacing two words at once: "My 'giraffe' reaches into my 'battleship.'" Then switch verbs too: "My 'horse' 'guffaws' into my 'painting' to 'glorify' my 'petunias.'"

Try: "I mangle the doorknob." Then: "Tom the Tango instructor depletes the writhing doorknob." You may take this exercise to the ridiculous: "Fine Frank cobbles the crystals to flatten the baboon." If you take this exercise to the ridiculous with a person who is very young or very old (you define these terms), you can create great laughter.

Use the same sentence over and over, inserting different replacement words, until you become proficient. Eventually you will be able to replace words randomly as you begin to really notice the acts of unconscious "naming" that go on in your brain.

This game is very interesting to play with another person. It is a good game to play with a number of different people over time. If you play this game alone, you are likely to find yourself laughing out loud for no apparent reason as the game carries you into the creative state of mind!

DISCOVER NEW GAMES

Improvisation is a system in much the same way that architecture, building construction, and engineering are systems. Not only can we build houses with these systems, but the number and variety of houses we can build are infinite. We can also use them to build skyscrapers or bird houses, churches or temples, as well as houses, opera halls, theaters, business buildings, hotels, gazebos, tree houses, boats, greenhouses, tunnels, bridges, automobiles, airplanes, towers, highway interchanges, space ships, satellites, and integrated circuits. The list is infinite.

You can teach yourself to be able to generate an infinite number of Improv games and applications of Improv games. The Improv process itself can be used to generate new games and new application ideas.

Creating New Games

The designation "new game" does not require total uniqueness. A method for bringing your own style and personality to an Improv process is to select a game and "grow" a variation. At Improv conferences you will hear people describe new games. A common response to most new game descriptions is, "Oh, we call that. . . ."

There are truly "new" Improv games invented almost daily. Variations are made up whenever improvisers are at play. Time spent considering the structure of games and encouraging yourself, and the people with whom you work, to create new ones is a good exercise in developing your understanding of the whole process.

Inventing New Games

You can invent a game by selecting a game type to study very carefully to figure out how it works. The basic game types include line games, roll-through games, two-person games, circle games, and three-to-seven-person games. After you understand the game, then focus on finding applications for that game type that go beyond performance and fun. Applications in learning and pedagogy are especially rewarding to develop. Change around the set design or make other structural or logistical changes to the game type you have selected. By playing with a game type using this discipline, you may develop whole new games, which seem to surface as though by magic.

Final Thoughts

Daily disciplines are vital to creating your own creativity. You may use the ones I've suggested or you may find disciplines of your own. I especially recommend that you find a playful substitute.

Creating new games and inventing new games will keep your Improv discipline alive and supple. Doing this will also enhance your use of Improvisation itself.

A BREATH OF FRESH AIR

Breathing is a kind of discipline. When breathing is well-regulated and working as it should, it enhances your ability to stay in the current moment. It energizes your activity, and it helps you make the best use of The Improv. Good breathing is a key element in creating your own creativity.

When breathing we must both give (exhale) and receive (inhale) in equal measure. Sometimes we find ourselves always giving of ourselves: giving time, energy, emotional support, money, and more. You may have noticed that unless you receive some measure of return you can become burned out, exhausted—even bitter. On the other hand there are times when we seem only to take and take and not to give back. Eventually, this also isolates us; we can become bloated, yet never full. Imbalance in either direction can keep us from working in current time. It can make our efforts a struggle rather than a joy.

The longer we hold our breath, the more carbon dioxide we produce and maintain in our bodies. As the carbon dioxide builds, we begin to experience toxic responses. As we approach toxic shock, we panic. Actually, the instant we start to hold our breath, our cells begin to shut down activities not related to the search for oxygen. Our thinking slows, metabolism fluctuates, our heartbeat increases, blood vessels begin to constrict from the extremities inward, blood pressure fluctuates, adrenaline flows, and attendant endocrine responses ensue. Panic sets in and eventually we will pass out.

When breathing stops, even for an instant, the body does not care whether it is because of a decision or the result of an accident. The body takes severe steps in a prescribed and ancient order that leads to unconsciousness and maybe even death.

Beyond the power to hold one's breath, it has been calculated that the average human breathes only 80 percent of the time. Furthermore, we tend to use only about 60 percent of our lung capacity. This is not a conscious act. Even on a very bad day, we do not say, "I don't like the world today. I am going to withhold my precious carbon dioxide." On a given day we may say, "I am unworthy." However, we do not say, "I refuse myself the gift of oxygen. I shall not breathe in today."

What we tend to do instead is to hold our breath for short periods of time as part of bad breathing habits. We tend to breathe in and hold our breath for awhile. Or we breathe out and hold it, perhaps as a sigh, depending on our own particular habits. Unless you are trained in one of the breath-awareness disciplines, this process is usually unconscious. Part of the process of making The Improv your own is to begin to notice your own breathing habits.

A SHORT BREATHING EXERCISE

Take a breath and don't let it out. Take in another breath. Then another, without letting your breath out. Try taking still another breath. Another? At some point you can't do it any more. OK, let your breath out and breathe normally for awhile.

Try doing this in the other direction. Exhale. Don't take in another breath. Exhale again. Again. Can you exhale once more? Probably not. All right. Breathe normally for awhile. Notice that you must breathe in and out in approximately equal measure.

Whatever your personal breathing habits, if imbalance is the result, your body will fight it. It will rob you of energy and clarity. Imbalance in your breathing will disturb the synchronization of your body, mind, and spirit. If you are not in sync with your breathing, you will be out of time elsewhere.

In order to make Improvisation truly your own and to create your own creativity, you will do well to attend to your breathing. Learn to breathe fully and continuously. Learn to use your breath as a tool to keep yourself completely in the moment. There is a great deal of information available on breathing practices. Depending on your interests, try looking to the fields of sports, music, dance, meditation, yoga, and the martial arts for more guidance.

A BALANCE BETWEEN GIVING AND RECEIVING

In order to achieve the ability to create our own creativity, we must strive for an essential balance. At the same time, in many areas of our lives we must separate giving from receiving. Often we give emotional support to our family and friends in their times of need and then must wait for our time of need to receive support in return. We must give young children emotional support and cannot expect emotional support from them while they are young.

Sometimes we work for our money in one endeavor and gain our personal satisfaction elsewhere. When we work for ourselves or in new jobs, we often must give for rather a long time before the rewards are returned. This is equally true of education and training.

Many jobs have both positive and negative aspects; satisfaction may be had by focusing on the positive. Often in our employment there must be a separation between give and take. Yet if balance is not eventually achieved, the results can be harmful.

If you take joy in the process of work, you can gain the most from it and do the most with it. Joy can maintain the best general balance in your life. Joy and satisfaction in the process of living create a sense of balance and ultimately a sense of well-being. In using The Improv for any of its purposes, it is a very good idea for you to receive joy and satisfaction from the process itself. Part of your job is also to help others find joy and satisfaction—to achieve balance in the process as well.

If joy and satisfaction are not present during the process of learning and change, the events themselves can become a negative experience and participants may lose the will to be open. Without joy and positive feedback, the probability that information will be retained or real behavior will be changed is reduced dramatically. Without involvement and interaction in the process itself, the probability of future application—doing something real with the information—is reduced.

As Improv executives we must lead the way by doing. We must walk the talk, stride the ride, live the lesson, face the facts, vibrate with the vision, swing with the steps, wallow in the wonder, gallop with the goals, triumph with the truth, breathe the breath. . . . You get the idea.

ABOUT "JOE"

Early in my Improv career, a young man showed up at our workshop. I shall call him "Joe." Joe was in his mid-twenties. Some years before he had been in a serious accident that had left him with the mental and emotional age of a bright twelve-year-old. He lived in the back of a store and supported himself by keeping the store clean.

Joe had seen an Improv show and decided that he wanted to learn how to do it. Before he came by, Joe had bought a new suit made of brown and beige plaid polyester. He came dressed this way to the workshop.

By the standards of the young people playing at that time, Joe was slow and had a limited frame of reference. To the younger people, he seemed more than a little bit strange. Many were uncomfortable in his presence and others did not like to play with him. Every time Joe came to a workshop or show he wore the same plaid suit. Every time he also came with the same open heart, the same friendly smile, the same conviction that he could do the work. He always arrived with a smile, patience, willingness to laugh, and a quiet tolerance of those who shunned him.

Before long Joe settled in and everyone found ways Joe could be on the stage without disturbing performances. Some used him in a somewhat cruel fashion, almost as a stage prop, in order to get laughs. Being on the stage when people were laughing was ambrosia on which Joe feasted. He had a bigger heart than the rest of us, and the source of the laughter did not matter to him. The limelight was an elixir that produced a dawn of new feelings, and he simply basked in it.

After awhile everyone became more tolerant, more adult, more kind, and eventually protective of Joe. The cruelties came to an end as he became a member of our "family." Joe found his niche in The Improv. He was a natural "straight man." He had all the freshness and enthusiasm of a twelve-year-old with the wisdom of one challenged beyond the average. He grew. His strengths became stronger, his weaknesses diminished. He was a joy and pleasure to play and work with. Joe became an inspiration to us all. He was there for the process itself.

The Improv Plateau

All who improvise must face plateaus. Wit and intelligence, natural funniness, and even raw talent will all run out after awhile. Eventually our public face gives way to our deeper self. I have had the pleasure of knowing some extraordinary "wits" and talents who have come to The Improv ready to float through it. However, when people are working two, or three, or more workshops and two or more shows every week, even extraordinary wit and talent runs out after a few months—or a year or two at the most. Each time the wit, and brain, and intelligence, and talent, and luck, and pattern adherence run out, there is an "Improv Plateau." The player must reach inside for more resources. It is here that the creativity has its source. It is here that you can make The Improv your own.

The Improv Crisis

Somewhere between a month and six months into the process, everyone goes through the "Improv Crisis." This is a crisis that requires releasing all resistance and entering into the unknown world of pure Improv creativity. This point can be pushed by a trained and practiced Improv facilitator so that an early Improv crisis, the crisis of achieving freedom, can occur at a significant level within a few hours.

The Improv crisis looks similar each time and with each person, regardless of how and when it is achieved. It looks a bit like fear and panic. The eyes may lose their focus, palms become sweaty, the heart beats faster, breathing speeds up, and dizziness may occur. The crisis often shows itself as resistance, confusion, or hostility. The person in the transition later talks of disorientation, loss of time sense, heightened sensory perception, and a feeling of breakthrough and relaxation.

With enlightened facilitation, with a participant-centered approach—including personal involvement and leadership—with adherence to the rules, theories, practices, purposes, forms and spirit, the Improv executive can guide the participants through this crisis and directly to personal and social creativity.

The miracle of Joe was presented to me at the beginning of his second year of play. Some new, very talented, and bright young people joined the Improv workshop group. One evening a fairly new player came to the "Improv crisis." Her wit, her intelligence, her extraordinary depth of reference, her talent, her innocence, her control, and her patterned responses all failed her and she was lost, perhaps for the first time in her life.

That evening Joe took the stage with another experienced player and he brought down the house. All he did was follow the rules, walk the path, open his big heart, relax into the moment, and play wholeheartedly. Jonathan playing "What is there that we have never seen before?" reminds me of the way Joe flies through The Improv.

The young woman in the crisis whispered out loud to herself, "If Joe can do this, I can do this." A bond was created, not just between Joe and the young woman, but between the young woman and the spirit of The Improv, the spirit of creativity, the spirit of life. The simultaneous simplicity and complexity swept her off her feet. When she next took the stage, the glaze in her eyes turned to a sparkle, her hesitancy turned to commitment, and her mind released its control and gave power to her whole being. Down came the house once again.

In order to use Improvisation effectively as an executive business tool, you will have to go through your own Improv crisis. If you use the form well, you will go through the crisis more than once. Each time you go through the crisis you will find yourself on the other side of a personal or professional limitation or barrier.

To activate the creativity of The Improv and to make it your own, you will have to spend time with it over the years. Improvisation, whether for leading, teaching, playing, or for making a living, is a lifetime study. It begins with your breath and goes through the disciplined practice of all its elements, in small, successful, incremental steps toward the ancient human vision of progress. Proceed with joy and with a playful spirit.

Epilogue

In 1979 it was my great pleasure to meet the great architect, inventor, writer, and philosopher R. Buckminster Fuller. I had read pretty much all that "Bucky" had published and loved his ideas and his thinking. His speaking was as eloquent as his writing, as inspired as his geodesic dome. At the end of the meeting there was a reception line.

I waited my turn, and when I finally met him I shook his hand and gushed about his work. I must have acted like a rock-and-roll groupie. He listened kindly, nodding and smiling. Then, with a gentle and sincere voice he said, "That's very nice. Thank you. Now, forget about me and go do something." I suggest to you the same thing now: you just forget about me and go do something.

Bibliography

Arch, Dave. *Showmanship for Presenters: 49 Proven Training Techiques From Professional Performers.* San Francisco: Jossey-Bass/Pfeiffer-CTT Press, 1995.

Bandler, Richard. *Using Your Brain for a Change.* Moab, UT: Real People Press, 1985.

Barton, Robert. *Acting, Onstage and Off* (2nd ed.). New York: Harcourt Brace College, 1993.

Boyd, Neva L., & Dagney Pederson. *Folk Games of Denmark and Sweden.* Chicago, IL: H.T. FitzSimmons, 1915.

Boyd, Neva L. *Handbook of Games.* Chicago, IL: H.T. FitzSimmons, 1945.

Bridge, William H. *Actor in the Making.* Boston, MA: Expression, 1936.

Campbell, Don. *The Mozart Effect.* New York: Avon Books, 1997.

Coleman, Janet. *The Compass.* New York: Alfred Knopf, 1990.

de Chardin, Pierre Teilhard. *The Phenomenon of Man.* New York: Harper & Row, 1959.

Duchartre, Pierre Louis. *The Italian Comedy.* New York: Dover Publications, 1929.

Hartnoll, Phyllis. *The Theatre: A Concise History.* London, England: Thames & Hudson, 1968.

Hayakawa, S.I. *Language in Thought and Action.* New York: Harcourt, Brace & World, 1964.

Johnstone, Keith. *Impro, Improvisation and the Theatre.* New York: Theatre Arts Books, 1979.

Korzybsky, Alfred. *Science and Sanity: An Introduction to Non-Aristotelian Systems and General Semantics.* Lancaster, PA: Science Press, 1933.

McCrohan, Donna. *The Second City.* New York: Putnam, 1987.

Mitchell, Don, Carol Coles, & Robert Metz. *The 2000 Percent Solution.* New York: American Management Association, 1999.

Nachmanovitch, Stephen. *Free Play: Improvisation in Life and Art.* Los Angeles: Jeremy P. Tarcher, 1990.

Neeld, Elizabeth Harper. *Seven Choices.* New York: Dell, 1990.

Partch, Harry. *Genesis of a Music: An Account of Creative Work, Its Roots, and Its Fulfillments.* New York: DaCapo Press, 1974.

Pearce, Joseph Chilton. *Magical Child Matures.* New York: Bantam, 1985.

Pike, Bob. *Creative Training Techniques Handbook.* Minneapolis, MN: Lakewood, 1994.

Spolin, Viola. *Improvisation for the Theater.* Evanston, IL: Northwestern University Press, 1963.

Spolin, Viola. *Theater Games for Rehearsal.* Evanston, IL: Northwestern University Press, 1985.

Stevens, John. *Invincible Warrior: A Pictorial Biography of Morihei Ueshiba, The Founder of Aikido.* Boston, MA: Shambhala, 1997.

Sweet, Jeffrey. *Something Wonderful Right Away.* Toronto, Ontario: New Books, 1978.

von Oech, Roger. *A Whack on the Side of the Head.* New York: Warner Books, 1983.

Whitelaw, Ginny. *BodyLearning.* New York: Penguin Putnam, 1998.

About the Author

Robert Lowe is the founder and chief executive of *Improvisation, Incorporated,* an educational consulting firm specializing in the use of Improvisation theater techniques for organizational development and business and professional communication. His clients have included The Southern Company, AT&T, Medtronics, Inc., Georgia Pacific Corporation, the Government Services Administration, Metro Atlanta Rapid Transit Authority, the Southeastern Regional Association of Girl Scout Executives, Centers for Disease Control and Prevention, Georgia Baptist Medical Center, the Fulton County Staff Development Council, Mitchell and Associates, and the Center for Puppetry Arts.

In his twenty-year exploration of Improvisation, Lowe has been an observer, a player, a teacher, a director, and a pioneer in the uses of Improvisation for purposes other than performance. He was the founder and artistic director of Atlanta's *The Next City Comedy Theatre* and has been the director or a key player in a number of other Improv troupes, including *The Let's Try This Players* of the Georgia Institute of Technology, which has been introducing Improvisational creativity to high-tech students for more than ten years. He has taught Improvisation and stand-up comedy, public speaking and presentation, and community and personal advocacy in a variety of venues. Robert's *Improv Comedy Workshop*™ with graduation performance has placed dozens of "just plain folks" on the Improv stage facing live audiences. His work in Improvisation is known in twenty countries outside the United States.

Robert Lowe has been a management consultant, a public speaker, an adjunct professor, a corporate vice president in financial services, a national sales representative, a program analyst, a project director, a welfare supervisor—in the San Quentin district of Northern California, a customer service manager in South Central Los Angeles, a U.S. Navy officer, a legal services paralegal and community educator, and a legal secretary. He has been a Boy Scout executive, a corporate collector, a carpenter, an electrician, a political activist, a community activist, an advocate for handicapped accessibility, an actor, a dancer, a meditator, a teacher of children, a poet, an historian, and a philosopher. He is also an Eagle Scout, which pleased his mother and father to no end.

Robert has been a teacher with the Department of Communication at Georgia State University for twelve years, teaching "human communication, public speaking, business and professional communication, voice and articulation, acting, and special studies in improvisation," where he has been honored as Outstanding Part-Time Instructor. He is currently involved in academic research into Improvisation as a human communication tool, in a program leading toward a Master's degree in Communication, and a Ph.D. degree in Human Communication.

Lowe is a Nidan (second degree black belt) in Aikido with over twenty years on the mat and more than seven years specializing in the teaching of children. His articles have been published in *Aikido Today Magazine* and *The Journal of Asian Martial Arts.*

He is a husband, the father of a fine boy who is eleven, and the stepfather of an extraordinary twelve-year-old young man and a fifteen-year-old who impresses him more than she knows. Robert spends some time each day in grateful thanks to God for all that is.

More than anything else, Robert Lowe is a man who one day more than twenty years ago found the power of focus on the current moment and has been unwilling and unable to let it go for even a minute since then. When he talks about The Improv, and about creativity, and about the human spirit, and about the power of spontaneity his eyes light up, the air crackles, and his feet only barely touch the ground.

Robert grew up in a neighborhood which had one of the highest juvenile crime rates in America between 1950 and 1970. There were youth gangs in the schools before it was the fashion and motorcycle gangs on the streets where he learned to walk in hope. He worked in poverty communities in South Central Los Angeles during the "first" Watts Riots. Through the Vietnam war era of revolution, he has seen the world come up abruptly against itself only to find the desperate need of some real personal, internal, and creative human work. Lowe feels that through the eighties and the nineties and into the 2000's the need for this work has become mandatory.